Parenting the difficult child

Parenting the difficult child

Florence K. Rogers

Chilton Book Company
RADNOR, PENNSYLVANIA

Published in Radnor, Pennsylvania, by Chilton Book Company
and simultaneously in Don Mills, Ontario, Canada,
by Thomas Nelson & Sons, Ltd.
Library of Congress Catalog Card No. 78-14649
ISBN 0-8019-6783-x
Designed by Adrianne Onderdonk Dudden
Manufactured in the United States of America

1 2 3 4 5 6 7 8 9 0   8 7 6 5 4 3 2 1 0 9

This book is dedicated to all the wild and wonderful kids who drive adults crazy and do many other things, and to their beleaguered parents. But especially it's for Benjamin, who's worth more than ten less spectacular kids; for Emaline Sprankle and Bud Oehrli, good people who can put it together in the classroom; for Sister Carmelita, who could teach standing on her head if she had to; for Lee Brubaker, who still thinks kids are very special people; and for Josie Dunbar Pennebaker, who told me to put up or shut up. Bless us all, because we need it.

Contents

PART TWO

Preface

This book was written primarily for parents—parents whose children are hyperkinetic, learning disabled, hyperactive, troublesome in school, unruly at home, difficult to manage, and/or any combination of the above, specifically diagnosed or not. It was definitely written from a parent's point of view, and it is my most sincere belief that I have treated both parents and children sympathetically. I certainly meant to.

I also hoped to compile information on the hyperkinetic or difficult child's dilemma that would be useful to professionals. I may not have treated the professionals that deal with hyperkinetic children as kindly as some of them deserve. However, I very strongly feel that many professionals, by systematizing and classifying (and perhaps, ostracizing) these children, have compounded their problems and created a situation that is detrimental and severely curtails their potentials.

While dealing with the problems of classification and labeling of children, I was confronted with a problem of my own—how to distinguish this particular group of children whose symptoms, degree of involvement, individual situations, and problems differ from those of other groups of children with or without specific types of problems. After rejecting most designations for one reason or another, and after considering the possibility of coining a new term, I resigned myself to the use of "hyperkinetic," with the full knowledge that the majority of these children are not hyperkinetic in the true sense of the word. As a matter of fact, they are so very different from each other that it's difficult for me to think of them as a group: They are children with learning disabilities, hyperactive children, hard-to-manage children, children with slightly elevated activity levels, children who are truly hyperkinetic, children whose only problems arise from the school situation, children who start off in life as "difficult" infants, children who can't seem to learn to "behave," and children who have a tendency to be impulsive. They may or may not have problems with motor or perceptual development. They may or may not have developed emotional problems. Intellectually, they run the gamut from retarded to gifted. Their socioeconomic status and their home lives are as varied as their symptoms.

I have tried to condense a great deal of material on the subject of hyperkinesis into a manageable and informative guide for parents, including a very brief history, a little terminology, and definitions of some of the concepts, which parents may find useful (the first seven chapters). Because of their brevity, some of the explanations may seem incomplete or somewhat shallow. Should the reader feel the need for more information on a particular subject, I refer him to the bibliography.

This book is based on fairly comprehensive research in the fields of psychology, education, medicine, and a review of the popular literature. Although the opinions are my own, and therefore the distillation of the material researched is my own, there remains the fact that there is a great deal of published material that tends to support my views.

The second half of the book deals with day-to-day situations and problems which are fairly common to parents of difficult children. These chapters are arranged chronologically. Although the problems of hyperkinesis persist over time, there are age-specific situations that many parents will undoubtedly encounter.

My thanks and appreciation to my long-suffering friends who had to listen to me expound on the problems of hyperkinesis while I was researching the book; to my editor who pointed out my inconsistencies and disorganization; to a great typist who deciphered hand-written annotations on the manuscript; and to my children, all of whom successfully survived the research and writing episodes.

My apologies for the use of the word "he" to refer to the hyperkinetic child. Although many more boys than girls are hyperkinetic (approximately five boys to every girl so blessed), "he" is used for the sake of brevity, not because of its implied gender.

Before my children find fault with me, let me make it clear that I never thought of them as "difficult" or anything else so categorically restrictive. I have thought of them as gifted, obstreperous, superlative, exasperating, maddening, yes. Hyperkinetic, disturbed, or overactive, never.

Parenting the difficult child

The Difficult Child

Nineteen years ago, I began to be aware of the problems associated with a childhood condition that's been called minimal brain dysfunction, learning disability, hyperkinesis, hyperkinetic impulse disorder, and various other synonyms. My second daughter, Gerry, an exquisitely beautiful, healthy, happy, gratifying baby, started to walk. She was delicate but wiry, cheerful, very determined, and eight months old. I remember thinking, as I watched her not-so-uncertain steps rapidly lengthening into a splendid racing stride, "That's trouble." It was.

My beautiful daughter is now twenty. To her mother, she is still exquisite, healthy, relatively happy, sometimes pleasant to be with, and astonishingly intelligent, although somewhat misdirected. I think she's going to be all right but, believe me, it's been a fight all the way: fights between the two of us, between her and other people, between me and others, and involving various combinations of me, her, and others.

I truly had no desire to add to the geneticists' theories concerning hereditary personality traits, but somehow my youngest child, Ben, another of those marvelous, perfect babies, heaved his charmingly fat, solid little body onto remarkably sturdy legs at an early age. (The bodies were different, but the determination was the same.) The pediatrician was very reassuring. "No, no," he said, "These big, fat, placid babies are never troublesome." Ho, ho! The baby fat turned to muscle, the stride quickened appreciably, and I remember thinking, "This couldn't happen to me twice, could it?" It did.

Are both of these children learning disabled or hyperkinetic? Do they have some irreparable impairment, brain damage, or dysfunction?

Medical and psychological evaluation indicated that, on the whole, both children were physically and emotionally sound, evidenced superior motor skills, and were gifted in intelligence. The worst symptom found was that my daughter was ambidextrous and therefore did not have a dominant hemisphere in the brain, which is sometimes considered a "soft" neurological sign (see Chapter 2). Learning disabilities, such as confusion between left and right, and certain reading problems, are believed to result from mixed dominance. If such problems ever existed for Gerry, they were so minimal that no one ever noticed them.

Despite evidence of emotional stability and good physical health, there were many, many problems. There were school problems, peer problems, and problems with other adults. There were tremendous complications between us as parent and child. Sometimes, when there were no real problems, somebody invented one that didn't exist, thereby creating a further problem.

Unfortunately, there are people who have and who will continue to label these children and children like them with designations indicating a wide, nebulous range of impairments and deviant behaviors far in excess of reality. What such labeling does is to allow the adult to explain easily his lack of success with the child. What it does for the child is questionable, although it can be detrimental in the extreme.

It has become fashionable to subsume a wide range of behaviors and personality traits, properly or improperly, under headings such as minimal brain dysfunction, hyperactivity, and learning disabilities. While hyperkinesis and learning disabilities do, in fact, exist, incidence is limited and the proportion of the school-age population actually so affected is probably not growing very rapidly, although the widespread, casual application of these labels would lead one to believe otherwise. Surely the incidence is not growing as rapidly as some authorities would have us believe. It appears that we are indulging in a variation of a favorite intellectual pastime—suppressing deviant behavior. As a species, we have a rather long and notable history distinguished by our attempts to stamp out deviance, and we've worked hard to get rid of pagans, witches, sinners, and other assorted heretics. My concern here is not with the roots of heresy. My sympathy lies with the poor heretic, the one who does not conform—and with the parents of the heretic.

What about the parents? Well, this seems to be the reversal of the biblical mandate about the sins of the father. In this case, the sins of the child are heavily visited upon the parents. The sad part is that there are, of course, no sins, no sinners, and no heretics. There is a child who deviates from somebody's version of normal, and there are parents who are confused, anxious, worried, harried, and sometimes very angry.

Parenthood is never an easy task. Being the parent of one of these children is doubly difficult. The normally rocky road from infancy to adulthood begins to resemble a mine field to which some inventive and perverted genius has added deep, well-camouflaged pits, icy patches to make the footing impossible, and barbed wire barricades.

Parents, on the whole, are really not prepared for what is called the "hard-to-manage" infant. Such a baby is extraordinarily demanding of time and attention, doesn't sleep as much as babies are supposed to sleep, screams at the smallest frustration or irritation, is difficult to soothe when upset or tired, startles at the slightest disturbance, and wakes from a sound sleep at the smallest noise. Moreover, such a child wants, and demands, lots of stimulation, amusement, and attention but reacts badly to too much stimulation. He's physically active and very strong, so he can't be put down just anywhere. Without proper management, he can work himself into a state similar to colic. The child is just not a terribly satisfactory baby. Taking care of him—giving him as much care as he seems to want—is more of a task and less of a pleasure than the parents had anticipated.

As a toddler, he exhausts his caretakers. He has more energy, more curiosity, more self-determination, and more ingenuity than the parents thought possible in one child. (It's like having triplets with one body.) The child is more resistant to parental control, more self-willed, and has pronounced negativistic tendencies. As for temper, he probably has a very short fuse, and his outbursts of anger are quite direct. An older sibling who doesn't immediately surrender a toy the child wants is apt to get smacked in the head. Consideration, cooperation, and sharing are concepts that are alien to his nature. As long as things go the way he wants them to, however, he is usually cheerful, lovable, and affectionate.

Fighting and bickering among the child and his siblings becomes commonplace. It goes on regularly, protractedly, and frequently, with an excessive amount of reporting on the child's activities. "He won't let me do my homework!" "He took my ball away from me!" "He hit me!" (However, crucial events are never reported. No one ever says, "He's sticking a knife in the toaster!"—until it's too late.)

The child seems to get into an awful lot that he shouldn't, and a considerable bit of damage and destruction results owing to curiosity and inventiveness. I've come up with a theory that explains this phenomenon: Any one person who does a lot of things will numerically do more wrong than a person who does fewer things. He may get into trouble 20 times a day, but it's not fair to compare him to the kid next door who only does 20 things all day (because he's lethargic due to an underactive thyroid) and only 3 of the 20 happen to be wrong. The highly active youngster may do 300 things, so 20 is a pretty good average.

With great fortitude, the parents usually socialize the child (it used to be called "bringing the kid up right") to the point where he doesn't somehow kill himself or anybody else. And so they manage to limp through the preschool years at great emotional cost. Except when the condition is so severe that the child is literally ricocheting off the walls, parents are more inclined to see him as a huge pain in the neck rather than as a serious problem. However, the child is often irritating, hard to manage, disruptive, noisy, fidgety, and frustrating to an extreme. Having to cope with him on a day-to-day basis—actively cope, that is—drains the parents' physical and emotional reserves, with little compensatory satisfaction. The parents, naturally enough, seriously begin to question their parental abilities.

With so much going on, it becomes increasingly difficult to separate the "right" from the "wrong," the child from his behavior. Even if the parents can direct their accumulated anger toward the behavior, and not the child, sometimes the child cannot sense the difference. In other words, the child's behavior erodes the parental approval and acceptance that the child desperately needs and wants.

The entire family becomes involved in a situational cycle in which they all, in effect, get the short end of the stick. The child feels rejected, picked-on, and singled out for punishment. (He often is.) The parents feel inadequate and angry. (If the child's behavior does not improve, the parents must be doing something wrong.) Brothers and sisters feel neglected and resentful. (They do know whose fault it is that the parents are upset and angry.) The home situation may become quite chaotic and unbearably tense. (And everybody knows who's the culprit.)

When the condition is severe and the parents are not able to manage the child in any way, they may seek medical and/or psychological help. There isn't much help out there for them. Medicine offers drug therapy, but making a decision to put a three-year-old on amphetamines is extremely difficult. Most psychologists don't really know what to do with a kid who's ramming around and tearing up the office.

Meanwhile, despite all efforts and good intentions, the parents are frustrated in their attempts to make the child behave like other children. As their child-rearing techniques prove ineffective, they turn to the experts, whose opinions range from the extremely permissive and democratic to the totalitarian and terribly repressive, with a few quasi-religious theories thrown in for good measure. Parental floundering from one method to another establishes a pattern of inconsistency, which further muddies the water and leaves everybody guessing where the limits are on any particular day. Their repeated failures to modify the child's behavior, of course, compound whatever feelings of inadequacy and guilt they already have, making them less assured and less certain of their abilities than they were to begin with.

So the days go by, sometimes good, sometimes bad, and the parents push and pull, sometimes peacefully and sometimes forcefully, heaving their very unwilling two-ton rock of a child up the hill through early childhood. (Pushing a two-ton rock up a hill and raising a hyperkinetic child require the same qualifications—commitment, endurance, and perseverance.)

When the child finally enters school, the problems of early childhood pale by comparison. This is a child the school system is not equipped to handle. He is not a group-oriented child, and he can be very disruptive in a group situation, which the parents have already observed, no doubt. Needless to say, the child is frustrated and irritated by the regulations imposed by the new system, and, in a group of twenty-five of his peers, his behavior will deteriorate rather than improve. No, he doesn't want to get in line. No, he doesn't want to join the show-and-tell circle. No, he doesn't care what the others are doing. He's presently doing something *he* wants to do. No, he doesn't want to learn to print his name. No, he doesn't want to sit quietly and listen to the story. It's a dumb story, anyway. And if you call him that name again, he'll punch you in the nose!

After some time, the parents become aware that the process of education is certainly on-going, but what the child is learning is not his ABC's. He is busily perfecting his techniques for disruptive behavior in the course of which, by antagonizing his teacher and classmates, he will be negatively reinforced in his behavior and attitudes.

Now what happens? Well, the parents are usually called in for conferences, which all too frequently turn out to be dumping sessions rather than problem-solving dialogues. The representative of the school system, a teacher, principal, or guidance counselor who naturally feels he must protect himself and/or the institution, seems more concerned with absolving the school than with trying to figure out what's going wrong. The only way to absolve one party, of course, is to affix the blame on the other, namely, the parents.

It is sometimes difficult to distinguish the possible causes of aggressive behavior, but there is a deplorable tendency to classify children's unacceptable behavior as part and parcel of an "emotional disturbance," whatever that means. Now, since everybody knows that emotionally disturbed children are the direct result of a "bad" home, there is the implication that something is wrong with the parents or they wouldn't have a problem child. Something in the child's home life is the cause of his unacceptable behavior in school. Right?

Not necessarily, but the parents will have a hard time convincing the school personnel that they are adequate, loving parents and that their child does not have some deep-seated emotional problem. If the parents already have doubts about their parental abilities, those feelings are now being confirmed. Even the most self-confident parent will occasionally find himself sitting in a corner muttering to himself, "What am I doing wrong?"

For many years, I had a problem understanding why other people became so upset and defensive when dealing with this kind of child. Finally, I realized what a blow to one's self-esteem it must be to be confronted and challenged by a child. First of all, it's very unexpected. Second, since we commonly regard children as our inferiors (or at least our subordinates) it's a direct attack on our authority, prestige, and power to be thwarted by someone who is so obviously not as knowledgeable, not as capable, and certainly not as big. (Remember the jokes about the 110-pound weakling who challenged the 200-pound muscleman? Try to remember how amusing it is the next time you're challenged by a 45-pound dynamo.)

Whatever is going on in school, the parents are often asked to "do something" about it—from a distance, of course. They are asked to reward and punish behavior over which they have no control or authority and for which they are not responsible. (The child is rarely able to make concrete estimates of the situation that would help parents understand what is going wrong, so any chance to understand the behavior is nonexistent.) If the parents feel powerless to control the child's behavior at home, an attempt to exert pressure on the child in the school situation can only further jeopardize their sense of authority.

At this point, the more heavily the parents have invested emotionally in their child, the more adverse their reaction. From a limited perspective, the parents are inclined to take one of two disastrous approaches. Either they internalize and assume total responsibility for the child's behavior, making superhuman efforts to correct and control that behavior (thereby releasing the child from responsibility and freeing him to act just as impulsively as he wishes), or they become overwhelmed with their own feelings of inadequacy and exonerate themselves as parents by shifting the total responsibility and blame from themselves and the school onto the child, thus classifying him as "bad" or "sick."

There are alternatives, but they aren't always apparent to parents caught up in the turmoil of raising a hyperkinetic child. What makes these alternatives so hard to see? Well, let me presume that the parents do not ritualistically beat their child every day, and so have few mechanisms for unloading their anger and frustration. These feelings have been accumulating over a period of time, and so every minor incident assumes greater proportions than it should, which adds fuel to the fire. The accumulated anger and guilt make it hard for parents to make sound judgmental decisions. It's far too easy to fall into emotional potholes.

It's easy to accept somebody else's decision, especially if the other person is an "authority," regarding the handling and disposition of the child.

If the child's behavior is bad enough, sometime or another somebody will probably suggest that he be evaluated—medically and/or psychoeducationally. Since, at an early age, hyperkinetic children do not usually manifest either physical or emotional impairments, the results of the evaluation are infrequently definitive. The child is pronounced sound in body and mind, which is all very nice, but it certainly indicates to the parents that, if there's a problem and nothing is wrong with the child, then there must be something wrong with them. It has to be the fault of the parents, who in reality have done some things wrong and are not ideal parents.

Now, we all know that there are many factors in the home life of a child that can cause unacceptable behavior. There are, among many others, lack of discipline, parental spoiling, tension, conflict, divorced parents (I think the term is "broken home"), sibling rivalry, working mothers, marital discord, and alcoholism. If the parents have not already been looking around in their lives trying to find out what was wrong with them, either as individuals or as a couple, they are now encouraged to do so.

In the natural course of events, the parents will likely find something in their family situation that can be construed as the causal factor. They can then concentrate their time and energy on patching up their own deficiencies or resolving their own conflicts, which will no doubt be beneficial to their child, providing they are able to effect positive changes in their handling of the child along with resolving their conflicts or whatever. However, since the parental problems were not the immediate cause of their child's behavior to begin with, parental self-improvement will not eliminate the child's problem behavior, although it may alleviate it.

It takes an enormous amount of parental self-confidence, which the parent-child situation has undermined, to be able to stand up and say, "Hey, listen! I'm a pretty good person and a pretty good parent. There's nothing so terribly wrong with me, and there's not so much wrong with the kid. I'm not disturbed, and he's not disturbed, but I'm not so sure about you, fella!" Naturally, as the self-confident parent stalks out, the other party is confirmed in his opinion that there is something wrong. "Well, with parents like that, what can you expect from the kid?"

As the school situation deteriorates (and it usually does, especially in the areas of peer relationships and academic achievement) and the child becomes more and more unhappy and frustrated, he brings home more and more of his deviant behavior, and the parent-child relationship deteriorates, too. The child has perfected his disruptive techniques and can have an adult standing on his head in thirteen seconds flat. His perceptions of himself in relation to his universe have become distinctly negative. The parents have no surcease from the problems and tensions created by the child's behavior.

Eventually, the school and child may make some adjustments and survive in a state of armed truce. The child may elect to "tune out." The minute he enters the classroom, he drifts off into his own fantasy land, emerging only for skirmishes with peers and adults, until the final bell rings. Of course, he never hears the first word—or the last—of instruction, and any learning he does takes place by some process of osmosis. This usually results in a lot of flack about incompleted work and poor grades, and the parents may become a trifle perturbed.

Despite the truce, periodic outbursts occur, particularly as the child and his peers are often openly antagonistic. Unfortunately, these children come to believe they are picked on by other children, mainly because they are. Other children soon learn that they can have a lot of fun by pushing the proper buttons and watching the fireworks. All one has to do is push the button "dumb," for instance, and the kid starts swinging and disrupts the class, which was very boring, anyway.

About the time the parents feel some relief, as they see the child settling down, they are informed that he is failing academically or that he has just viciously attacked another child twice his size "for no reason," since the bigger kid "didn't do anything." As a result of the child's erratic behavior, teachers and other adults often expect the child to be the instigator in any situation. It is difficult for the parents to convince anybody that behavior doesn't happen in a vacuum and that the child may have been provoked.

In due course, the child becomes aware that there's something wrong with his behavior, that somehow he's different from his peers, and that his methods and techniques are less than successful in achieving what he really wants. He sees the world, including his own parents, as being hostile to him. The world, including his parents, usually are, in varying degrees.

During the late primary school years both parents and child are sometimes overwhelmed by confusion, frustration, guilt, and hostility. The parents' arbitrary handling of the child, because of their indecision as to how to handle him, often leaves him bereft of structure and purpose when he most critically needs to be aware of the limits and potentials of his life. The parents can no longer see him as separate from his behavior. Irritation, exasperation, and a pattern of response best described as "What have you done wrong *now?*" further erode the child's shaky self-esteem. There are some periods of relative quiet during which the parents may attempt to renegotiate their relationship, correct their management techniques, and better support the child's rather feeble attempts at more constructive behavior. But, because of his negative self-assumptions, the child usually actively resists parental attempts to improve the relationship, which results in further parental irritation and exasperation.

So, with much head-shaking and perplexity, the parents shove their unruly and unrulable child into preadolescence and junior high. Moving such a child into a new school, with new teachers, new peers, and new expectations, is something that shouldn't happen to any parent. Perhaps the child learned to get by in the fairly sheltered environment of primary school. Perhaps he achieved a measure of acceptance from teachers and peers. Perhaps he was able to establish some sort of support network for himself, which he has now had to leave behind. Whatever the reasons, he usually reacts to the new situation with the behaviors he used in kindergarten. These behaviors weren't acceptable then and are less tolerated now.

Middle school or junior high school years are supposed to be a time of transition. For the hyperkinetic child, one must ask, "Transition to what?" Very often, despite a high level of intelligence, the child manifests dramatic evidence of his inability to concentrate, his lack of self-control, and his frustration with a situation he regards as a form of punitive captivity—school. In other words, he fails in his class work, does not pay attention, does not do homework, fights, abuses and irritates others, and, in general, demonstrates just how unhappy and negativistic he is. The parents are aware that their child is not happy and that he is probably in great emotional pain. What can they do? Suffer with him.

Since his lack of dedication to the process of education is quite noticeable, the school again applies pressure to make him achieve and conform. The parents are misguidedly induced to supervise and oversee the child's homework, activities, and attitudes. It becomes increasingly difficult to disclaim responsibility for the child's work, particularly since they can foresee the consequence of school failure. Parents tend to drive themselves around the bend by asking themselves silly questions like, "What in the world will become of him?" "What is he going to do with his life?"

If it hasn't happened yet, to make matters worse, because of poor achievement the child is often placed in a special education class for "slow learners," the retarded and the truly disturbed. This is the ideal place for a child to learn less and less and to become more and more negativistic about himself. (The child may have a recorded IQ of 140, but the teacher sees achievement, not intelligence, in the classroom. If the child is in eighth grade but working on a third-grade math level, it's easy to think he can't learn because there's something, namely, stupidity, preventing him.) Most parents, of course, are well aware that graduates of special education classes hardly ever get into the colleges of their choice, not to mention much of anything else, except minimal, poorly paying jobs.

The days when the child simply careened off the walls are suddenly remembered with nostalgia, as the parents desparately ask each other the important question, "How are we going to get the kid through school?" Their problem becomes critical when the child reaches the age where, because of the problems and frustrations he faces daily and hourly in the school situation, he announces that he's going to quit school as soon as he can. He's had enough, he thinks, and he's not too far from wrong.

Sometime during middle adolescence, the parents, exhausted and more than a little tired of the struggle, are faced with pulling themselves back together as best they can and making another sustained effort. Asking for another sustained effort isn't fair, of course, but then none of this was, was it? The issue isn't justice, anyway; it's success.

Later during adolescence, maybe because the child is more mature, some changes do take place. It used to be thought that some process of maturation "cured" hyperkinesis. Now, authorities argue that hyperkinesis just goes on and on. Nevertheless, the child seems better able to cope with his problems on a rational basis, able to find solutions, and able to apply them in a more positive manner. The parents are called upon to walk the very fine line between guidance and control. The child is in dreadful need of parental acceptance and support to bolster his morale and is better able to make use of them; at the same time he is moving into the realm of adult freedom and responsibility. The usual complications and furor that surround this period of growth are protracted and intensified. The conflicts are sharper, more direct, and louder.

Without very positive reinforcement from his parents, the child will be all too ready to accept himself as a nonsuccess, a loser all the way. Is success possible? Can this child grow into a reasonably successful adult? Can a parent realistically hope for an affirmation of achievement as a parent?

The answer must be qualified, because not everybody agrees on a definition of success. Some children are apparently easy to guide to the goals their parents deem suitable. After all, children do respond, within reason, to parental expectations. Some children seem to glide into appropriate slots, where they function, if not remarkably, adequately. Trying to shove a hyperkinetic child into a convenient, conventional, but wrong, slot is disastrous.

Perhaps that's what parenting such a child amounts to—finding a little space in the world for him where he can function, guiding him into a place where he's not "up against it" all the time, helping him find the areas where he's competent and can succeed (there are many), and writing off the nonsuccesses and failures with a minimum of fuss. Is that success? Define success.

Part One

1 A Statement of Premises

In case you haven't noticed, the subject of hyperkinesis and related impairments is a hot, new trend in the social sciences. Since the mid-1960s, the number of children of school age identified as having one or more behavior patterns that are included under such labels has grown to rather astounding proportions. Depending on whose research report is being used, estimates of the number of children so described (but not necessarily diagnosed) range from a modest 5 percent of the school-age population to a staggering 20 percent.*

* There are a few examples of absurdity sprinkled through these surveys. For instance, in one city in the Midwest it was found that 53 percent of the boys and 30 percent of the girls in the school population were considered by their teachers to have problems with "restlessness."

Although it is generally agreed that 10 million children *labeled* hyperkinetic-learning disabled is a conservative estimate, 15 million may be closer to the truth and, with the new preschool screening programs, predictions indicate that 20 or 30 million school-age children may be identified as having some combination of hyperkinetic-learning disability *symptoms.* (There are over 50 million children in grades K through 12.) There have always been some children with learning disabilities and/or hyperkinesis, and there probably always will be, but haphazard labeling is no help. Some authorities feel that 2 to 3 percent is a more rational estimate of the number of children who are in fact hyperkinetic or learning disabled.

Hyperkinesis may be hot, but it's not so new. Other writers have pointed out that restlessness and impulsivity were decidedly character traits of the early American settlers, some of whom became national heroes. Certain learning disorders have been ascribed to a number of famous people. There are references made to Albert Einstein and Thomas Edison as being notable failures in the classroom. My favorite candidate among historical personages is Genghis Khan. He's a good example of a man who moved around a lot but still managed to be highly successful in his endeavors.

Diagnosing historical figures is a great parlor game, but beside the point, the point being—is one out of every five children hyperkinetic? Not likely. No more likely than one out of five being delinquent, emotionally disturbed, addicted or any other catch-all phrase you can invent that would indicate deviant behavior.

After proper passage through a developmental stage, during which it was designated by terms such as "being bad," "incorrigibility," "predelinquency," "minimal brain damage," "minimal brain dysfunction," "overactivity," "hyperkinetic impulse disorder," and many more, hyperkinesis has now reached maturity as a full-blown epidemic, like whooping cough did before immunization. Unlike whooping cough, however, hyperkinesis is a loose, rather vague collection of behaviors rather than a systematic and diagnosable syndrome (i.e., a constellation of recognizable symptoms) which can be identified and treated. The diagnosis of hyperkinesis is often a subjective evaluation made by someone who is not trained and has insufficient knowledge of the characteristics and behaviors that would make such a diagnosis adequate, not to say correct.

The causes and cures of whooping cough are well known, as is the immunizing agent. The causes and cures of hyperkinesis are unknown. There are many theories concerning the causes, but there are no definite, surefire cures. The entire subject is wide open to investigation, interpretation, and argument.

What we are confronted with is a hard-to-manage and

troublesome child, his distraught parents (at some point, other upset adults also make an appearance), and a lot of literature on hyperkinesis in the fields of education, psychology, and medicine. A lot of the literature is repetitive, inconclusive, and unnecessary, but a lot of it is rational, practical, sound, and far-reaching. What happens to practical, conclusive professional literature? It doesn't seem to have much impact. Perhaps it is lost in the deluge of verbiage along with the most important factors—the child and his parents.

I have some very strong opinions about hyperkinesis, as will become more apparent, but it seems only fair to begin by setting out some basic assumptions.

THE CONCEPT OF NORMALITY

The first assumption concerns the possibilities of human behavior—the range of individual differences. I sincerely hope that schools and universities are still teaching, in their introductory psychology courses, that human possibilities and variations are limitless. Every individual has some measure of every possible human trait, of which there are many. It can never be, "He's got it, and I don't." It has to be, "He has more of it than I do." The same characteristic that makes the paranoid delusionary keeps most of us from crossing the street in front of large, fast-moving trucks.

Hereditary, inherent characteristics are limited secondarily by impositions of the environment. Some of us are born with capacities to be more intelligent, creative, active, timid, placid, suspicious, tall, fat, inquisitive, or whatever. Some of us have a hereditary propensity for certain kinds of mental illness, for living longer, for contracting certain diseases, and the list goes on and on. Environmental factors, such as nutrition, parental expectation, educational opportunities, contagious diseases, and accidents limit the extent to which these traits are developed. The environment, therefore, can limit the development of certain characteristics; it cannot prevent their growth entirely, except in rare circumstances. A deprived environment can depress intelligence, but it cannot extinguish it. Conversely, an extremely good environment can help a retarded child maximize his potential, but it cannot lift him into the gifted range of intelligence.

Human characteristics are distributed along a continuum. According to a statistical theory (which may now be found invalid), if these characteristics were plotted they would assume a bell-shaped curve, with the greatest number of individuals represented by the peak of the curve. This peak is considered "normal." In some cases, an arbitrary number or term has been assigned to this peak, as in the case of intelligence, where the norm is considered to be 100 IQ points.

It should be obvious that "normal" does not necessarily mean "optimal." An IQ of 140 is better than an IQ of 100. In other cases, less than normal is considered more satisfactory, such as the child with less than a normal amount of curiosity who will probably be thought of as a model pupil and his parents' angel, because he doesn't ask too many questions.

It should also be fairly obvious that many human characteristics cannot be measured categorically and are defined arbitrarily, since the definitions are based on subjective reporting or evaluations. For instance, intelligence can be measured and defined to a certain extent. No one has been able to catalog the operants of what is called intelligence, nor are they able to define the constructs intelligence tests measure.

To put it briefly, then, there is a wide range of human behaviors and characteristics, and deviation from the norm is not necessarily bad, wrong, or sick. It can be better, acceptable, desirable, or just plain different—and it should also be permissible.

Hyperactivity is considered a deviation from the normal. Since the norm for activity has yet to be established (and I doubt that it can be, especially as purposeful, positive activity would have to be separated from purposeless, random activity), the definition of hyperactivity must depend on each individual's idea of what is normal.

OPTIMAL LEVELS OF STIMULATION

The second assumption is based on a theory which, when simplified, states that every individual has an optimal level of sensory stimulation and that the individual attempts to achieve this optimal level, which varies from individual to individual and fluctuates within an individual. Some people are postulated to require more stimulation than others to achieve this optimal state.

My hypothesis is that some of what is described as hyperkinetic behavior or overactivity is a reaction on the part of the individual to attain the optimal level of stimulation he requires at a given moment.

Some writers have used the word "hypereactive" to describe this response to what the individual may sense as an understimulating—in other words, boring—environment. I seriously considered using "hypereactive" in place of "hyperkinetic," but it seemed that there were already enough words being used to cloud the issue.

It's my contention that children do hypereact—because they crave stimulation and simply have not acquired the judgmental abilities to ponder the consequences of their acts. By the time they become aware that some of their behavior results in unhappy or negative consequences, patterns of behavior have been established that are extremely difficult to eradicate.

Adults who are understimulated—or just plain bored—usually find things to do that will compensate. An adult who is bored by his job can look for another job; however, a child who is bored in the classroom usually cannot look for another school.

DIAGNOSING HYPERKINESIS

The third assumption is that too many diagnoses of hyperkinesis are made on too little evidence by too many people who know nothing about the condition. As we shall see in

Chapter 5, a diagnosis of hyperkinesis must be based on a thorough examination of the child, complete with a personal history and school reports, and should be made by someone or several people with a thorough knowledge of the subject.

All too frequently a child who is hard to manage, at home or at school, or who exhibits a high activity level is diagnosed, on incomplete evidence, as hyperkinetic. Parents are likely to be given rather forceful directives, by physicians and school personnel, concerning the treatment of such children, based on sketchy evaluations. Sometimes the diagnosis is predicated on implications, not on an evaluation. It should be pointed out that many professionals, including physicians, teachers, guidance counselors, and psychologists, are not qualified to make a diagnosis of hyperkinesis because they lack training, knowledge, and direct experience with hyperkinetics.

The evaluation is only as good as the evaluator and his expertise, and both are always open to question by parents. Your family doctor might prescribe amphetamines for your child because his teacher says he is hyperkinetic and needs drug therapy to stay in school—an irresponsible practice that is discussed in Chapter 9. Neither may know a thing about hyperkinesis and its treatment, and parents have a right—and responsibility—to question their expertise. No treatment or therapy, of course, should be undertaken on the recommendation of someone who is not qualified to make a diagnosis.

Relative to the matter of evaluation, there are three other points that should be clarified. First, parents have the right to decide whether or not they think a particular program or therapy will benefit their child. Parents know their child better than anyone else, although some authorities think parents are evasive, forgetful, or out-and-out deceitful when reporting past events, which makes their input suspect. (Teacher reports are supposedly less subjective and, therefore, more accurate.) There are programs and therapies that are not effective with hyperkinetics, there are therapies that are not consistent with the goals and aims of the parents, and there are therapies that the parents will find are not beneficial to their particular child. There are also therapists, and I use the word loosely to cover the practice of psychiatry, psychology, education, and medicine, who are so closely tied into their individual theories of therapy that they can't see the forest for the trees.

Which brings us to the second point: the individual therapist. There are therapists who are superb, and some who are competent; there are incompetent therapists, and there are a few who should have been hung years ago. (Therapists are also people who can make honest mistakes in judgment, but that's another matter entirely.) Estimating the professional competence of a person evaluating or treating your child is a problem of the first magnitude and will be considered in Chapter 4.

The third point concerns the content and extent of the evaluation itself. What components go into an adequate, accurate, *safe* evaluation? Each case is individual and different, as unique as the child himself. As a rule, the less severe the symptoms, the more rigorous and thorough the evaluation should be. A classical case of true hyperkinesis, which occurs infrequently, is pretty easy to determine on evaluation.

A complete evaluation includes an extensive medical evaluation, with a neurological examination if indicated. There are authorities who feel that a neurological exam doesn't help establish whether or not the patient is hyperkinetic. This is probably true, but it will rule out other possibilities, such as brain lesions. Other components needed are psychological testing and interviews, case histories from parents and teachers, and examinations by specialists (such as speech and hearing therapists and specialists in visual problems). A complete battery of tests is not always necessary, but it's better to rule out relatively simple, easy-to-treat problems before accepting the label of "hyperkinetic." For instance, wide fluctuations in blood sugar, as in hypoglycemia, can cause erratic mood swings and manifest itself in unacceptable behavior. Pinworms can make it impossible for a child to sit still for very long.

A superficial physical examination is not likely to uncover physiological impairments or dysfunctions that might affect the behavior of a child. In a similar vein, cursory psychological testing is almost always inconclusive.

Psychoeducational tests, measuring devices, and scales are the psychologist's tools of the trade. The sum of the results of such tests is a profile of the individual tested: They provide indications—signposts—as to what is going on within the individual. Somehow, though, the whole is still greater than the sum of its parts, and the individual is a lot more than the numbers obtained by adding his test results.

There are good testing devices and bad testing devices and some that don't even make any sense. There are many books on the subject of psychological tests—what they mean and don't mean, what to look for, what they can measure and what they purport to measure, and how their validity was established in the first place. All of them advise caution when interpreting test results. Test results and scores are open to interpretation by the tester. Heaven defend us all from those who trust whole-heartedly numerical results and their own interpretation without being able to see the child as a totality apart from his scores.

The trend toward mass testing or screening of preschool children is a little scary. Just what is it that we hope to accomplish by screening all preschool children? Are we really going to "fix" all of them or are we just going to label them and forget them?

Major disabilities will, hopefully, be detected in due course. As for minor disabilities, there are some interesting questions. Where will all the therapists come from? Who will pay for these programs? (I doubt that they will survive too many requests for larger and larger appropriations.) How good are the tools used to diagnose, treat, and remedy disabilities? We have yet to prove that we can adequately deal with—and provide funding for programs for—children with major handicaps and disabilities.

Some authorities view with alarm the tendency to tinker with children, as if they were cars with faulty carburetors, and fix up all their problems. In the meantime, there are some people who think the emphasis is on the wrong aspect of the problem and, rather than spending time and money diagnosing children, it would be better to spend our efforts on providing better screening devices, better training for the adults who work with children, better research, and better therapeutic techniques.

THE PARENT-CHILD RELATIONSHIP

The fourth and last assumption concerns the emphasis of this book. Most writers on the subject of hyperkinesis neglect one very important aspect—the parent-child relationship, which is usually the first thing that falls apart when a child behaves inappropriately or doesn't live up to expectations. It is accepted that a chaotic, tense, angry environment aggravates the condition and makes the child's behavior worse. The fact that the behavior of the hyperkinetic child creates much of that chaos, tension, and anger seems to be overlooked.

Yet the parent must be the child's first line of defense. No one else can help him if his parents can't or have given up and won't try. (It doesn't matter if you give up three times a day, as long as you keep trying.)

This book is concerned with what parents can do to help themselves while they try to help their child, so that some of the love, acceptance, concern, and approval can survive the chaos, tension, and anger.

Perennial parenting is tedious. Parents are not superhuman. They are ordinary, fallible creatures who, in the normal course of events, make a lot of mistakes, do a lot of things that they shouldn't, and never get around to doing some things they ought to. Even small mistakes can assume overwhelming proportions in the sometimes strained relationship between parents and a hyperkinetic child.

When a "problem child" becomes the focus of family life, the problem has become institutionalized, which means that, without much foreseeable change, it is likely to be around for a long time. Too often, all parental energy and attention are devoted to this child, to the detriment of other children—not to mention the parents' own interests and abilities and their relationship to each other. (It would be interesting to research the question of how many divorces a problem child has triggered.)

A parent who devotes all his energy to his problem child soon hasn't much left to give the child except more of the problem. Since the child is hard to manage, the parent tries harder and harder to manage the child. Paradoxically, the same amount of effort devoted to helping the child learn to manage himself would have some positive payoff.

The child is *not* a formless lump of clay which the parents or other adults can mold to their wishes. The parent does not "act" on his child. The parent and child interact, with the child doing his own "acting" at least 50 percent of the time. (Sometimes 75 percent, depending on the child.) The child has an individual personality, with his own predilections and preferences. Children are not "small" adults. They neither think nor act as adults do, nor should they be expected to. The child is not a domestic animal or a wild beast. He can be taught, but he cannot be trained. Children are young, inexperienced people who have a lot to learn about adult concepts of responsibility, consequences, right and wrong, and other notions.

Since they are people, children have rights, which often conflict with parental rights but do not negate parental rights. (It's fairly obvious that the parents and the hyperactive child will have a problem establishing priorities on rights). The child should not be allowed to tyrannize his parents, nor should the parents infringe on the child's rights.

Everybody has a right to be himself, within limitations, to learn what he is, and to make what he can of himself. Learning to be oneself is the process known as adjustment. Adjustment does not mean learning to be like somebody else, or conforming to another's patterns of behavior. It means learning to handle the individual's special abilities and vulnerabilities within the limitations imposed by society.

Unfortunately, "adjustment" is a word like "agreement" or "cooperation." It is often taken to mean "You should do what I want you to do." Everybody makes adjustments on a continual basis, some good and some not so good. There are situations to which some individuals cannot or have a hard time making adjustments. Inability to adjust to a specific situation is not necessarily an indication that there's something wrong with the individual. There may be something wrong with the situation.

I also think it's perfectly all right for a person not to like some other people. I refuse to believe it's healthy to teach a child he should like everybody. People do conflict and there are personality clashes. Adults have learned tolerance and avoidance techniques. The devices for avoiding personal contact with other people are not intuitive, and tolerance is acquired only after many years of experience. A child who doesn't like other people is apt to be direct and abrasive. Perhaps we would be more effective in helping the child learn to control his behavior if we stressed social amenities, and let him make up his own mind whom he likes and dislikes.

While we're on the subject of likes and dislikes, let me briefly mention the typical parental reaction to hyperkinetic children, which is apt to be one of dislike. It's difficult for parents of hyperkinetics to separate the child from his behavior and to remember that they like the child while disapproving of his behavior. (Keep in mind that it's probably more difficult for the child to understand this concept. It becomes virtually impossible for him to understand once he enters school and is confronted by teachers and peers who won't even try to separate him from his behavior and will, therefore, reject him in totality.)

I'm not sure it's realistic to separate a person from his behavior, and it's quite possible that when we tell ourselves that we separate the person (whom we love) from the behavior (which offends us), we're just not quite honest about the whole thing. I think it's more honest—and it should not be guilt-provoking—to admit that a child's behavior has exasperated us to the point where we simply can't take any more of him, for the time being, at least, rather than to insist we love the child when we are on the verge of homicide.

Parental reaction to the hyperkinetic child is apt to be both angry (punitive) and excessive. Since most parents know the child needs their love and approval (which they do not show very often) and doesn't need their anger and excesses (which he probably sees a lot of), parents wind up with an almost overwhelming burden of guilt. I have found that guilt is a useless commodity. Besides being useless, guilt is mighty uncomfortable. I think parents of difficult, hard-to-manage children must rid themselves of many of their guilt feelings before they can realistically appraise themselves in relation to their child.

While I advocate that parents be honest with themselves, being brutually honest with the child is not always the best policy. Keeping quiet may be. When the parent has punished the child for misbehavior and he screams at him, "You don't love me! You hate me!" maybe it would be better to turn and walk quietly away rather than to stop and think about it.

On the whole, it's sometimes difficult to restrain a torrent of opinion, feelings, a list of 300 things the kid has done wrong, and downright abuse. (No, you won't feel better if you cut loose. You'll probably feel guilty and miserable later.) It's far better to keep the issue at hand sharply defined with a minimum of verbiage. Lengthy bouts of arguments, debates, and reasoning should be avoided. When the child says, "The world hates me!" neither three million reasons nor a lengthy, logical argument will convince him he's wrong. Maybe he isn't. Nor is it particularly helpful to point out the many things he does to make the world shun him, no matter how justified the parent may momentarily feel.

Parents of hyperkinetic children usually have a lot to feel guilty about; they carry around more than their share of bad feelings. Many of these feelings are unrealistic and unjustified, based as they frequently are on an idealized concept of parenting.

Trying to help parents get rid of bad feelings—guilt, inadequacy, anger, frustration—is really the whole point of this book.

2 Naming the Game

NAMES AND LABELS

If I had to define the word "label" as it applies to people, I would say it is a definition by function which, on a societal basis, implements communication, in that it enables one person to communicate with another on a relatively impersonal basis without first having to determine what that person is or what he does.

Labels are quite handy. I don't have to spend a lot of time getting to know people to find out what it is they can do for me. My ophthalmologist examines my eyes; the electrician fixes the wiring; the mechanic replaces worn brake shoes; etc. Given the right label, I can have reasonable expectations as to how these people will function for my purposes, and that is all I need to know as long as they function on a reasonable level of competence.

Other labels are broader and, although based on function, include emotional responses predicated on the roles and responses expected from someone so designated: mother, sister, husband, child, daughter, and father.

Then, there are labels that designate, or purport to designate, a particular level of functioning: genius, retarded, schizophrenic, immature, adult, underachiever, learning disabled, hyperactive. All these labels describe a deviation from the norm—in most cases, an unacceptable deviation.

Such labels are intrinsically dangerous because they don't give enough information about the person labeled. They are used to pigeonhole people, not to define them. The danger lies in the kinds of expectations we come to attach to the people so labeled. A mildly retarded child and one who is severely impaired do not function on the same level, and it would be grossly unfair to expect the severely retarded child to perform as well as the mildly retarded child. It's also unfair to expect the mildly retarded child to do less well than he is capable of doing, simply because he is retarded. There are many other reasons to reject the entire concept of labeling based on level of functioning, especially the labeling of children.

The problems inherent in the classification of children have reached such proportions that the Department of Health, Education and Welfare has undertaken an extensive and fairly comprehensive study of labels used for children, and we shall have to wait and see how they eventually resolve the issue. In the meantime, Nicholas Hobbs has written a fascinating book entitled *The Futures of Children,* which should be required reading for all parents, teachers, specialists, and professionals who work with children. Hobbs, discussing some of the subjects that can be only briefly summarized here, writes:

> Classification and labeling serve several purposes not immediately obvious: to maintain the stability of the community and of its institutions, to control the allocation of resources and govern access to them, to reduce discord in school and neighborhood, to preserve majority values and expectations, and to allay anxiety generated by the presence of a deviant individual (pp. 19–20).
>
> . . . children themselves can be profoundly affected by categorical labels and the expectations generated by them. To call a broken bone broken never widened a fracture . . . But to say that a child is mentally retarded, or emotionally disturbed, or antisocial, or even visually handicapped is to require him, in

some measure, to be so. To some indeterminate extent, labeling requires behavior appropriate to the label (p. 20).

What these observations add up to is this: There is a substantial community-serving component in policies and procedures for classification and labeling exceptional children and in the various kinds of institutional arrangements made to take care of them. "To take care of them" can and should be read with two meanings: to give children help and *to exclude them from the community.* [italics added.] (p. 21).

Labeling is dangerous, destructive, counterproductive, and pointless. Any possible benefits accruing from a classification system are immediately voided by the harm done.

Classification systems have no inherent value, except to statisticians, whose main concern is numbers, not people. Commonly, professionals attach labels to people to enable them to better understand the situation and therefore propose appropriate treatment. This is pure and simple nonsense, unless one believes that all hyperkinetics are alike, that each paranoid is like every other paranoid, and that all delinquents are carbon copies of each other.

WHAT IS HYPERKINESIS?

Whatever hyperkinesis is, it's not a unified entity. The medically oriented, and some other professionals, tend to regard it as a disease syndrome. But hyperkinesis is *not* a disease. Leprosy is a disease. Medical appellations have so far helped to solidify the "differentness" of the hyperkinetic child in the public's mind. Further obfuscation of the subject is achieved by the use of various designations by professionals to describe similar symptoms. Medicine leans toward "minimal brain dysfunction," with a few still throwing out the horrifying "minimal brain damage" to stupefied parents. Education tends to use "learning disabilities." "Hyperactivity," "hyperkinetic," "overactivity," and "hyperkinetic impulse disorder" are used by many, often interchangeably. To find out what is meant by any of the designations, one must ascertain what behaviors or symptoms each individual thinks of when using a particular designation.

This is almost impossible. To date, over 500 separate behaviors, symptoms, and characteristics are subsumed under the general heading "hyperkinesis–learning disability–minimal brain dysfunction." Some of the many, and seemingly contradictory, symptoms are:

hyperactivity (overly active)
hypoactivity (underly active, listless)
spotty intellectual deficits
irregular intellectual achievements
high incidence of left and mixed laterality (left-handedness or ambidextrousness)
confused perception of laterality (right versus left)
general awkwardness
slowness in finishing work
reading disabilities
spelling disabilities
writing disabilities
speech disorders
visual disorders
psychomotor disorders
easy fatigability
thumb sucking
nail biting
head banging
teeth grinding
slow to toilet train
explosive
low tolerance for frustration
sleep abnormally light
sleep abnormally deep
socially bold and aggressive
antisocial behavior
physically immature
physically advanced
very sensitive to others
poor adjustments in large groups
poor peer relationships
impaired ability to make choices, particularly among many choices
failures in living
propensity to feel stress
inability to appraise adequately
inability to plan realistically
stress-prone
inattentiveness
short attention span
short interest span
not able to persist at abstract tasks
distractibility
impulsiveness
poor motor integration
deficit in perception of movement
deficit in perception of time
deficit in perception of space and form
aggressive
greedy
impatient

cruel to animals
prone to temper tantrums
overreliant on companionship
inability to postpone gratification
jealous
jerky
twitchy
temperamental
stubborn
independent
academic lag
belligerent
disobedient
fights more than normal
quarrels with siblings
immature
difficulty in coping with changes
renders drawings of people simplistically
persistent in baby talk
generally more fearful
low self-esteem
emotional deviance
more anxious
defiant
unable to take correction
inability to complete projects
difficult to get to bed
hard to get to sleep
wakes early
dances, wiggles hands
leaves classroom without permission
moves from one activity to another
unpopular with peers
talks too much
wears out toys and other objects
breaks things
gets into things
unpredictable
unresponsive to discipline
destructive
meddlesome
accident prone
clumsy
unable to control himself
socially immature
inclined to daydream
negativistic
erratic
excitable
withdrawn
lacks social perception
tendency to perseration (repetitive action)
nonadaptability
bad dreams or nightmares
bed wetting
demanding
lies
steals
cheats
masturbates
compulsive
impaired sphincter control
sexual acting-out
fire-setting
clinging
diminished pain response
inclined to regress
unable to experience pleasure
insatiable
unable to organize hierarchically
bossy
impervious
resists acculturation (socialization)
self-centered
makes weird sounds

hard to manage
always on the go
sassy
controlling
resists control
clingingly affectionate
touch-me-not
impervious
scholastic underachiever
tends to stereotyped behavior
persistent
irresponsible
not adaptable
intense in reaction
facility for projecting blame onto others
doesn't understand punishment
inclined to nag and whine
need explicit directions
easy to fool; gullible
asks a lot of questions
chooses friends who are younger than himself
worries excessively
selfish
episodes of high fever
runs away
voice poorly modulated
migraine headaches
episodic violence
lack of drive
poor posture
hair twiddling, skin picking
inappropriate voice tones; flat tones
inappropriate sexual patterns
digestive problems
excellent memory
can't see wholes, only fragment
unable to discard irrelevancies
unable to reason
poor value judgments
unable to organize
unable to sustain efforts
poor sense of humor
lack of imagination
nervous
shallow
doesn't assume responsibilities
tends to psychotic decompensations
incapable of empathic reactions
needs certainty
compulsively touches things
cannot be diverted from an action
does things dangerous to self and others
panics easily
can't cope with new situations
uses irregular grammar or incomplete sentences
has difficulty relating experiences
confused by large group activity

The items in this list were taken verbatim from various articles and books on the subject of hyperkinesis. I've tried to eliminate duplication and retain as much of the original meaning as I could.

Having read the list, would you say your child was hyperkinetic? (Having read the list, would it not be possible to say that, at one time or another, we are all or have been or will be hyperkinetic?)

The imprecise use of insignificant verbiage ("emotional deviance" and "failures in living") makes it more difficult to define hyperkinesis. A stubborn, independent, bossy, impervious child is not necessarily hyperkinetic, although he may be hard to manage. Is he likely to be called hyperkinetic? Possibly.

At the same time, more and more children are demonstrating the hyperactivity, distractibility, and impulsivity commonly associated with the impairment, without evidence of any physiological and/or psychomotor deficits. Can it be that children, as Hobbs pointed out, gradually acquire the characteristics we expect them actually to have when we label them hyperkinetic? Is it simply a case of more and more professionals recognizing the symptoms as hyperkinesis, or are they making mistaken diagnoses? Is a new, environmental factor creating an outbreak of hyperkinesis among our children? Or is it some combination of these factors?

The truth of the matter is that not much is known about hyperkinesis, except for the most severe cases. Because of the great interest in the subject (and, I might add, advances in fields which might throw some light on the subject, such as genetics, biochemistry, and neurology), no doubt research will answer many of today's pressing questions in the foreseeable future. In the meantime, let's take a look at what is known, with the understanding that research is just as likely to prove me in error as not.

The disorders, loosely grouped under the term "hyperkinesis–learning disability" are probably not a single entity but several separate impairments, closely related, varying in degree, but sharing no common cause, cure, or treatment. Some of the impairments overlap; some do not. Many authorities feel that the causes of the disorder are physiological. Many of them see the cause as a dysfunctioning of the brain, which is the result of organic damage, detectable or not. (See, we haven't come very far from "minimal brain damage" after all.)

There are, decidedly, many correlations between

hyperkinesis and a variety of other impairments: abnormal EEGs (recording of brain waves), soft and/or hard neurological signs (such as poor development of fine muscle control, clumsiness, etc.), learning disabilities, psychomotor disturbances (an inability to coordinate action with thought), a history of epileptic seizures, and signs of neurological delay. A positive genetic history (evidence that other members of the family had similar impairments) correlates with hyperkinesis in about one-third of the cases studied.

Correlations also exist between hyperkinesis and such prenatal, birth, and postnatal conditions as difficult birth, oxygen deprivation at birth or shortly thereafter, maternal nutrition, maternal infection, maternal medication (drugs obtained by prescription or otherwise), smoking during pregnancy, infant trauma or infection, prematurity, low birth weight, and more. It is generally supposed that one of these factors, when it occurs, by causing a minimal amount of damage to the brain, produces hyperkinesis. Since there are many more children who have survived such occurrences without incidence of hyperkinesis than there are children who have not, the matter may not be quite so simple. It is important to remember that correlation does not imply a cause-and-effect relationship between one factor and another. Two factors can exist side by side without one being the direct cause of the other.

Classic or textbook cases of hyperkinesis do exist. Although they are few and far between, it is probably a good idea for parents to know something about true hyperkinesis. The classic condition has three components: hyperkinesis with its accompanying behavior characteristics (also known as hyperkinetic impulse disorder), soft neurological signs, and learning disabilities. Any child can have one, two, or three of these distinct components.

SYMPTOMS OF TRUE HYPERKINESIS

The purpose of the following discussion of distinct symptoms is to make the problem manageable for parents so that they can insist upon a specific diagnosis of *actual impairments,* stressing degrees of impairment, and look for realistic treatment suitable to the degree and kind of deficit.

Hyperkinetic Behavior

More than 50 percent of children labeled hyperkinetic evidence no signs of learning disabilities or neurological involvement. Estimates vary, of course, from researcher to reseacher, but with the growing awareness of the condition and its symptoms, it's likely that more children will be diagnosed on the basis of their behavior, especially their school behavior, alone.

The ingredients of hyperkinetic impulse disorder naturally vary from individual to individual and fluctuate from day to day. And there's a lot of disagreement about what actually constitutes a symptom. The following are commonly thought to be essential components of the disorder:

Hyperactivity, both physical and verbal. This means not only more activity and restlessness but also the inability to engage in specific activities or stay with a particular object or activity at appropriate times. The fact that a high degree of activity, when it is purposeful, meaningful, and directed, is not necessarily a form of hyperactivity is becoming accepted and understood. Such activity is not a cause for concern. It is only purposeless, undirected activity that need give us pause.

It's important to make the distinction between unfocused activity when one is doing something one wants to do, and unfocused activity when one must do what one doesn't want to do. Certainly, it's a lot easier to concentrate on an activity that is interesting or amusing or has some other rewarding components. It's a lot harder to concentrate or focus on a dull, repetitious, or otherwise uninteresting task, especially if it's the kind of activity that's being done simply because "it has to be done." Children are often expected to focus their attention when it's really not easy for them to do so. Some of the demands made on children to sit still and be quiet, stop fidgeting, etc., may be completely out of line with the child's age, abilities, and requirements. My sympathies are with the bored-to-tears six-year-old terror who can't sit still, not with his underactive, understimulating teacher or his inconvenienced, irritated-by-all-this-fidgeting parents. I recognize the need for the child to learn the acceptable behaviors that every other child must learn. But why these particular behaviors—sitting still and being quiet—have to be such end-alls is a little beyond my comprehension, unless it has to do with adult convenience.

Poor impulse control. This includes the inability to tolerate frustration or to delay gratification, poor judgmental and planning abilities, recklessness, and the inability to perceive consequences, and accounts for much of the so-called antisocial behavior. In other words, even in situations where the child knows what he should or should not do, he is unable to control his behavior. He acts instantaneously without reflection of any kind. It's as though the decision-making processes were short-circuited, resulting in a direct relay from impulse to action.

There is almost never a conscious decision involved in this child's impulsive behavior. One should avoid the mistake of blaming him for wrongdoing as though he made a deliberate decision to act wrongly. Yes, he knows he shouldn't hit the kids smaller than himself. Then, why did he do it? There's probably no reason, he just did it. If he had stopped long enough to think about it, he likely would have remembered that it was wrong and might not have done it.

Short attention span and high level of distractibility. These two are, for all intents and purposes, indistinguishable. Both derive, I believe, from the child's inability to focus his concentration on any one object or activity. If his cognitive abilities were focusable, he would have a longer attention span and be less distractible.

Since the child is unabel to focus, he is distracted by the most minor external or internal stimuli: another toy, another child, someone talking, something he sees outside the window, his own thoughts and reactions, almost anything. It's easy to see how this distractibility becomes a serious handicap in school.

This tendency, plus a high activity level, results in the kinds of behaviors that drive parents to distraction. The child rushes from one activity to other, appropriate or inappropriate, good, bad, or indifferent. The harder parents try to get him to settle down to peaceful, purposeful activity, the more frenzied his activities may become.

Increased emotionality or lability. Lability means that the child reacts more violently, often unpredictably, with spontaneous mood swings predicated on minimal stimuli. Lability is associated with the inability to control impulses, and it is difficult to distinguish one from the other. Either one or both of them result in the aggressive acting-out behavior that is often the chief complaint of those who must cope with the child. There is a tendency to overexcitability, irritability, and seemingly compulsive behavior.

Since these children recognize the unacceptableness of their behavior, much of the overexcitability and irritability seems to stem directly from their tremendous efforts to stop and redirect their activities, which, when coupled with external stimulation, can result in increased tension, escalating excitability, and activity.

It has been said that the hyperkinetic child has weak "ego boundaries" and cannot see himself as a distinct entity with limitations and with control over the entity without these boundaries. My feeling is that, on the contrary, the child distinguishes himself and his unacceptable behavior easily and is definitely aware of the effect his behavior has on the rest of the world. Increased awareness tends to make the child extremely preoccupied with the complicated mechanics of his behavior and their results, and he gradually becomes more and more self-centered, unable to appraise the effects of his behavior realistically. He becomes extremely negativistic, overly sensitive to criticism, disapproval, and rejection directed toward him, angry and bitter at his lack of success, and more inclined to emotionality—as does anyone who finds themselves in a situation where failure is guaranteed.

Resistance to acculturation. This fine-sounding phrase means the child is hard to manage, resists pressure to conform to adult standards of behavior (principally because he can't conform), and generally doesn't do what other people think he ought to. He is often described as being controlling, independent, and obstinate and probably develops these tendencies out of self-defense. I seriously doubt that most of these children are as independent as they seem or are comfortable with this pseudoindependence. It is more likely that they haven't learned techniques for seeking approval and support in socially approved ways.

Some authorities go on endlessly with lists of deficits and symptoms that seem to me to be secondary effects of a hyperkinetic condition rather than true symptoms. For instance, poor interpersonal relationships are often mentioned as being an integral part of hyperkinesis. It seems obvious that relationships will degenerate as a direct result of the child's behavior and in time it will be difficult for him to establish good relationships. Two things are required before a person can effectively negotiate good relationships: first, he must know how; second, he must have some successes on which to base his expectations. The child who has seldom, if ever, found himself in a good, solid, successful relationship does not know how to achieve one, and he doesn't expect anything different from what he already has experienced—irritation, anger, disapproval, hostility, rejection, and disappointment.

Similarly, low self-esteem is frequently mentioned in connection with hyperkinesis. Since I can't accept the premise that a child is born with low self-esteem, I must conclude that he grew that way—as a result of his interaction with others from whom he did not acquire the self-image of a successful, accepted person.

It is most difficult to sort out causes and effects, especially as the child gets older. Eventually, many hyperkinetic children develop emotional problems that are hard to distinguish from the neurotic and psychotic. It is always important to keep the newly acquired problem behavior sharply demarcated from the original set of symptomatic behaviors. Without this demarcation, too often the treatment is aimed at the new symptoms and not at the original cause. As an example, working on a child's poor self-concept may be beneficial, but not so beneficial as helping him correct the behavior that resulted in the negative interactions that decreased his self-esteem.

This emotional overlay has serious implications for the treatment of the older hyperkinetic child. ("Older" means any age past infancy.) Confusing the original hyperactivity and impulsive behavior with learned responses such as anxiety, a negative self-image, or attention-seeking behavior is easy to do. The difficulties of distinguishing primary factors from secondary emotional disturbances should never be understated.

Learning Disabilities

Hyperkinesis is a common cause of school underachievement, but it is not a specific, definable learning disability. Major learning disabilities, on the whole, are somewhat easier to diagnose because the diagnostic tools are available and because the disabilities can usually be objectively observed and are amenable to treatment. Many minor disabilities are never diagnosed, treated, or corrected.

As I have said, the hyperkinetic child may be learning disabled. The child with learning disabilities may or may not be hyperkinetic. A learning-disabled child who is hyperkinetic is more apt to receive attention, most of it unfriendly, than one who is either hypoactive (quiet, underactive) or more typical in activity levels. The hypoactive child is likely to be passed on from teacher to teacher, grade by grade, without his problems being treated or corrected, despite the fact that he cannot do the work and is therefore not being educated. A little intervention and treatment in the early grades can often make all the difference in the world.

Learning disabilities come in many shapes and sizes, and in all degrees and combinations. There are many educational specialists and psychologists who have been trained to diagnose and treat specific disabilities. The federal government is currently pouring a lot of money into special programs designed for children with handicaps such as learning disabilities. Many school districts that have never had programs before are delighted to institute programs for such children, procuring monies from the government based on the size and extent of the program. This is all wonderful, except that often a lot of people are involved who really don't know what they're doing. Those who work in specialized areas such as mental retardation or learning disabilities must, or should have, the proper training and knowledge. Since the accelerated press for special education programs is a recent phenomenon, specialists are in short supply. Administrators with experience and/or knowledge of the field are even rarer. Suddenly, a teacher who twenty years ago took a few courses in remedial reading is considered a specialist in diagnosing and treating learning disabilities. Even with the best intentions in the world, school districts suffer from a lack of qualified personnel, lack of expertise in setting up and running such programs, and the conservative and prevalent notion that special education is reserved for the stupid, the sick, and the damaged, who should be set apart from normal children and never allowed back in the classroom, thus avoiding the risk of contamination. The temptation to get federal funds, considering the rates of dropping enrollments and school closings, while at the same time justifying the school system's existence, is irresistible.

Nevertheless, children with specific learning disabilities need specific treatment, and where and how they get such treatment, how best to get it while avoiding social stigma and arriving at the best possible course of treatment, are problems that must be attacked by parents.

The first hurdle to overcome is to understand the vocabulary. It is unfortunate that many specialists do not take the time to explain the technical jargon to parents—or use it to mask their own deficiencies. I remember vividly the mother of a child who had not learned to read telling me with obvious relief that the problem had been diagnosed:

"He has dyslexia." When questioned, the parent could give no concrete information as to how severe the problem was, exactly *what* the problem was and how it affected the child's ability to read, how it could be remedied, and what, if anything, she might do to help. Nor had she been told if there was a specific treatment program available for her child, where to look for help, or whether or not remediation would correct the problem, partially or totally. The professional who met with this parent should have, of course, been prepared to give her at least some of this information. (If nobody tells you, ask!)

Without going into the many configurations and combinations of specific disabilities, let's look at the main categories.

Anomia, a spelling disorder. Whether the child can or cannot spell correctly in his mind, the message doesn't get through in oral or written form.

Aphasia (dysphasia), a language disorder. There are basically four different aspects of aphasia. The child cannot (1) understand or (2) express either (3) spoken or (4) written language.

Apraxia (dyspraxia), a psychomotor disorder. The child is unable to translate sensory input into motor activity—or the appropriate motor activity. This can result in poor visual-motor coordination, general clumsiness, or poor fine or gross muscle control.

Diplopia, double vision.

Dysarthria, a defect in articulation or speaking. The child may have difficulty prounouncing certain sounds or he may have problems putting his thoughts into words, and anything in between.

Dysgraphia (agraphia), a writing disability. The child may be unable to translate ideas into written words or sounds.

Dyslexia (alexia), a reading disability. Like green paint, dyslexia covers almost everything. The child may be word-blind or unable to distinguish left and right, or he may see everything as a mirror image. Dyslexia includes many specific disorders such as aphasia and anomia, and many more that are less common. To say a child is dyslexic says very little, without evaluation of the specific deficit and its severity.

There are many other specific dysfunctions, such as perseveration (the inability to shift from one stimuli to another), disassociation (the inability to organize things into unities or wholes), and figure-ground pathology (the inability to discriminate the figure from the background). Besides these, there are disabilities in the integration of perceptions, malfunctioning in the process symbolized by: sensory input → integration → output. The sensory input may be totally sound, but the flaw lies somewhere between the input and the response (output).

Reading and writing disabilities are fairly well understood, and a good deal is known about remediation. Auditory and cognitive dysfunctions are relative obscurities, probably because they are almost impossible to measure, hard to evaluate, not amenable to easy remediation, and less common than some of the other disabilities.

The potential for semantic difficulties is apparent. The learning disability must be carefully analyzed and measured if appropriate treatment is to be initiated. The extent and type of treatment depends on the severity of the disability and how much it affects the total child. Many children have overcome and compensated for learning disabilities which were never detected. However benign, neglect is not to be recommended. The child will develop his own compensatory techniques in time, some of which will be more trouble than the original problem. The younger the child when treatment is initiated, the better the chance for a total cure. It would be better for everybody if the child spent a year in speech therapy or remedial reading in first grade rather than undergo four years of partially successful therapy in high school.

Neurological Involvement

Very few children diagnosed as hyperkinetic give evidence of neurological involvement or impairment. However, cases of true or classic hyperkinesis usually evidence some neurological dysfunctioning, subsumed under the heading "soft neurological signs." (It is important to make a distinction between "brain damage" and "brain dysfunction." Damage, on the whole, can be ascertained through examination, and the site of damage can usually be demonstrated, e.g., in cases of severe cerebral palsy. Dysfunction is most frequently presumed to exist not because of neurological evidence deduced from examination, but from symptomology.)

The soft neurological signs are impaired visual-motor coordination (eye-hand, for example), poor balance, body rigidity, clumsiness, poor fine or coarse muscle coordination, inability to eye-track, strabismus (one or both eyes turn in or out), choreaform movement (spasmodic or twitchy, jerky movements), lack of laterality (not markedly left- or right-handed), and others not so frequently found. Many of the neurological signs relate to a specific learning disability and are presumed to be more or less the cause of the disability.

Neurological signs are more likely to be present in children in whom hyperkinesis and/or learning disabilities are pronounced, although there are exceptions to every rule.

Some children with either hyperkinesis or learning disabilities have abnormal EEG's. However, only about 60 percent of children with mild to moderate EEG abnormalities demonstrate any other symptoms of a hyperkinetic or learning-disabled condition.

Rarely does the neurological examination of a hard-to-manage child define or localize any malfunctioning or deficit. Despite some opinions to the contrary, what the neurologist can't tell us is quite important. An inconclusive neurological report should direct our attention to other factors. Sometimes, knowing what isn't wrong is nearly as important as knowing what is.

Of course, the lack of findings from a neurological examination does not mean the child is perfectly allright. It simply means that the parents ought to continue to try to isolate the physiological or environmental factors that are aggravating, if not causing, the child's behavior.

Why are neurological examinations rarely definite? I suspect that there are two reasons. First, there's still a great deal that has to be learned about the brain itself, its functioning, chemistry, and peculiarities. Second, neurological measuring devices may need to be refined and improved, and more information must be compiled against which individual measurements can be compared. Too many people regarded as functional and normal have abnormal EEG's and other so-called neurological signs. Obviously, there's a tremendous need for a great deal of research and refinement.

I would like to add a word of caution. Parents considering neurological examination for their children should rely on well-qualified, experienced neurologists, preferably those with training or experience in pediatrics. There are a deplorable number of handbooks in circulation at the moment, which attempt to promote the local doctor as a combined neurologist, special education diagnostician, psychologist, and social worker, all rolled into one handsome package.* The possession of an M.D. or Ph.D. does not confer special powers on any one; it takes specialized training and experience to make a specialist.

ARE YOU HYPERKINETIC?

What, then, is hyperkinesis? Many functional normal people, including you and me, could be labeled hyperkinetic, depending on the particular diagnostician's list of symptoms and types of indexes used. The world is filled with

* Since getting copies of several of the neurological examination data included in these handbooks, I have persuaded everybody I know to perform some of the tests suggested as indicative of soft signs. Nearly everybody I know, all of whom are reasonably intelligent and functional people, have a problem "passing" some of the tests. As an example, see how well you do on this one: Close your eyes. Extend your arms at shoulder height directly out to the sides. Now, with your eyes tightly closed, attempt to make the tips of your index fingers touch directly in front of you as you bring your hands around in front of you with arms still extended.

people who have a wide range of deficits, dysfunctions, talents, abilities, personalities, temperaments, strengths, and weaknesses who have had to learn how to put it all together and live as successfully as possible. If one accepts the fact that people are all different, that each individual is unique, then one must accept the fact of divergent behavior. If we are all unique, then we do indeed live in our separate realities. To attempt to define and catalog these realities is pernicious in the extreme, particularly when the definitions are as subjective as the realities.

Having established that a lot of us are hyperkinetic, the next thing to ask is whether being hyperkinetic is so bad? Frankly, such children have a lot going for them. On the positive side, they are usually direct and forthright. They have unusual stamina and energy. They are generally pretty fearless, which ought to be a good thing to be. They are inclined to be independent and assertive and are more likely to be controllers than controllees, which are all qualities admired in adults. They are usually bright, very inquisitive, quite inventive and creative, extremely perceptive, and sensitive. They are deeply affectionate and fiercely loyal to those they love. They are generally strong-willed and do-or-die determined people. They are physically strong and adept. They will try anything and are capable of intense efforts to do whatever they set out to do. They are exuberant, boisterous, and a lot of fun, and if those aren't good qualities, I'll be double damned.

The next time somebody offers to tell you how awful or abnormal or troublesome your child is, count up all his good points, the really marvelous things he can do, and just start enumerating them one by one in great detail. Tell how you're astounded by his intellectual curiosity, how you marvel at all the things he can do on his own, how he puts the strangest things together and makes incredible inventions. This technique is not guaranteed to encourage further discussion, but it usually makes the parents feel a lot better. (Besides, it doesn't hurt to remind yourself that the kid isn't all bad.)

Whatever the reasons, no one has bothered to count

and document the positive, good characteristics of the hyperkinetic child. Yet, the good points are what parents must work with. Concentrating on eradicating or changing inappropriate, unacceptable behavior results in painting a very negativistic, one-sided picture of the child—for ourselves, for him, and for others. It's far healthier to help develop the positive aspects of his personality. The emphasis should be on increasing the attention span, not reducing distractions; teaching the child reflective techniques, rather than trying to stop his impulsiveness; helping him accept his differences, rather than enlarging on them; helping him find and expand his capabilities, rather than harping on his deficits and weaknesses.

To accept the fact that the child is hyperkinetic—with or without learning disabilities or neurological deficits—is completely different from a passive acceptance that to be hyperkinetic is terribly wrong. So, the kid's hyperkinetic. So what? The immediate, solvable problem is not that the child is hyperkinetic. The immediate problem is what can be done to help him.

RESISTANCE OR DENIAL?

By resisting the implications of labels, categories, and diagnoses, I do not mean to minimize the problems associated with hyperkinesis. These problems are very real. They are not trivialities that can be outgrown or treated offhandedly. They are usually serious, long-term problems. Over the years, the orchestration may change, but the tune remains familiar: New problems arise from the original disorder.

Resistance to labeling is not the same as denial of the problem. To resist labels is to hold open the doors of opportunity and growth. To deny the problem's existence is to slam the door and lock it from both sides.

Further, to admit to yourself that your child is hyperkinetic is one thing. To let somebody else label him "deviant" is quite another. Therein lies the danger.

The entire concept of screening and labeling young

children should be viewed with skepticism. If the screening and categorizing process can be useful to your child, by making available to him programs, therapies, specialists, and educational opportunities that would not readily be available otherwise, then it can be beneficial. If screening and labeling the child result in his being dumped outside the mainstream of society, educationally or emotionally, without any attempt to remedy the condition and return him to the normal situation as quickly as possible (whenever this can be done), then screening and categorizing are only harmful and should be resisted at all costs.

The current, healthy thrust in special education is toward what is called "mainstreaming": taking the child out of the regular classroom only when absolutely necessary, using special remedial or resource teachers in conjunction with regular classroom teachers, keeping the child in special education the shortest possible time, and remediating specific deficits that keep him out of the classroom. Critics of mainstreaming can point to many shortcomings in the practice, but when did practice ever live up to expectations raised by theory? Compared to what education offered before mainstreaming, the concept offers much promise for the learning-disabled child.

Children who are hyperkinetic–learning disabled should never be placed in classrooms with the emotionally disturbed or retarded. There is no way that such a placement can remediate specific deficits. To so place them merely brands them irrevocably as unfit for society, while it confirms their negative image of themselves.

Placing the hyperkinetic–learning disabled child in special classes designed for him can be beneficial. Contrary to popular belief, however, even young children are aware of subtle nuances, and the nuances of special education are not especially subtle. There is social stigma attached to special education children. Whether the benefits outweigh the detriments is an issue that must be decided for each child.

I recall vividly, many years ago, listening to a diatribe from an elementary school principal, listing my daughter's many notable instances of unacceptableness. I didn't like the tone of the conversation. I asked her what we could do, and she really had no answers, just more complaints. After a while, it dawned on me that everything she said indicated her belief that the child should be removed from society (i.e., the school), that the child was more of a problem than they could handle, and that she wanted me to do something with her, something she could not specify and that I would have been unwilling to do, anyway. This is the attitude that prevailed, and it is prevalent today. It's the attitude that prevents the hyperkinetic child from achieving his potential and from improving and growing as rapidly as possible. It's an attitude that has to be changed when possible, manipulated when it serves the child's best interests, and resisted, confronted, and confounded otherwise.

3 Some Causes and Cures—Maybe

Since knowledge is somewhat limited, a discussion of the factors that cause hyperkinetic behavior, simple or compounded, will be brief, and may not be conclusive. Nobody has definitive how's and why's. There are decided indications of links between hyperkinesis and other physiological and/or environmental factors. While few clear-cut cause-and-effect relationships have been established, the need for further research and indications of directions for research are apparent. For the present, the subject of causes and cures should be approached with a completely open mind and no preconceived attitudes.

ORGANIC FACTORS

There are many studies that link the events that might cause minimal brain damage (or dysfunction) to the infant (before, during and immediately after birth) to hyperkinesis, but to infer brain damage from such a link is to add insult to injury. While it's entirely possible that there is some relationship between hyperkinesis and a difficult pregnancy, difficult birth, and/or neonatal injury or infection, too many children escape unscathed from such circumstances to make the matter cut and dried.

Frequently, brain-*damaged* children (in which there is provable, definable impairment) are hyperkinetic, some to an extreme almost beyond belief. For this reason, in the absence of ascertainable damage, it was postulated that the appearance of hyperkinesis was the result of some undetectable minor sort of malfunctioning called minimal brain dysfunction. This theory, which has many adherents, has never been proved, and I doubt seriously that it can be.

The theory that hyperkinesis is the result of a chemical or metabolic brain dysfunction has been advanced and certainly merits careful, full-scale research efforts. It is generally thought that some abnormality in the metabolic process leads to an imbalance of necessary chemical agents, resulting in depressed inhibitory functioning or increased excitatory function, or some combination of both. Translated, this means that a certain substance is lacking or inadequate in the centers of the brain that would control or inhibit behavior or the centers that stimulate behavior.

The use of stimulant drugs to treat hyperkinesis is based on this assumption—the drug compensates for a deficiency of some substance in the brain. But the assumption of a deficit and the compensatory actions of drugs are not proven. Drug therapy and hyperkinesis is a subject of such serious implications that it will be treated at length in Chapter 7.

The most rational—and simplest—organic theory advanced concerning minimal dysfunction is one that postulates that the dysfunction is related to maturational delay or irregular maturation. (Whether or not the delay or irregularity is related to a chemical or metabolic imbalance is another question.) There is research to support the notion that hyperkinetic children are somewhat immature or are immature in certain areas of development when compared to their age-mates.

Ideally, science assumes that the simplest explanation is always the best, and I believe the theory of delayed maturation has more to offer than an involved, unproven theory concerning chemical imbalances.

My own experience indicates that hyperkinetic children show developmental irregularity or specific lags in maturation. They often respond with behaviors and reactions that are more appropriate to younger children. They do not, as a rule, demonstrate equivalent maturity in all areas. Intellectually and physically, they are often superior to their peers. In other areas of development such as abstract thought language development, inhibitory regulation of behavior, etc., they are noticeably irregular or delayed in achieving levels of competence.

The theory of maturational delay does not mean the child will automatically "grow up" some day, although he will certainly continue to mature. Various components or abilities will continue to be somewhat retarded in development. Specific situations the child confronts should be tailored to his many levels; he must be encouraged to respond appropriately, and he will continue to need help in overcoming specific delays where and when they occur.

There is a concurrent theory that states that there is an optimal maturation level at which specific learning occurs (e.g., learning to crawl, talk, write, etc.) and that before or after this optimal time learning is either impossible (before) or difficult (after). This is true in the case of learning disabilities, for instance, which are far harder to correct at a later age than they are if detected and treated in early childhood. One can presume, then, the learning of accculturative techniques, such as inhibiting direct and immediate action, will become more difficult in relation to the child's age. In other words, after the optimal time, learning a specific approved behavior will be more difficult for the child and will probably take longer to become a part of his everyday repertoire of behaviors. Therefore, it is reasonable to expect a maturational lag to continue to exist to some extent, although it can be modified and abridged.

OTHER PHYSIOLOGICAL FACTORS

There are a number of factors (vitamin and other deficiencies, physiological imbalances, and intolerances for certain substances) that seem to be associated with a state that at least resembles hyperkinesis. Hypoglycemia, for example, which is basically the inability to metabolize large doses of carbohydrates efficiently and which leads to elevated blood sugar levels, can produce symptoms of hyperkinesis in some children.

Nutritional deficiencies, including vitamin deficits, have been investigated by only a few researchers in relation to hyperkinesis. Since a higher proportion of poor, urban children are affected than their presumably better-nourished suburban counterparts, several investigators have hypothesized that nutrition, or lack of it, may play some part in producing a hyperkinetic reaction. (Hyperkinesis has also been linked to poor maternal nutrition, which suggests that further research in this area could be fruitful.)

There are published reports on the treatment of hyperkinesis with vitamins, etc.; however, I would discourage the indiscriminate use of vitamins as therapy unless some deficiency is ascertainable.

GENETIC FACTORS

There is a good deal of evidence to indicate that there may be some genetic link between the hyperkinetic child and his forebears, evidence of what is called "polyfactorial transmission" or "polygenetic factors." That is, hyperkinesis is the result of some combination of several genetic factors, rather than of a single gene or chromosomal deficit or abnormality. However, not all parents with high activity levels produce children that resemble them, nor do parents with low activity levels produce sedentary types. Unraveling the knot of genetic transmission is a very complex problem, but recent developments make it plausible that someday there may be definitive answers.

Another theory that's been advanced is that some combination of genetic factors predisposes certain people to react adversely to environmental factors. There is some evidence that such predispositions exist, but isolating the factors is the problem. A more fruitful approach might be to try to identify the environmental factors that exacerbate the condition. As a matter of fact, several such factors may have been already determined and will be discussed later.

TEMPERAMENT AND CHILD-REARING PRACTICES

Temperament and child-rearing practices fall very neatly between organic and environmental causes of hyperactivity and relate to both. More and more, researchers are focusing on something variously known as "temperament," "cognitive style," or by some similar designation having to do with inherent characteristics or personality. (The old heredity-versus-environment argument has finally been resolved. More rational people are willing to admit that people are a combination of the two factors: a personality that came prepacked and the influence of experiences.)

Instead of the wonderful, placid, formless baby, whom parents and other adults plan to shape according to their preferences, we are now confronted with a very real, dynamic individual with built-in likes and dislikes, predilections, preferences, sensitivities, needs, and a lot of other things we never bothered to think about. Add to this the possibility that hyperkinesis is a reaction to understimulation—based on the assumption that some individuals seem to crave more stimulation than others and that hypereaction is an effort to reach some optimal level—and we have a very complicated situation.

A highly active child whose parents are prone to passivity and minimal amounts of activity will stick out like a sore thumb, while the same child, born to parents with high activity levels, may be whimsically accepted as "a chip off the old block." The less active parent will be sooner overwhelmed by the rambunctious child, while the active parent is likely to permit activity levels that will prove to be unacceptable later.

If a child with a need for great motility or a lot of stimulation were allowed to develop naturally, within the framework of easy acceptance of his needs, wide latitudes for his activities, and firmly established limits (imposed more for the sake of safety than his parents' convenience), then perhaps he might not develop some of the negative aspects of hyperkinesis.

Many of society's child-rearing sanctions, however, are predicated on adult convenience or preference. The first reaction of many adults to a troublesome child is apt to be disapproval and punishment, rapidly followed by avoidance (if possible), rejection, and hostility.

The parent-child interaction is self-reinforcing—it perpetuates itself—whether it's a happy or damaging relationship. The infant whose excessive activities have resulted in much parental attention, negative or positive, has been taught to think that continued activity will result in further attention. Parents who have come to think of their child in terms of his excesses will continue to treat him accordingly. The child will, of course, react or act upon other adults much as he does with his parents.

There is reason to believe that a number of hyperkinetic children, particularly those whose only manifestation is behavioral (without learning disabilities or neurological evidence), are simply children whose activity or stimulation levels fall in the high range. The blame for continued or deteriorating behavior on the part of the child must be attributed to faulty parent-child or adult-child interaction patterns which began in infancy and will continue unless corrected.

A number of researchers have observed that modern American child-raising techniques are primarily negative and punitive. Many child control techniques are based upon the removal or absence of a positive parent-child interaction. The emphasis of parental management is to curb disapproved behavior rather than to encourage approved behavior.

It should be obvious that negative child management applied to a highly active, highly impulsive child leads to increased frustration and attention-seeking activities on the part of the child and increased punitive and negative responses on the part of the parents. Parents and child meet in a head-on collision, between parental expectations and infant personality. Further negative interactions result in the parents trying harder and harder to sooth, placate, curb, and control the child, to which the child reacts by redoubling his efforts—hypereacting—to achieve stimulation or motility. As the child grows older, he becomes more able to get into things and harder to manage, so the parents work harder to prohibit his actions and make him conform to acceptable standards.

ENVIRONMENTAL FACTORS

Lead Levels

There is a definite, positive relationship between lead levels in the body and hyperactivity. Children who have suffered lead poisoning commonly respond with patterns of hyperkinesis. Recently, research has shown that hyperkinesis and elevated lead levels, below the toxic point, are related. Though cause and effect have not been established, researchers tend to believe that lead causes hyperactivity and may be ingested in substances such as lead-based paint or inhaled directly from the atmosphere where it is released in large quantities by cars using leaded gasoline.

Lead poisoning in children is commonly treated with an agent that removes lead from the body through the excretory system. Whether this is effective in the treatment of hyperactivity has yet to be determined, although animal experimentation has shown that the effects of high lead levels are reversible; that is, hyperactivity can be decreased.

Radiation Stress

One of the most fascinating subjects of conjecture and research in recent years has been the area of radiation stress resulting from the use of conventional fluorescent lighting and unshielded TV cathode tubes. There have been numerous studies, usually conducted within the classroom setting, demonstrating that hyperkinetic behavior decreases as a result of changing the method of lighting. As a matter of fact, activity levels decreased for all children.

Avoiding radiation stress resulting from exposure to improperly shielded or leaky TV cathode tubes is relatively uncomplicated but may prove troublesome. Parents can request information about the cathodes in specific models directly from the manufacturer. Generally, the newer the set, the less likely it is to leak radiation. Since the late 1960s, manufacturers have taken a few precautions to eliminate the possibilities of such leakage. Should the cathode tube be imperfectly shielded or leaky, then the solution is to separate the child from the TV set, which may be a troublesome operation.

Nearly all school buildings (and all public buildings such as libraries and post offices) are lighted by conventional fluorescent tubes. This poses quite a problem for parents who may suspect their child's activity level is affected by fluorescent radiation. Modified fluorescent lighting is available (tubes have long ultraviolet waves, lead foil shields over the cathodes, and a wire screen to ground radio frequencies), but getting the school board to install this type of lighting is a little impractical. Parents may want to research the subject and discuss the possibilities with their physician and school authorities to see what potentials and what dangers do, in fact, exist.

Food Additives

The third environmental factor is one of major interest: food additives. Almost everybody is aware of the controversy about food additives and may have heard of the work of Dr. Ben Feingold, who postulates that salicylates and some other compounds, although they are not allergens (i.e., they do not produce an allergic reaction, like hives, in the classical sense), nevertheless are the direct cause of certain biochemical reactions that produce symptoms of hyperkinesis.

According to Feingold, elimination from the diet of artificial coloring, artificial flavorings, and BHA and BTA (preservatives), all of which are found in almost 80 percent of commercial foodstuffs, produced "favorable" to "dramatic" results in 60 to 70 percent of the cases studied. (I should mention that a number of common foods are restricted during an initial four to six week "drying out" period. The reader is directed to Feingold's works for a comprehensive description of the diet.)

A number of researchers have attempted to substantiate the effectiveness of the diet. Unfortunately, there are factors that make research with uninstitutionalized children very difficult. It's very easy for either the parents or the child to break the regulations and invalidate the findings. Any school-age child can be tempted by "forbidden fruits" and will occasionally succumb to an overwhelming urge for a piece of candy or chewing gum.

However, there are enough case studies and clinical evidence to indicate there is some basis for expecting a favorable outcome from the diet. At least some improvement has been noted in about 60 percent of children whose diet has been restricted. Meanwhile, more research is being done, and positive results are coming in.

Let me put it this way—the diet works for us. After more than a year, I am convinced it has been of tremendous benefit to my son Ben. There has been a noticeable change, including a decrease in aggressive or belligerent behavior, a reduction in purposeless activity (although he's still a very active person), a lessening of irritability and excitability, and a reduction in impulsive behavior. His learning capacities have increased (from a second-grade reading level to a fifth-grade level in one school year), he is far happier and more positive about himself and his abilities, he is much more reflective and able to handle difficult situations, and he is more sensitive to other people. What is most striking, however, are the impressive advances in his ability to focus his attention and to concentrate his energies for extended periods of time.

It was only after the fact that I was able to see that the

child had been "speeding." As he expressed it. "I just have to hurry!" Since he was a very unhappy and miserable child, well aware of his condition and its consequences, and aware that he had little control over his actions, he was amenable to trying a diet "that might make you feel happier and less angry."

Still, adhering to the diet is a problem. Most convenience foods, and a lot of other things, are prohibited because of their composition. A greater amount of time must be spent in food planning and preparation. Besides, on the whole, unadulterated foods are more expensive. All members of the family must agree to cooperate by keeping prohibited foods out of the child's reach. Changes in dietary habits, I understand, are sometimes resisted by family members.

Once the dietary restrictions prove beneficial, I think most children are willing to make whatever small sacrifices they must to avoid temptations, like soda and candy bars. I am very proud of Benjamin's ability to watch-dog his own diet and to refuse proffered goodies that he knows he shouldn't have. He's only too happy to explain that he's on a "natural food diet." Oh, well, terminology doesn't matter, it's the spirit that counts.

I have come across something interesting that I haven't seen mentioned in the literature in connection with food additives, namely, increased growth rate. In a little over a year, my eight-year-old son has grown four inches and gained twelve pounds. I have only briefly discussed growth gains with other parents, so my results are inconclusive. However, such a large gain leads me to speculate on the peculiar effects of food additives on particular people and ask if they do not act much like amphetamines, depressing appetite and growth while increasing excitability and activity.

If you try the Feingold diet and find it is not particularly beneficial, keep in mind that there are now approximately 4000 food additives and, according to Feingold, any compound, natural or artificial, intentional or unintentional, can produce an adverse reaction in somebody. Food sensitivities and allergies of various kinds have been shown to be related to several forms of emotional illness. It's not a bad idea to rule out allergens through a series of allergy tests, although the process can be quite expensive.

If the child behaves hyperkinetically only sometimes, or on specific occasions, the parents might want to keep a "dietary diary," carefully recording exactly what the child eats at a given time, to see if some pattern of reaction does indeed occur.

Environmental Stress

The fourth, and last, environmental factor involves the environmental stress reaction. I was delighted to find that there is some evidence (suspicion might be a better word) to support my contention that the impositions placed on children in our society tend to exacerbate the problems posed by a high activity level or a mild condition of hyperkinesis.

The typical school-age child is expected to sit quietly for six hours a day, pay attention in class whether he's interested or not, never be rowdy, boisterous, or noisy, and to accept achievement as the reward for his hard work. After school, he is further encouraged to be quiet, seen but not heard, watch TV, play subdued games, stay out of the way, and generally not to cause a commotion or be disruptive. He has most likely been bussed to and from school. He has had little opportunity for physical activity, outside of gym classes, and he has no chores to do that would require exertion or concentrated activity on his part. Hardly ever is he told to go out in the yard, even if the space has been provided for him by caring parents, and shout until he's hoarse and run around until he's ready to drop.

To make matters worse, many people live in congested urban areas and many people raise children in apartments, where quiet must be maintained.

The child with a high activity level requires an outlet for that activity. Without an appropriate outlet, the activity can become quite destructive. It is for the parents to decide whether activity will be productive, directed activity, which can be managed and directed by the parents, or if they are willing to just let the child go around raising hell wherever he can. Since the child is no longer required to chop wood, hoe the vegetable garden, haul water from the well, feed the livestock and milk the cows, and other assorted tasks that used to absorb one's energy, it behooves the parents to substitute suitable activities, depending on the age and interests of the child: riding a tricycle at three, playing soccer at eight, and painting the garage, for an appropriate reward, of course, at twelve.

Since it is axiomatic that the active child requires more active supervision, it is often easier to involve the child in the task at hand than to try to do whatever one is doing and at the same time keep an eye on what he's doing. I might add that hyperactive children are often very happy to perform manual tasks, where they can find success and satisfaction. "Manual" does not translate as "boring, repetitive, and menial"; it refers to jobs that require some physical activity or exertion. For example, washing the dishes is pretty dull work, but scrubbing the basement or porch floor with lots of suds, a broom, and a mop, waterproof boots and all, and rinsing it with the garden hose, may be appealing work for the active child.

Postulating organic damage or dysfunction is and has been a serious impediment for the hyperkinetic child. While ascribing his behaviors to factors beyond the child's control may relieve the onus of his behavior—which I doubt it does in any large measure—it does not increase the possibility that researchers, educators, psychologists, and parents will turn their most productive efforts to seeking other causes or remedies, or view the child in a positive, growth-oriented way.

Since research indicates that a number of factors seem to bear directly on hyperkinesis, is it not logical to question the theory that hyperkinesis is an entity with an organic cause? Would it not be more logical, and more practical, to think of hyperkinesis as a state that may result from a variety of causal factors, some of which may be manipulated, eliminated, decreased, and/or modified?

Accepting a theory of organic damage or dysfunction is a self-limiting, self-fulfilling premise. It's one thing to accept organic disabilities when the disability is evident: The child was born without legs or feet. It's quite another to accept a disability per se that is unsubstantiated and based on a theory which has yet to be proved. Organic dysfunction undoubtedly causes hyperkinesis. Exactly how many children with hyperkinetic symptoms are organically dysfunctional remains to be seen. In the meantime, it is more prudent to check out the environmental factors that might contribute to the child's hyperkinetic behavior.

4 Coping with Professionals

Attempting to deal with professionals on an equal basis, rather than on a father confessor to retarded child level, is a delicate and tricky operation. There is usually the feeling that a professional knows more than the parents (not necessarily true), that the professional is less emotional and therefore more rational (possibly true), and that the professional can better help the child than the parents (not true). Parents are the most effective agents in remediating their child's behavior. Any parent who consults a professional is trying to help his child and is in the best possible situation to do so.

PICKING PROFESSIONAL PEOPLE

It's extremely hard for parents to make judgments concerning the professional competence and suitability of professionals who are to be involved in the lives of their children. In order to help make such a judgment, begin by asking yourself a number of questions. What do you think of this particular professional as a person? How do you feel about him? Are you comfortable with him? Do you feel defensive? Do you understand what he's talking about? Is he trying to make himself understandable? Does he take the time to talk with you and explain what's going on? If he outlines a program of therapy, do you understand the techniques and possible consequences? Has he defined concrete and appropriate goals for the child? Has he involved you as parents in the therapy and suggested what you can do to help? Or are you totally in the dark?

Very often, parents feel vague misgivings about a particular professional but continue under his direction simply because they don't know what else to do. They doubt their own ability to evaluate people. Don't. If you have doubts and questions, confront the professional and try to clear the air. If he cannot resolve your doubts and make you feel more comfortable, it might be smart to look around for someone else. Nine times out of ten, these vague feelings are, in fact, real, and your distrust has some justification.

Even if you respond positively to the professional as a person, you should inquire about his professional qualifications, reputation, and competence. Qualifications are fairly easy to ascertain. Ask him about his training. Do you think his training has been thorough, or did he just take a couple of courses in college and there isn't anyone more qualified to fill the post? Has he had actual, hands-on experience with your particular kind of problem? What did he do? How did he handle it? What was the outcome?

Ascertaining competence is very difficult. Time, of course, will tell whether the professional is effective in dealing with your child's problem. If your child has been in speech therapy for six months and there is no sign of improvement, you can be relatively sure that something is wrong. This method of proving competence, though, is very time-consuming and tends to be expensive.

Personal referrals are a good way to locate therapists. However, if you don't know anyone who has had to seek their services, there is no reason not to ask, politely, of course, and as tactfully as possible, for references.

You can check to see if the professional has done any writing in journals or magazines. What about his affiliations with schools, institutions, hospitals, clinics, and professional organizations? The psychologist who evaluated my son is a well-known founder and director of a reputable school for learning-disabled children, and I assumed, correctly, that he would know a disabled kid when he saw one.

If a professional hasn't time to talk to you, or puts you off, don't take up any more of his valuable time; just leave. I don't mean that he should sit still for three hours while you catalog every major and minor event in the child's history, or that you should call him twice a day for professional advice, but within reasonable limits he should be willing to devote some time to explanation and discussion.

He should be willing to stay in touch with you and make periodic progress reports. Without progress reports, how can you judge whether or not any progress is being made? Even if you can see improvement in the child, you should have the therapists' feedback. Is *he* satisfied with your child's progress? Are things going along as he expected? Are there any new complications? Has the prognosis changed? Can he put a time limit on therapy or has his estimate of the time required changed?

Now, simply because the parents are at ease and feel good about a particular professional does not mean that the child will automatically establish rapport with this person. The child may not like the therapist, or he may not like the idea of therapy. It's also possible that the professional will not like your child or particular types of children.

Trying to find out what the child thinks about the professional isn't easy. Children often answer direct questions with the answers they think adults want to hear. So, if you ask your child, "Do you like Dr. So-and-so?" chances are the young patient will say he does.

On the other hand, it is important to listen to any comments and complaints the child may make, no matter how far-fetched or inconsequential they may appear to be at first. There may be something going on that the child cannot explain, so he mentions some strange, little thing that doesn't sound very important. Parents should track down these comments and find out what they really mean. Suppose the child comes home, after his twenty-first session of therapy and says, "We never do anything. We just play games." This comment might mean any number of things: Therapy is going well but the child doesn't really like the idea of therapy; therapy has been going well but, in the past few weeks, the child has stopped talking and relating to the therapist; therapy has never gone well, and the therapist and child have always just played around, only now the child is bored with the games; etc.

It's very easy for therapists to project their own feelings and experiences onto their clients, especially children. The therapist who had a troubled childhood, and has never resolved his own conflicts with his parents, tends to identify with the child, who may be having problems with his own parents because of his unacceptable behavior at home. The child, of course, in an effort to please the therapist, starts to respond to the therapist's unconscious clueing and develops symptoms conforming to the projections. The conflict with his parents may become the subject of therapy, rather than the child's behavior which is the root of the parent-child discord.

Several years ago, I became the inadvertent fourth party in a quadrangle involving mother, therapist, a teenage girl, and me. The child tried to make me play the therapy game. After avoiding a number of her attempts I decided it would be easier to confront the situation and informed her I did not agree to assume the role, but agreed to talk with her, with the understanding that I would probably wind up defending her mother and giving her the parental point of view, which she might or might not like to have. The child was seeing a therapist because of severe conflict with her mother and, after several conversations, it became apparent that her complaints were directed against the therapist, who seemed to overidentify with the conflictual problem and who seemed to be helping her build a case against her mother rather than resolving the conflict. In other words, too much empathy, too much sympathy, and not enough reality. Having been able to vent her angry feelings toward her mother, this child was now mature enough to feel the need to do something constructive about the situation. She seemed to feel that the therapist was in effect holding her back rather than supporting her efforts to make changes in her attitudes and actions.

There are certainly many good, effective people in all professions, and there are many people who work well with hyperkinetic and difficult children. But it is a sad fact that adult reaction to hyperkinetic children can also be punitive and excessive. Apparently, the hyperkinetic brings out the worst in some people. There are some who are upset with the child's open expressions of anger, which they see as very wrong and very sick, and these people become terribly anxious when their control mechanisms are not effective in handling the child.

Working with a hyperkinetic child is trying, exasperating, and physically taxing. Some people simply can't or don't want to put forth the amount of effort required. Some others are threatened by the child's independence and assertiveness. It really doesn't matter why or wherefore, and there should be no difficulty in accepting the fact that some therapists, teachers, and other professionals do not work well with hyperkinetics. Just find somebody who likes to be in the same room with an extremely challenging child. There are many.

THE EDUCATOR

Several years ago, I visited a good number of private schools in our area, trying to find the "perfect" spot for my son. His kindergarten teacher (a very effective woman) and I had several conversations on the subject, comparing notes and sharing information on various schools. Finally, she summed the situation up beautifully: "You're not looking for a system of education. You're looking for one, single teacher for Ben, and a good teacher can teach standing on her head."

That's true. A good teacher is effective in almost any circumstances, in any environment, in any setting, working with any theory or philosophy. A good teacher is more comfortable and more effective in a setting compatible with his own teaching methods (i.e., an open or a traditional classroom setting), but he could teach "standing on his head" if he had to.

Parents will generally have enough problems with the process and system of education without looking for more. Exposing the child to a noneffective or hostile teacher is asking for too much.

The easiest way to short-circuit some of the problems that can arise is to find one good teacher for your child to begin with. (Convincing the authorities to allow the child access to that teacher is another matter.) A teacher who sincerely likes the child and is interested in his welfare will be most cooperative in passing him on, hopefully, into good hands. Since the teacher is in a position to know both the child and the other teachers in the school, he will be able to make a fairly rational decision as to his successor. Particularly if he has been successful in handling your child—and teaching him—the teacher will be careful to see that the child is assigned to another teacher who is seen as sympathetic, compatible, and willing to work with him. (The actual administrative policy for assignment of pupils varies from district to district; sometimes an administrator handles difficult placements, and sometimes it is done quietly on a teacher-to-teacher basis, without official sanction.)

What kind of person is a good teacher for the hyperkinetic child? First of all, he must be self-confident. He cannot be threatened by the child, or it's all over. He should be fairly relaxed in the classroom and should be at ease with children and secure in the knowledge of his ability to work with them effectively. For this reason, it is better to avoid an inexperienced teacher who is not yet sure of his effectiveness and has not developed or polished his techniques. I'm sure that some inexperienced teachers are very good, but I prefer for them to polish their techniques elsewhere.

A very clear distinction should be made between rigidity and discipline, which many people mistake for the same thing. A good teacher for the hyperkinetic must be able to maintain control, impose discipline with a minimum of disruption (the child is disruptive enough for both of them), and yet be flexible enough to see and meet the special needs of the child. Unbending insistence on a stern code of behavior is rigidity, not discipline. The hyperkinetic child needs discipline, as well as standards, limits, and goals. He cannot survive rigidity. He is likely to explode when confronted with expectations he cannot hope to meet, and he cannot live up to rigid codes of behavior.

A good teacher likes children, likes his job, understands children and their uniqueness, and accepts their varying abilities, needs, and limitations. He accordingly attempts to direct his teaching toward the particular group of children that make up his particular class, not toward a theoretically derived class composition that has no basis in reality.

As a rule, men who teach elementary grades teach young children because they want to. (They could move up into the more prestigious junior or senior high levels if they wanted to.) I hate to sound like a sexist, but men are more inclined than women to be more tolerant of hyperactive boys. Perhaps, they view much of the activity as similar to their own childhood experiences. So a male teacher is usually a good choice for a hyperkinetic boy.

Never believe that all teachers are selfless and totally dedicated to molding the minds of young children. Neither should you accept the notion that teaching is just a job, like working in an office or repairing streets. Anyone who works with children should, and probably does, have a commitment to that work, and those who do not should look for another occupation, willingly or not.

Long-time teachers should be scrutinized very carefully by parents of hyperkinetic children. The veteran can often be described as "having one year's experience teaching and repeating the same mistakes for thirty years." There is the further problem that older teachers may have some difficulty coping with a large class that includes two or three highly active children. All of this is not axiomatic, of course. There are sixty-year-old teachers who can run rings around thirty-year-olds and are still as fresh and open-minded in their approach as on the day they began teaching.

What other sterling qualities should a teacher of hyperkinetic children have? A fair amount of energy, an outgoing personality, a loud voice when necessary, enough intelligence to a least keep up with children, and a sense of humor. A teacher who wants to sit behind the desk and doesn't move around a lot tends to let the kids dawdle and fool around; one who is slow on the uptake and passive in interaction with the children, and whose appearance, mannerisms, and tone of voice are lifeless and dull, and/or whose demeanor is sour, is not a prime, grade-A candidate for teaching this child. The parent should look for a teacher with energy and authority in the classroom, one who keeps things moving, one who keeps the children occupied and working, and one whose classroom is a stimulating and busy place to be.

A good teacher for the hyperkinetic is one who is able to define limits in advance and enumerate them clearly, spelling out what is permitted and what is not, and who then expects the child to stay within these limits. When the child strays beyond the boundaries of acceptable behavior, the good teacher does not regard this straying as an attack on himself, but sees it as a childish infraction of the rules.

A teacher who sees an infraction of the rules as a personal attack by the child upon his own ego or status probably should be dismissed. Since teachers are normally not dismissed, your only recourse is to remove your child from such a classroom before he becomes convinced that he is, in fact, attacking the teacher, that he has some special power over adults (he does, but it's better not to let him know it), and that this power can be used viciously at will.

The Open versus the Conventional Classroom

The major differences between open and conventional classrooms, besides some differences in physical layout, is the teacher's state of mind. Basically, an open-classroom philosophy allows the teacher to abrogate his authoritarian position. (The physical setting of the classroom tends to minimize an authoritarian position.) Teaching materials and day-to-day planning focus on the immediate and creative, rather than on prescribed lesson plans in which teachers are inclined to become bogged down with facts, figures, schedules, and tests.

The role of the child within the context of the educational experience is positively enhanced by simple recognition of the fact that it is more important for children to learn than for teachers to teach. The teacher's role in the open classroom is *not* curtailed; it is changed.

It's not so much a difference in teaching method or theory as a difference in the way teachers view their own role in the process of education. Obviously, there are as many different kinds of open classrooms as there are teachers to teach in them. Mainly, the teacher will be "open" to the extent that he can function without traditional props to bolster his authority, rules, and regulations. Teachers in conventional settings manage to open their classes, and some teachers in open settings impose rigid rules and regulations.

I think it needs to be said that emphasis on the child's role in the learning situation cannot be equated with total democracy (or anarchy). A good liberal education will not fail to include the basics, such as reading and writing. It should, however, go beyond that, and encourage creativity, individuality, and the ability to think.

There have been any number of studies demonstrating that hyperactivity is less apparent—or decreases—in the open classroom setting. There are several obvious reasons why this may happen, the first being that the child is better able to keep himself occupied if he has some choice as to his particular activities. Nine times out of ten the hyperkinetic child will choose to do something rather than be bored. The next obvious point is that the activity level of all children in open classrooms rises somewhat, which tends to obscure the sharp line educators tend to draw between normal and excessive amounts of activity. The third factor is the teacher himself: The open-classroom setting probably attracts a more flexible, more democratic, less authoritarian personality, who tends to see the individual needs, abilities, and achievements of each child rather than viewing the class as a collective. This teacher is less perturbed by activity than a teacher who is rigidly structured. The fourth point is that the open classroom allows for more physical movement, which may relieve the hyperkinetic child's need to be active. It has been noted that, if the child is allowed brief periods of activity interspersed with nonphysical activity, and if allowed to leave his seat for brief periods when frustrated, anxious, or restless, he will respond by being generally less restless and less prone to acting-out when asked to comply with attentive, quiet behavior.

The teacher in the open classroom must be a highly disciplined person, of course, or the classroom will turn into chaos. However, the teacher's need for a highly structured classroom environment should not be confused with self-discipline or the ability to maintain discipline. Some teachers need the artificial means of a structured classroom in order to promote that nebulous thing called "discipline." Some don't.

A *rigidly* structured classroom is a very inappropriate place for the hyperkinetic child. He will inevitable fall far below the accepted standards of behavior. The best possible situation is one in which a well-defined, well-established structure allows some freedom for the individual child's idiosyncracies, including freedom of mobility, motility, self-expression, and needs. A teacher who insists upon performance beyond the child's abilities will drive him into hysterics.

More and more teachers in conventional classroom settings have opened up their classes. They've rearranged the furniture, set up study and activity centers, and made the room look less formal. They allow more flexibility in the teaching schedule, so that level of interest becomes more important than keeping track of the time. They tend to arrange the time so that children can pursue their own special interests. They permit more movement and mobility in the classroom, as long as it's not disruptive. They emphasis rewards for good work and deemphasize grades, competition among the children, and low achievement.

The best way to find an open-classroom teacher in a conventional school is to make arrangements to observe the teacher at work. How does the teacher handle the class? Is he dogmatic or democratic? Does he maintain a physical distance from the children or is he an active participant in their activities? Is the classroom subdued, chaotic, or moderately humming with activity? Are any of the children working on their own special projects or interests or is everyone tightly tied into the scheduled material? Is the teacher's presentation of the subject matter interesting? Do the children quietly sit and listen or are they encouraged to participate? You'll need to spend at least a couple of hours observing classroom interactions before you can answer these questions. Don't settle for a quick tour of the school's facilities and a half-hour in the classroom, unless the teacher is so good that you can make up your mind about him instantaneously.

When Something Goes Wrong

By the time parents are informed, classroom problems are usually well formed and blossoming. At this point, they have little choice—they must intervene. They must make every effort to find out what the problem is, how it can be alleviated, and how far the teacher is willing to negotiate. If, for some reason, the problem cannot be solved or alleviated through and with the teacher, the next step is to refer it to the principal, who is a very important person in the drama.

According to many principals and school administrators, there is little most of them can do, being constricted and constrained by "policy." As a matter of fact, most principals have some power of discretion and are quite capable of doing a little finagling when it suits them. The principal is the guiding light of a school and can make or break it. It's a good idea to get acquainted with your principal and make an assessment of his personality and effectiveness. A good indication of the principal's orientation is how he is greeted by children in the hall. If the kids are glad to see him and are anxious to talk with him, he is probably child-oriented. If the kids are not too exuberant in their greetings and don't care to be noticed, he's probably system-oriented. A firm but fair disciplinarian will be greeted warmly; a punitive, capricious demagogue will be avoided.

When discussions with the teacher are unavailing, or the parents come to believe that some of the problems are created by the teacher's handling or mishandling of the child, the best thing the parents can do for the child is to remove him—have him transferred. This advice may sound extreme, but it is predicated on the belief that no one can expect improvement in the child's behavior without concurrent remediation on the part of the teacher.

Moving the child from one classroom to another, or from one school to another, goes against the grain of most administrators. Nevertheless, it is sometimes necessary. For instance, let's presume that, for one reason or another, the child has made some definite gains, his behavior has improved noticeably, and the parents feel he is ready to make more gains in classroom behavior and performance. However, the teacher reports no improvement, even after the parents have pointed out instances and types of improvement. The teacher still believes the child is not capable of working at grade level and is not willing to help him catch up. The parents ascertain that the child's school behavior has not improved as much as his home behavior, and that he is feeling "picked on" because the teacher does not recognize his efforts. The school year has six or seven long, tedious months to run, and the parents are convinced that the teacher either has unrealistic expectations of the amount of improvement the child can manage or is unwilling to undergo a change of attitude. The parents can leave the child where he is, allowing him to further build his negativistic attitudes as a student—a nonachiever who can't learn—and wait and see what happens the following year, or they can try to move him to a classroom where his achievements and improvements will be recognized and where he may earn some success as a student and recognition of that success.

The hyperkinetic child is usually in such dire need of any approval and appreciation that any efforts or improvement on his part may merit, that I suggest looking for a better placement immediately.

Moving the child from classroom to classroom in the same school can be accomplished. Moving the child to another school is sometimes comparable to moving the moon and stars from their orbit. The first problem is to overcome the resistance of gravity—in this case, dyed-in-the-wool, till-death-do-we-part bureaucrats, of which most school district administrations abound.

One final word about education. Our system of education has been sharply criticized of late, often by people who are in a position to know what they're talking about. So many children are not being educated for multitudinous reasons that it is becoming apparent that the system is too systematized, the conventions too conventionalized, and the norms too normalized to accept—much less educate—any child who falls outside a very narrow range of acceptability. Add to the standard bureaucratic inefficiencies and ineptitudes the problems created by urban overdevelopment, ineffectual teaching training, centralization of a large number of children under one roof, general public apathy concerning the quality of education, lack of funds, and dropping enrollments, and it appears that schools are weighed down by internal and external difficulties that will in time, if left unresolved, bankrupt the system.

Too many good teachers who would like to do a better job than they're doing—and who know how to do a better job—are prevented from doing so by such factors as inappropriate or lack of materials, administrational policies which dictate the content and method of instruction, the convenience of other teachers and staff, shortage of support or therapeutic personnel, and a general lack of knowledge or training. Too many teachers are becoming combination babysitter-jailors. Nevertheless, many good teachers manage to survive the system, and it's these teachers the parents must look for.

THE COUNSELOR OR SOCIAL WORKER

Most people who go into guidance counseling, psychology, or social work want to make some contribution to society, which isn't a bad reason for such a decision on the whole. Once in a while, though, one runs into a "do-gooder" whose noble purpose has slopped over into sentimentality and who has come to overrate his training and/or abilities. (The do-gooder can be easily recognized because he normally goes around loudly proclaiming, "I want to help you.")

Because of a overwhelming desire to help, the do-gooder often exceeds his prerogatives: diagnosing, prescribing, labeling, adjudicating, making suggestions, conferring blame, and in general creating havoc and destruction, based on a lack of credentials, training, expertise, and experience, abetted by scrambled wits. Do I sound harsh? Well, the do-gooder can do a lot of damage, some of which is difficult, if not impossible, to repair.

When my son entered kindergarten, we ran into a do-gooder, the guidance counselor of the school he attended. The following dialogue is excerpted from an actual conversation between said counselor (G.C.) and myself (F.R.):

G.C.: Benjamin is a very disturbed little boy.

F.R.: Well, it's a very disturbing situation. He's very unhappy in school.

G.C.: But he's so angry all the time.

F.R.: That's true. Something's making him angry. I'd like to know what it is, because now he's coming home very upset and unhappy.

G.C.: He's not like this at home?

F.R.: No, he's not. I've never seen the behavior you've been telling me about. I've heard he's acted up for other people occasionally, but I've never seen anything like you describe.

G.C.: We'd like you to agree to have him tested.

F.R.: I don't know about that. I'd have to think about it a while.

G.C.: Why?

F.R.: Because I'm a psychologist by training, and leery of tests, that's why.

G.C.: Do you know the tests, understand them, I mean?

F.R.: Yes, that's why I'm a skeptic. Which ones would be used, and who would do the testing, anyway?

G.C.: The regular tests, I suppose, and XYZ Testing Associates. [This particular group, I discovered, did not have a reputation for reliability.]

F.R.: Which tests specifically would be used?

G.C.: Well, I'm not sure exactly which ones. Which do you object to?

F.R.: Let's make a deal. You tell me which ones are going to be used and I'll tell you which of those I object to? Okay?

G.C.: If you won't agree to have him tested, I don't know what we can do for him.

F.R.: Before we go through all this, I'd like to see him placed in Mrs. C.'s [the other kindergarten teacher] class for awhile. I'd like to see how he behaves.

G.C.: We can't do that.

F.R.: Why not?

G.C.: Because David [my older son] had Mrs. C. last year.

F.R.: What's that got to do with it?

G.C.: Well, school policy is never to put the second child in with the same teacher.

F.R.: Oh, nonsense!

G.C.: I don't see where it would make any difference.

F.R.: How do you know it wouldn't? I want to see if Ben would be happier with Mrs. C. Don't tell me you won't make exceptions in special cases, at a parent's request for a teacher.

G.C.: No, we don't.

F.R.: Then I don't agree to have him tested.

G.C.: But he's emotionally disturbed. He needs help.

F.R.: Bull! He's not emotionally disturbed. How the hell did you come up with that one?

G.C.: His teacher has kept a list of all the things he's done wrong.

F.R.: *His teacher has done what?*

G.C.: I asked her to keep a record of the things he did.

F.R.: Oh, boy! Somebody's nutty around here and I don't think it's me.

G.C.: What do you mean?

F.R.: Lady, there's a name for people who make lists of things that other people do wrong and we both know what it is. It's paranoia.

G.C.: I asked her to do it, so I would know what Ben was doing.

F.R.: Fine. Did she keep a list of all the things he did right?

G.C.: No.

F.R.: Why not? It seems to me to be a pretty one-sided picture.

G.C.: Ben has severe problems and needs to be helped.

F.R.: Good. Ben may have problems and need help, but one of his biggest problems is his teacher.

G.C.: Miss S. is a fine teacher. There have never been any complaints about her as a teacher. She never had a child as disturbed as Ben before.

F.R.: Undoubtedly. The fact remains that there is something here in the school that's upsetting him. I didn't know what it was and I really began to wonder if there was something wrong with him.

G.C.: I don't think you understand that Ben is totally out of control. We don't know what to do with him.

F.R.: Well, the only thing that you could do, you won't do.

G.C.: What is that?

F.R.: Put him in Mrs. C.'s class.

G.C.: We can't do that, and if you won't agree to letting us test Ben, we really can't do anything for him.

F.R.: That's becoming more and more apparent.

G.C.: What?

F.R.: Never mind. So, now what?

G.C.: Well, we can't do anything unless Ben is tested. I can't understand why you resist that. I don't know how Ben is going to be able to stay in school without help.

F.R.: That's a good idea. I'm not sure he should stay in school. At least where he is now.

G.C.: What do you mean? Are you going to take him out?

F.R.: I don't know. Maybe.

G.C.: Will you at least consider having him tested?

F.R.: Oh, of course. I consider lots of things. It gives me

something to do in my spare time. You've certainly given me some things to consider today.

G.C.: I can't tell you how important it is that Ben be tested. We can't do anything until . . .

F.R.: Hey, I just had a great idea! Speaking of tests, let's all be tested; you, me, the teacher and Ben. Let's see who comes out better.

This lengthy discussion had already covered the topics of Ben's "broken home," his relationship with his "absentee" father, my working, his relationship with his brother and sisters, his relationships with other children, his attitudes toward school, and a few other minor points, such as placement in a school for severely disturbed children.

I had made a very grave mistake and fallen into the trap of the lady's sincerity. She was indeed sincere in her desire to help Ben but was totally incompetent and unable to do so. Besides overstepping the boundaries of propriety, this misguided counselor made several appalling mistakes that need to be pointed out. She made a diagnosis on insufficient evidence, all on her own, even before psychological evaluation. She relied too heavily on one person's reportage—the teacher's. She misinterpreted the symptoms. Obviously, somebody had told her that "broken" homes produce angry, frightened children who are emotionally disturbed. (Either her training or her lack of ability to profit by that training were seriously flawed.) She overprescribed remedial action, recommending placement in a school for the severely disturbed on the basis of an incomplete and erroneous diagnosis. Even if the child were emotionally disturbed, such a placement would have been questionable.

The implications of the "wrongdoing list" still disturb me, and I must question the fact that it may not be unusual for school personnel to set about gathering evidence, like the attorney general, against a child who is giving a teacher grief. There is something very wrong, "paranoid" was the word I used, about such a hysterical overaction to the misbehavior of a young child. What is particularly upsetting is the fact that many authorities recommend that pediatricians base a diagnosis of hyperkinesis on evidence collected from school personnel.

The story has a happy ending—after a school holiday Ben was quietly transferred (not officially) to a private kindergarten with an excellent, exuberant teacher and lots of teacher's aides. The problem behavior disappeared after a few trial runs by Ben, which were half-hearted and which nobody, not even Ben, took seriously. There were bad days, sporadic incidents, and minor catastrophes, of course, but the words, "emotionally disturbed," were never heard again.

Why was the guidance counselor so bound and determined to declare my son emotionally disturbed? I don't know. Maybe she thought she was right and I was wrong. Frankly, a few doubts had crossed my mind from time to time regarding his emotional stability. While I could entertain some doubts, however, the counselor had a completely closed mind: She believed she was right. Actually, she did us both a favor—she pushed me into making a speedy decision and finding a good kindergarten teacher. Ben's records were never transferred and, while he is now a student in the same school district, somehow his first kindergarten records have been lost and are not a part of his permanent file.

The entire system of education in the United States would have long since collapsed if permeated with personnel like our friend. It is not. Most guidance counselors, social workers, remedial therapists, and teachers are not of this ilk.

Parents are encouraged to be candid with people associated with the school systems, mental health agencies, and whatever, in order to "help" the child. The danger of this, though, is that the child is too easily classified and labeled, and the label will remain attached indefinitely. Information is too readily discussed, disseminated, and subject to abuse. Supreme Court decisions have made it impossible for teachers to include derogatory comments on school records, since these records are now supposed to be open and available to parents. However, these decisions do not affect the files of guidance counselors and such, which are supposedly confidential and for the use of the counselor only.

YOUR OWN RULES OF THE GAME

There are rules for every game, as we all know. Unfortunately, parents often do not understand or appreciate the rules of the game most educators, psychologists, and social workers tend to play. The following are suggestions for handling and more or less staying on top of conversations and discussions in connection with your child. I do not guarantee that these techniques will endear you to anybody, but they may prevent you from being conned.

Preknowledge. (Or don't go into the lion's den without a gun.) When parents are told that "there are problems," they should try to make an educated guess about the tenor and subject matter of the consultation. This means, try to find out exactly what is to be discussed; find out everything you can about the other party; try to figure out what your child may or may not have done.

Try to elicit information from the child. If you have to, promise complete amnesty for any misdeeds, but try to get his side of the story *first.* If the child is willing to confide—without fear of repercussion—you may find out that he is misbehaving, but that other things are going on that are not exactly kosher. Try to get specifics—exactly what he is doing and exactly what the other person does as a result. "He picks on me" may be the truth, but it's not much help.

Rehearsal. (Or practice makes perfect.) This may sound simple-minded but, when you've decided what you want to say or what points you want to make, go over them in your mind, rehearsing how you want to say them. It's sometimes very difficult to remain calm and dispassionate—sometimes it's hard to find an opportunity to speak your piece—so it's important to have your thoughts well organized. (Chances are the other person won't.)

If you've had previous discussions with the other adult, you should be able to figure out the best approach and how you want to present your ideas.

A positive approach. (Or the art of counterdemands.) Normally, when parents are called in for a conference, the other party wants the parents to do something. To prevent parents from agreeing to unreasonable or questionable demands, or seeming to agree, they must be prepared for a positive approach.

If confronted with suggestions or demands that are new to you, and you have had no time to consider them, it is not unreasonable to insist on taking the time to reflect. Never acquiesce unless you do, in fact, agree with the other person's statements. If you feel doubtful, you have a right to some thinking time.

Then when the parents have decided what they want, or what they think ought to be done, they must deal in positive, goal-directed specifics. They should be able to explain what they want done, how it can be done, and how to implement the procedure or methods. They must, as much as possible, stick to positive recommendations, be just as nice and polite as humanly possible, and steer clear of criticism, judgments, reflections on the character of the other adult and other subtleties that will impede progress.

As an example, let's hypothesize about a teacher who thinks all children are or should be "nice" boys and girls and should be able to be quiet and sit in their seats for long periods of time without causing classroom disturbances, should not be loud and boisterous, should not fight and squabble, etc. This exemplary teacher has called a conference with the parents, not so much to seek solutions but to complain about the behavior of the child. She wants to air her grievances—she probably has some, but airing grievances does not automatically resolve the problems. The parents have met with the teacher before and realize there is quite a conflict between their child's capabilities and the teacher's expectations. There is nothing to be gained by going in unarmed, because it isn't realistic to expect the teacher to make concrete recommendations as to how *she* can improve *her* classroom interaction with the child, which is a necessary step in alleviating the problem. The child is ready to attempt to improve his behavior but won't be able to continue the efforts if the classroom interrelationship continues to deteriorate. With this goal in mind, it is up to the parents to make positive suggestions as to the management of their child by the teacher. This should be done not by pointing out what she is doing wrong, although that can be a lot of fun if the parents are angry, but by making realistic suggestions, pointing out specific mechanics that are workable and practicable, trying to set up a more flexible schedule of work periods or a system of rewards, and attempting to provide some breathing space for the child.

Don't be afraid to make suggestions or recommendations. After all, they can only be vetoed. Cite authorities from magazines and newspapers, talk about alternative methods of therapy, point out what others have done or are doing that is proving successful. The written word seems to have more power than the spoken word, so showing the other person examples of what you're talking about that have been published is sometimes quite effective.

The positive stance. (Or how not to get caught being defensive.) You simply don't have to accept another person's estimate of your child if you don't believe it or if it's based on inadequate or incomplete data. Just don't sit there and nod your head as if you were agreeing when you're not. There is a marvelous English word that should be used more frequently—"no." If someone says something about the child you know is pure hogwash, try saying, "No. I really don't believe that."

Never try to explain away the child's behavior, particularly on the basis of his deficiencies, abnormalities, or illness. Don't let the deficiencies be maximized, even if they are explainable in terms of physiological problems beyond the control of the child. Don't feel guilty or subvert guilt to the child. Don't let another adult ascribe motives to the child—particularly adult-type motives which a child could not recognize or internalize.

Ask questions about the subject being discussed—penetrating questions if you can think of any on the spur of the moment. Even if the other person indicates you're asking dumb questions, don't be intimidated. If you don't know the answers to the questions, they're not dumb to you. Don't let any one pretend you're ignorant just because you don't understand the vocabulary or context.

Don't be too ready to confide your own doubts and fears about the child in another adult until you are totally convinced of his integrity, interest in the child, ability to do something positive, and awareness of the total situation. Nobody is going to wave a magic wand and take all the problems away, anyway. It is often such a relief to unburden one's feelings about the child that parents are inclined to forget that they are responsible for protecting, defending, supporting, and maintaining him.

Don't let anybody either minimize or maximize the problems. They exist. They cannot be brushed aside lightly—the child probably will not "grow out of them"—but they are not catastrophic.

Be as reasonable and cordial as possible, but make it clear that you are not there to have somebody dictate terms to you. Don't be awed by authority, prestige, or advanced degrees. You have a right to your own opinions, and they're just as good and as valid as anybody's. Many authority figures like to be patronizing. Remember, you are not a child or mentally incompetent. You are a reasonable, reasoning adult. If you can't stop the other person from being condescending, then tell him the truth—that being patronized irritates you, that you haven't been patronized for years and years, and that you are going to do your best not to be irritated.

A strong offense is the best defense. If you realize that the whole tone of the discussion is wrong, that nothing is being accomplished and that there is no hope of getting the other person to see your point of view, there's not much you can do except stop them—quickly. If they won't stop when you interfere diplomatically, indicate you're not listening by getting up and walking around.

No matter where the discussion meanders, insist upon bringing it to the point—a positive, constructive point. Don't allow irrelevancies to confuse or cloud the issues. If the discussion centers on your child's misbehavior in the classroom, confine it to that subject: how he misbehaves, why he misbehaves if you know, what the teacher does, what can be done to curtail misbehavior, what you can do, and what others can do.

Remember the child's rights. (Or everybody is not equal, are they?) Very often, the fact that the child has rights is overlooked, or forgotten, in the heat of discussion. The parents should decide exactly what those rights are in a given situation and keep them in mind at all times. If you have to, make a list and memorize it.

Basically, the child has a right to be treated like a human being, not as some inferior creature, whether or not he is deficient or disabled or anything else. He has a right to as much education as will benefit him. He has a right to be treated with justice and fairness. He has the right to develop his own abilities as much as he can, to be his unique self, and to resist infringement of his rights.

The child's rights cannot be abrogated because of his unacceptable behavior, although this often happens. The child is not a criminal from whom society must be protected at all costs. It is a fairly common practice among teachers to isolate a child who is giving them trouble. Commonly, this type of teacher does not see the behavior as an interaction between child and teacher but as stemming only from the child. Wrong.

Under the heading of rights, the subject of double jeopardy should be included. Double jeopardy is illegal under the law. It should not be allowed in connection with the child's misbehavior or punishment for that action. I have been requested at times to punish a child when he came home from school for misbehavior in the classroom. I'm sure the child has already been punished for the misbehavior, and if he has not, it's not my job to see that he is.

Speak up. (Or don't be afraid of an argument.) Parents are inclined to soft-pedal their comments—or worse, make noncommital comments—when authorities make ridiculous statements about their children, calling into question the parents' own prestige, abilities, or sanity. Respectable authorities, such as teachers, psychologists, and social workers, can get away with saying things that other people would get punched for.

Parents of hyperkinetic children often need the services and help offered by authorities in various fields and must put a certain amount of faith in the conclusions and recommendations made by these people. However, they are generally afraid to speak up, ask questions, and disagree when they are doubtful. I suspect they are afraid to disagree because, first of all, they feel the other person somehow knows more than they do and, second, because they're afraid the authority will find something wrong with them, especially if they seem argumentative or hostile.

Don't bother to be shy. Don't be afraid of disagreeing. Argumentativeness hardly ever got anyone committed to the funny farm. The worst that can happen is that you'll have to find another authority who agrees with you.

Priorities. (Or don't scatter your shot.) Concentrate on the points you wanted to make, even if you have to repeat them, rephrase them, and reiterate them fourteen times. Eventually the other person may notice you're trying to say something important.

Generally, the parents of hyperkinetics get a lot of complaints to contend with about unacceptable behaviors. The first step is to isolate particular behaviors or problem areas and deal with each one independently.

For instance, "misbehavior in the classroom" is a meaningless phrase and can't be remedied. Fighting, inattention, inability to concentrate, and reading or speech impairments are separate entities that can be handled effectively. The parents must ascertain which behaviors are unacceptable, which ones are causing the most trouble for the child, and which ones are likely to lead to a successful and speedy resolution, and deal with them individually.

What, actually, is the goal that should be achieved? Are there distinct, separable goals? What methods, therapies, or remedies are suitable to achieve these goals?

Responsibility for the child. (Or don't look at me, I didn't do it). It's difficult to remember that, while the child is not guilty in connection with his misbehavior, he is still responsible, to some extent, for what he does and does not do. Parents of hyperkinetic children have a tendency to overcontrol, and they are often encouraged to overcontrol, making infractions of the rules just that much easier because there are so many rules to infract. The impulsive behavior of the child tends to make adults believe the child cannot, or will not, understand that consequences result from his actions. One of the most important things this child has to do is to learn about consequences, and one of the worst ways to teach him is to overcontrol.

Parents are responsible for their relationship with the child. They are categorically not responsible for the relationship of other adults with the child. If another adult is having problems controlling the child, they are definitely his troubles, not yours, while your troubles are yours; and don't ever let the twain meet.

Even if it's thrust on you, don't accept the role of hatchet man. Do not agree to punish misbehavior that occurred in connection with other adults, and not in your presence or under your jurisdiction. ("Jurisdiction" is the key word here.) For instance, parents are often encouraged to oversee homework because the child doesn't do it. Since the parent did not assign the homework, will not reward or punish its completions or incompletion, he should never accept responsibility for seeing that it is done. Parents can encourage their child, find a suitable place and time for him to work, and check to see if he has the assignment and if he has completed it, but they are not required to stand over the child with a stick in hand forcing him to do homework.

It is sometimes made very difficult for parents to abjure responsibility for the child's actions. However, they must make a determination of areas of responsibility and then stick to that decision.

Put it in writing. (Or intimidation in printed form.) Insist that everything—evaluations, recommendations, test results, rules or regulations—be written and open for your inspection. Sometimes material such as the results of psychology tests are denied to parents on the basis that the parents will not understand them, but will be sent to a professional upon the parents' request. Fine. Find a professional who will share the results with you.

Do not accept verbal reports under any conditions. If the school administration insists the child's behavior is totally unacceptable, make them put their statements in writing.

When involved in discussions and conferences, make copious notes. A tape recorder is a rather intimidating device. Explain that you have so much on your mind that, naturally, you don't want to forget or overlook any important points that were discussed during the meeting.

All communications from the parents, all decisions and recommendations, or refusals to accept recommendations, should be put in writing. Needless to say, you should keep copies of anything you write.

Take witnesses. (Or marshaling the troops.) I have always resented the fact that the child is generally excluded from discussions and conferences that concern him. There are definitely times and places where I feel that the child should be a very necessary party to the discussion. It has been my experience that sometimes the presence of the child turns what could have been a futile exposition of the child's wrongdoing into a problem-solving, goal-oriented session.

Other adults resist vehemently and strongly allowing the child to be present during discussions of his behavior, and they generally can give excellent reasons for excluding him. The reasons for exclusion shouldn't bother the parents if they feel that the child's presence is necessary in any particular instance. It's amazing how perceptive children are, and sometimes they can make contributions to a discussion that are both helpful and positive.

It's better to take reinforcements into discussions and meetings than to go by yourself, even if the reinforcements are only observers and do not take an active part in the conversation. Not only are the "troops" somewhat intimidating, but they help confine the meeting to an exposition of the subject, without embroideries or other finery. A witness is also more likely to prolong the memory of the occasion and prevent distortion.

Traditionally, the mother of the child is the only one able to attend conferences and meetings, because she is the only one available during the day. It would be far better if fathers could arrange to take the time to be present, and active, at critical conferences. (The parents must decide to show a united front beforehand. This is not the time to argue parental differences.)

In rare instances, the parents may conclude that the child should be represented by a legal counselor or someone familiar with procedures and regulations that will be encountered, such as a lay advocate. It shouldn't be necessary to take your attorney to teacher conferences, but it may be in extreme disciplinary situations, such as expulsion from school, or in confrontations with juvenile authorities.

A TOUCH OF PARANOIA

Am I paranoid, you ask? No, but I'm terribly cautious. I wasn't so cautious before certain painful experiences made me realize that, in order to fulfill my role as parent, I had to reevaluate and reorganize my own attitudes and actions in relation to authority figures. I am certainly ready to give my confidence and cooperation to professionals, just as soon as they demonstrate they deserve them.

My primary responsibilities are to do what is best for the child, and that includes evaluating the caliber and impact of other adults who come in contact with him. It really doesn't matter if someone doesn't like me or thinks I'm uncooperative or stubborn or a fruitcake. As a presumed adult, it shouldn't be that difficult to bear a little disapproval.

Knowing how I should act and respond in given situations makes it easier for me to get the things done I want done and say the things I want to say, whether or not what I do or say changes the other person's attitudes or behavior. I always hope that, if I act positively, rationally, and authoritatively enough, something of what I say will stick in the other person's mind.

Unfortunately, coping with professionals who have to cope with hyperkinetic children is a pretty rough row to hoe. The best thing parents can do is to look for the good ones, tolerate the mediocre, and discard the poor ones as quickly as possible. Just remember that there are some truly fine, dedicated therapists, educators, administrators, and other child professionals out there. Look for them.

5 To Evaluate or Not to Evaluate

The decision to evaluate a particular child can be predicated on several factors: the degree or severity of the condition, the number of symptoms observable, and/or situational requirements that indicate the need for an evaluation to prove the child is not abnormal, to facilitate programs for treatment or therapy, or 100 other specific situational indications. In other words, the need for an evaluation is based on the condition of the child and the specific situations in which he finds himself.

A complete and adequate evaluation of the child, before a diagnosis of hyperkinesis or minimal brain dysfunction can be made, should contain, if possible, these four components: a medical examination, a psychoeducational assessment, an appraisal of the child's environment, and a behavioral assessment.

As each child is unique, so the evaluation process can vary from child to child, but a good rule of thumb is: The fewer and less evident the symptoms are, the harder it is to diagnose properly. If the child exhibits hyperkinetic behavior, one or more learning disabilities, and at least minimal neurological signs, it is a fairly simple process to eliminate whatever other possible causes might produce his symptoms and arrive at an adequate diagnosis. If the child merely evidences unacceptable behavior, particularly if his behavior worsens situationally (e.g., in school), diagnosis becomes more difficult. In either case, treatment should begin as soon as one can decide what it is that's to be treated. Keep in mind that there may be any number of causal factors in relation to hyperkinetic behavior.

THE MEDICAL EXAMINATION

There are three, and sometimes four, parts to a complete medical examination.

Clinical history. This should include a complete history of the mother's pregnancy, the child's birth, and the development of the child up until the present. It should also include relevant material about the family, such as whether or not other family members suffer from similar conditions.

There are many forms available for detailing the child's history, but unfortunately, many of them require simple "Yes" or "No" answers. A busy physician might not take the time to ask penetrating questions about problems which may have been answered positively.

A complete physical examination. Such an examination should include neurological, otological (hearing), and ophthalmological (seeing) examinations to rule out sensory defects. Many authorities feel this kind of physical evaluation is not necessary, but I firmly believe in ruling out any physiological imbalance or impairment that might be producing symptoms similar to those of hyperkinesis, e.g., thyroid malfunctions leading to over- or underactivity, allergies, hearing defects, and diseases of the nervous system.

There are now a number of indexes available that purportedly turn your local pediatrician into an instant neurologist. In the case of obvious neurological impairment, it is likely that the pediatrician will refer the child to a neurologist for further examination. However, for a pediatrician to hypothesize neurological dysfunction from these sketchy indexes, particularly since most pediatricians are not experienced in the field of neurology, is a highly questionable procedure.

There is an abbreviated "special neurological examination" included in Ciba Pharmaceutical's *Physician's Handbook: Screening for MBD,* that supposedly differentiates hyperkinetics from nonhyperkinetics. There is also a short form of the Lincoln-Oseretsky test, which also purports to distinguish between hyperkinetics and "normals."

Items such as the following are included in both short-form indexes:

1. Hopping on one foot and then on the other
2. Crouching on tiptoe
3. Standing on one foot
4. Walking backward six paces
5. Skipping
6. Alternating movements of the hands (slapping knees with palms and then with the backs of the hands)
7. Tapping the index finger on the thumb, both hands
8. Right-left confusion
9. Eye-tracking
10. Writing to dictation
11. Touching the nose with the index finger
12. Standing heel to toe with the eyes closed
13. Closing and opening the hands, alternately, with the eyes closed
14. Tapping (making dots on paper)
15. Sorting matchsticks from one box to another
16. Drawing vertical lines between sets of parallel horizontal lines
17. Placing twenty coins in a box

There are, of course, instructions accompanying the indexes, but these are likely to be irrelevant when given to physicians who do not have any knowledge of developmental levels, and not very helpful even to physicians with some knowledge of such levels.

For example, as a part of one test, the child is instructed to write to dictation and scored on the basis of "labored writing." The instructions specify that "drawing" the letters nicely is not writing per se. When you're seven, it is! When the child can reasonably be expected to have completed "drawing" cursive letters and has begun to freely write them is not specified.

Under "Spelling Errors," the authors of the handbook inform us that "the physician gradually acquires approximate norms for these." Good. Just be sure your physician has acquired these norms *before* he tests your child. (Remember, you do have the right to question the tester's training and experience, and the test's validity.)

Under the heading "Right-Left Confusion," is interjected the concept of "Immaturity," informing us that some aberrant concepts of left-right movements, "by the age of 7 ½" are "a sign of significant immaturity." There is, of course, no definition of "immaturity." What does it mean? The child can't learn left from right? His nervous system is immature? His body is immature? His ability to function according to direction is immature? Whose norms or scales were used to decide the age at which this behavior becomes immature?

There are many instances of this kind of equivocation. The instructions are very imprecise and leave too much to the discretion of the individual physician. It would be possible for almost any child, under the right conditions, being graded by a physician unfamiliar with developmental norms and lacking understanding and experience with children, to be diagnosed as dysfunctional.

It should be pointed out that no information on test reliability and validity is included in the handbook. Since most physicians are not familiar with psychoeducational indexes, it appears that the physician is left to presume that the indexes in the handbook are both reliable and valid.

Any neurological examination should be performed by a competent pediatric neurologist. I sincerely believe—or at least, I'd like to believe—that no physician would administer the Ciba neurological scale and, on the basis of that index alone, diagnose minimal brain dysfunction. (I want to emphasize how dangerous this index can be. The authors state that "MBD has been separated into three types: hyperactive, specific learning disability and the mixed type." In other words, Ciba's authors suggest an underlying central nervous system malfunction may be diagnosed whether or not neurological signs are apparent, which diagnosis could be founded almost entirely on teacher reports of unacceptable behavior.)

Routine laboratory tests. As in the neurological examination, these would rule out other causes of symptomatic behavior: lead poisoning, hypoglycemia, allergic reactions, and such. Sometimes such tests, while not definitive, raise suspicions—something isn't quite right—so that more specific testing can be initiated.

Specialized physiological tests as required.

PSYCHOLOGICAL AND EDUCATIONAL ASSESSMENT

Apparently, many psychologists and educators either are validating, or have validated and are using, measuring devices that will indicate (purportedly) anything from kindergarten readiness to psychosis. In almost every case there are published reports on the validity and the reliability of the tests as well as published criticism of the tests, the methods used to establish validity and reliability, and general disparagement of all testing devices.

My original intention was to describe the individual tests and comment on what they claim to measure, their validity, their reliability, and their weaknesses. It became apparent that a separate book would be required for that purpose, so to limit the discussion on tests and measurements, only the "tried and true's" will be commented on.

I have listed a number of commonly used measuring devices so that parents will have some reference point in discussing the child's evaluation and diagnosis. As an example, many of the screening devices purport to measure intelligence. Parents should not too readily accept results from one of these tests that indicate a low level of functioning. A full-range, individualized intelligence test is the only "safe" index of intelligence, because it discriminates between sensory impairments and level of intelligence, at least to some degree. It should be pointed out that many of these tests are "culturally contaminated." They are biased toward middle-class, white, verbally oriented children.

Screening Devices

The trend is toward screening school children, and the trend will undoubtedly continue, with more and more children being screened sometime during their school career. Screening has one purpose and one purpose only: *to isolate problem areas that must be examined and evaluated in individual sessions by specialists competent to make such evaluations.* Screening is not evaluation and is surely not diagnosis. Most screening devices will not give the specialist enough information to prescribe remediation. The few screens that are claimed to have diagnostic value must be administered by trained specialists.

Psychological, psychoneurological, or psychoeducational (whichever you prefer) evaluation is a lengthy, involved, time-consuming process. Including parent consultations, it may require anywhere from five to nine hours. Most screening is done with an eye to time requirements. The entire screening process, which is normally done in groups, may require less than one hour.

The following tests are more-or-less screening devices, which are presumed to measure components of intelligence, perception, levels of competence and, sometimes, emotional status. These are enumerated so that parents will be, hopefully, familiar with some of the common names. They are the Basic Concept Inventory, the Daberon, the Dallas Preschool Screening Test, the DIAL, the Jansky Modified Screen Index, the Kindergarten Evaluation of Learning Potential (KELP), the Kindergarten Questionnaire, the Meeting Street School Screening Test, the Metropolitan Readiness Test, the Preschool Inventory, the Preschool Screening System, the Riley Preschool Developmental Screening Inventory, the Yellow Brick Road, the

Vallet Development Survey, the Vane Kindergarten Test, and the Zeitling Early Identification Screening (ZEIS). Many school districts devise their own screening devices and pick and choose among the tests available in particular problem areas. So a screening might consist of the Slosson Intelligence Test (see below), various subtests from sensory and perceptual-motor testing devices, and various indexes from other screening devices. Such a screen's value depends on the capabilities of the person or persons who selected the subtests.

For some of these screens, it is claimed that a diagnosis and remediation program can be made from the results. Parents should be quite cautious of such diagnoses, and might well insist upon more refined techniques. Many screens were designed so they could be administered by untrained or minimally trained personnel, and I suggest that parents do a little reading in a social science library to gather information about the particular testing devices used on their child. A great deal of material concerning tests and screens is printed in educational and psychological journals, and most of the articles are not so technical that they are incomprehensible.

Cognitive Tests

Intelligence tests. The Wechsler Intelligence Scale for Children-Revised (WISC-R) is considered by many to be a most reputable and reliable intelligence test. It is divided into two basic parts; verbal and performance (nonverbal), and the two parts are further divided into subtests which measure different aspects of intelligence, some of which are sensitive to perceptual or sensory dysfunction. For young children, there is the Wechsler Preschool and Primary Scale.

The Stanford-Binet Intelligence Scale, which is predominantly verbal, has been criticized because it draws on learned or acquired knowledge. It is clearly unsuitable for deprived or linguistically dysfunctional children.

The Peabody Picture Vocabulary Test, the Goodenough-Harris Draw-A-Man Test, and the Slosson Intelligence Test for Children are also indexes of intelligence and are commonly used in screening and evaluation because they are easy to administer. The Goodenough is considered indicative of cognitive development but could easily be contaminated by emotional factors, such as a very negative self-image. The Slosson is an abbreviated, individual test that gives fairly good *indications* of intelligence levels.

The Bayley Infant Scales of Development and the Gesell Developmental Scales are good indexes for young children. The Cattell Infant Intelligence Scale and the Denver Developmental Screen, both popular tests, have been criticized as less reliable for predictive purposes.

Achievement tests. There are a good number of achievement tests, and some are used fairly regularly. The one serious fault of achievement tests is that they cannot measure certain very important variables—among them, motivation—and so, while they can tell us where the child stands now in relation to his peers, they cannot really predict his future performance, although some authorities like to think they can.

The Metropolitan Readiness Tests and the Metropolitan Achievement Tests measure and predict ability to succeed in school *fairly* accurately. The Wide Range Achievement Tests (WRAT), revised edition, a very popular test, has been the subject of criticism as to its reliability, validation procedures, and inadequate normative data.

The Peabody Individual Achievement Test, the Iowa Tests of Basic Skills, the California Achievement Tests, the Stanford Achievement Tests, the Hiskey-Nebraska Test of Learning Aptitude, and the SRA Achievement Series all are batteries of achievement tests that are commonly used. Since norms vary widely throughout the country, one should be extremely careful in accepting normative data on any achievement test.

Sensory and Motor Tests

There are a number of relatively accurate and reputable tests devised to isolate and distinguish specific dysfunctions or disabilities. They roughly fall into categories that discriminate sensory and motor abilities (visual, auditory-linguistic, and perceptual-motor or sensory-motor), social-emotional abilities, and conceptual or cognitive style. There are also tests that are used to diagnose specific school-related problems, such as reading or math disabilities.

Visual indexes. The Frostig Developmental Test of Visual Perception is the most widely recognized test. The Kohs Block Test gives indications of visual and sensory impairments. The Keystone Visual Survey is a recently developed test and is not as widely used.

Auditory-linguistic tests. The Illinois Test of Psycholinguistic Abilities (ITPA), the Wepman Auditory Discrimination Test, the Goldman Fristoe Woodcock Test of Auditory Discrimination, and the Test for Auditory Comprehension of Language are the most common diagnostic tools mentioned in the literature. Most of the intelligence tests, especially the WISC, the Peabody Picture Vocabulary, and the Gesell Developmental Schedules can be useful tools for diagnosing language difficulties.

Sensory- or perceptual-motor inventories. The Beery-Buktenica Developmental Test of Visual-Motor Integration, the Bender Visual Motor Gestalt Test (or Bender-Gestalt), the Purdue Perceptual Motor Survey, the McCarthy Scale of Children's Abilities, the Primary Visual Motor Test, and the Southern California Sensory Integration Tests are used frequently. The Bender-Gestalt is as tried and true as they come, having been formulated about 1938. There are also a number of form-board and pegboard devices, colored blocks, and shapes that are used to diagnose specific impairments, such as the Sequin Form Board.

Social-Emotional Measurements

The Thematic Apperception Test and the Children's Apperception Test are commonly used to measure the child's feelings about himself and others. The Rorschach and Holtman inkblot techniques may have application, depending on the abilities of the administrator, and may also be useful to diagnose sensory or visual difficulties such as figure-ground confusion or the inability to conceptualize visual stimuli as wholes. The interpretation of the results is highly subjective and therefore always open to question. These tests are usually as good as the person who administers them.

The Vineland Social Maturity Scale, a reliable and reputable measure of social maturity, is sometimes translated into a social competence IQ score. The Vineland was originally developed as a rating device for retarded children, whose abilities to perform many routine, everyday tasks, especially the kinds of things children need to learn in order to be able to take care of themselves, far exceed their measurable intelligence.

Children are rated on their ability to perform age-specific tasks and functions, such as tying shoes, dressing oneself, doing household chores, selecting and purchasing one's own clothes (on a budget), shopping at the grocery store, and traveling in one's hometown or home area on public transportation. The scale should be required reading for all parents. It's quite surprising how independent and responsible children can be expected to be. Reading the Vineland surely would inhibit a tendency to overprotect a child.

The Minnesota Multiphasic Personality Inventory has always been the center of dispute, and its diagnostic value seems to be related to the skills of the administrator, who needs to be both familiar with the inventory and its ramifications and skilled in handling children. Generally, I don't think it's suitable for young, immature, or language-deficient children.

There are a number of sentence completion and "what if" types of tests that purport to measure attitudes. Unless the tester knows the background of the child, the results can be misinterpreted quite easily. For instance, a child whose parents are divorced and who has little contact with his father will have problems completing sentences relating to a father figure. Without prior knowledge, the administrator could misconstrue the child's "incorrect" answers.

Cognitive/Conceptual Measurements

The Basic Concept Inventory purportedly measures level of cognition (ability to deal with thoughts). The Goldstein Tests are designed to measure concept formation. As for cognitive styles, there is a series of tests that measure field dependence-independence (the Early Childhood Embedded Figure Test) and reflection versus impulsivity (the Early Childhood Familiar Figure Test).

Specialized Tests

Most of these indexes attempt to diagnose the extent and prevalence of learning disabilities, and they are used when specific areas of dysfunction have been noted.

They include the Gray Oral Reading Test, the Reading Diagnostic Test, the Key Math Diagnostic Test, Raven's Coloured Progressive Matrices, the Durrell Analysis of Reading Difficulty, the Kottmeyer Spelling Test, the Porteus Maze Test (which also has other applications), Gates-McKillop Reading Diagnostic Tests, and tests for laterality (handedness).

Many of the tests mentioned above measure more than one aspect of human potential, such as the Gesell Developmental Schedules, which measure motor, perceptual, and cognitive development.

Many of the screening devices, such as the Jansky Modified Screening Index and the Vane Kindergarten Test, are based on adaptations of other testing instruments, such as the Bender-Gestalt and the Goodenough-Harris Draw-A-Man tests.

ENVIRONMENTAL ASSESSMENT

While there is tremendous emphasis on the child's behavior and a plethora of checklists for parents and teachers to rate the child, I have yet to come across a checklist that rates the parents, teachers, and other environmental factors that influence the behavior of the child. This seems to me to be a serious omission, so I'm going to make one up. Why not?

An environmental checklist should include a number of questions relevant to the child's place in society and how well he fits in, how he is viewed by parents and other adults, how his parents respond to him, what management techniques they use, and whether or not the parents are essentially capable of being supportive and helpful.

It is equally important to assess the child's feelings about himself. Is he able to confront his problem behavior and how does he see himself in relation to others? What are his real feelings about himself and his real worth?

The following checklist would be a helpful tool for professionals to use to be sure they have the total picture. Answered honestly (remembering that it doesn't help anyone to feel guilty, and that they probably haven't that much to feel guilty about, anyway) it could be helpful for parents.

Parental attitudes:

1. How do the parents feel about the child?
2. Are they relatively accepting or do they reject him?
3. Are they calm or anxious about the child? Are they indifferent?
4. Are the parents excessively restrictive or punitive toward the child? (Assess the methods of punishment, amount of free time, outside activities, number of times the child is punished per day, etc.)
5. What are their usual methods of punishment? How often do they act harshly or excessively?
6. How do they reward acceptable behavior?
7. How do they perceive themselves in relation to the child?
8. How do they think the child feels toward them?
9. How angry are they? At whom are they angry? Themselves, the child, or others?
10. Are they amenable to suggestions for improving management techniques?

11. Do they appear flexible—capable of changing their attitudes?

Parental expectations:

12. What do the parents see as the major problems?
13. Do they feel the problems are solvable or that the situation is hopeless?
14. What behaviors particularly upset them?
15. What methods have they tried to correct this behavior?
16. When they think of the future, do they see the child as predominantly successful?
17. Do they see the child as an inevitable loser?
18. Do they expect high achievement in school?
19. Do they look for improvement based on the child's abilities or on unrealistic assessments?
20. Do they reinforce the child's negative behavior?
21. What do they feel are the child's positive or strong points?
22. What do they regard as proper outlets for the child's hyperactivity?
23. If they had to predict a career for the child at the moment, what would it be?

Parental life styles:

24. Do the parents seem to be supportive when the child has problems?
25. Do they offer helpful, concrete suggestions for solving problems?
26. Are the parents active and outgoing, or are they pensive and quiet?
27. Do the parents enjoy physical work and/or sports, such as camping, fishing, tennis, skating, gardening, and do-it-yourself projects?
28. Do the parents enjoy only sedentary activities such as reading, watching TV, and playing cards?
29. Do the parents spend any time playing active games with the child?
30. How much time do they spend with the child in positive interaction?

31. Are the parents able to maintain a well-regulated but flexible schedule?

32. Could the home life be described as child-centered chaos?

33. Do the parents agree on matters of discipline, scheduling, rewards, etc.?

34. Are the parents mutually supportive, especially when the child behaves badly?

35. Do the parents appear to be flexible or are they inclined to rigidity?

Life space:

36. Does the child have plenty of space, indoors and out, to expend energy?

37. Does he have regular chores and responsibilities, such as caring for pets?

38. Is the home arranged to minimize accidental damage? Or is it cluttered and ornamental—un-child-oriented?

39. Do the parents encourage the child to participate in games and sports?

40. Do they provide a "quiet space" for the child?

41. How does the child get along with his siblings?

42. If the child is aggressive, how do the parents handle his aggression?

43. How does the child get along in the neighborhood?

44. Does he have age-mate friends?

45. How does the child behave in school? Better or worse than at home?

46. What is his relationship with his classmates?

47. What is his relationship with his teachers?

48. What is his relationship with other important adults?

49. How does his behavior affect his relationships with others?

50. What have the parents done to improve his relationships with others?

51. Does he behave better with some people than with others?

The child's view:

52. How does the child see himself?
53. What does the child feel about his parents?
54. What does he think his parents feel and think about him?
55. What does the child like to do?
56. Does he like school? Why or why not?
57. Who are the people he likes best? Why?
58. Does he ever feel unhappy? Very often?
59. What are the things that make him feel happy?
60. Is the child aware that his behavior is sometimes unacceptable?
61. Does he feel unable to change or modify his behavior, or does he feel capable of positive change?
62. What would he like to be when he's grown?

The reader should be able to see some of the points that need to be considered. How much of the child's behavior is caused by poor parental management? Are there supportive adults in his life who can help him? How pervasive are his problems? How much does he deviate from parental expectations?

It is totally inexcusable to assess the child's behavior without a careful assessment of parental attitudes and expectations, contingencies such as space and opportunities to discharge excess energy, and the child's own conception of himself. Obviously a child with an exceedingly poor self-image, created by punitive and hostile parents with excessive and unrealistic expectations, with few acceptable outlets for energy and activity, will probably be seen as more seriously symptomatic than the child with a good self-image, whose parents are relatively accepting (and hostile only on occasion) and who encourage him to acquire suitable outlets.

BEHAVIORAL ASSESSMENT

Behavioral assessment is an area of total confusion. Most of the scales used are recently developed, and some have not been completely validated or had their reliability established. On the whole, behavioral assessments don't seem to be much less subjective than my environmental index, and some of the questions are downright leading; that is, the respondent almost has to answer questions in such a way as to prompt a diagnosis of hyperkinesis.

The Werry-Weiss-Peters Activity Scale is broken down into seven specific behavioral situations, and the behaviors are more directly observable than some included in other scales. However, the response choices are severely limited: "no," "yes, a little bit," and "yes, very much." The narrowness of the range almost precludes a "no" response. The responses need to be refined and expanded. There's a lot of difference between "a little bit" and "very much."

The Bell, Waldrop and Weller Rating System is better as to the number of categories for response—there are eleven. However, the individual activities defined by each scale are ambiguous—they mean something to Bell, Waldrop, and Weller, but it's improbable that the average administrator will understand the subtleties. What is the difference between "frenetic play" and "nomadic play?" Under the heading "Induction of Intervention," the high-scoring child "very frequently plays in such a way as to make it highly likely a teacher in the area would feel compelled to intervene either to prevent injury to the child or others, or to prevent damage to physical objects." What does "frequent" intervention mean? 10 times? 12 times? 100 times? I don't know. It's also possible that the frequency of intervention has a lot to do with the personality of the person who intervenes, and not that of the child.

The Davids Rating Scale for Hyperkinesis lists only seven traits or behaviors to be rated on a six-point scale. Many of the descriptors call for subjective judgments, and the categories tend to overlap.

The behavior rating scale included in the Ciba Handbook is particularly biased. Besides the fact that possible response is limited to three choices, some of the questions are ambiguous. For example, under "Emotional Response," the parent is asked, "Compared with other children his age, is your child—slower, the same, or quicker—to anger? To cry? To laugh?" These questions presuppose knowledge of comparable age norms, and I don't think parents generally have such knowledge at their fingertips. (This might be a good question on a test of parental attitudes, which the scale is not.) The scale also includes a number of questions about school behavior, which the parents are asked to report not only subjectively but also second-hand. If the child's teacher says he talks too much or doesn't complete his work, what kind of validity can we ascribe to hearsay?

The Conners' Teacher Rating Scale and Conners' Abbreviated Teacher Rating Scale are widely used in the diagnosis of hyperkinesis. Both scale items and response choices are a little vague and imprecise. Responses describing degrees of activity range from "not at all" to "just a little," "pretty much," and "very much." Theoretically, depending on the proclivities and personality of the observer, any one child could be scored all over this scale by different raters. The Scale is divided into three categories: classroom behavior, group participation, and attitude toward authority. Many of the items include definitions. The abbreviated Teacher Rating Scale is composed of items from the full scale which purportedly distinguishes the hyperkinetic from others.

The Conners' Parent Questionnaire, ninety-three-item checklist, suffers from many of the same problems as the rating scales for teacher administration: ambiguity in language and imprecise definition of response. I fail to see why the responses cannot be phrased in numerical equivalents, so that the parent could decide how many times a particular activity occurred during a week or day and report that number.

There is also a Ciba Handbook School Report that includes, among behavior-oriented questions, questions regarding scholastic ability or achievement. Responses are limited and I would quarrel with the choice of words used in response: "poorly," "well," and "above average." "Well" is indeed a strange substitute for what so obviously means "average." This limited choice of responses forces a respondent to choose "poorly" if the child is not, in fact, doing "well." Almost as an afterthought, the authors ask the respondent to include information on special abilities, talents, and assets the child might have. However, since no other behavior checklist even suggests the child might have any talents, assets, or good points, I suppose Ciba's must be considered a small improvement.

Keep in mind that some authorities rely as heavily on behavior checklists as if they had been written by Moses on Mount Sinai, and there are a few who actually prefer such indexes to extensive medical and psychoneurological examinations.

I cannot help but feel that many of these checklists are "rigged." It's long been accepted that anyone can design a test that will prove what he wants it to prove. Fortunately, not everyone can establish validity (that the test yields consistent results, both throughout the test items and from one testing situation to another) for his index. Standardization of testing devices is a cumbersome, lengthy, and complicated process. Among other factors, normative data have to be established. I would love to see somebody try to establish norms for purposeful, positive activity.

Perhaps many of these authorities appear to be biased because they deal exclusively with the most symptomatic and extreme clinical cases of hyperkinesis; they tend to extrapolate their conclusions from that group and go on to apply them to mild and moderate hyperkinetics. After all, it's more than likely that most mild and a good number of moderate cases of hyperkinesis never are evaluated, never receive any type of therapy and, accordingly, are not included in the statistics, except in the academic environment, if they are unable to satisfactorily adjust to the demands imposed by the school structure.

This practice of extrapolating from a severely affected population and making generalizations about the so-called normal population is always a dangerous and impractical occupation. One can't draw conclusions from research with hospitalized psychotics that apply, for instance, to functioning self-sustaining populations. Such conclusions would be pretty invalid.

It may be quite possible to gather insights from severely affected individuals that can be useful in evaluating and treating those more mildly affected. What too regularly happens, however, is that "insights" become facts, and are applied as hard and fast, proven scientific data.

A broken bone is a fact, although there are many possible degrees of injury, from a small hairline fracture to an injury that involves mutilation. Hyperkinesis, the diagnosis of which is not always factual, has a far broader spectrum of involvement, so any generalizations derived from the study of the severely affected should be viewed with a good bit of skepticism.

THE DECISION TO EVALUATE

Parents tend to shy away from extensive evaluation. Besides the obvious deterrent—the expense—they are probably afraid the examination will reveal things they are ashamed of or feel guilty about, or they really don't want to face the fact that their child may be impaired or dysfunctional. Evaluation should not be such a fearsome bogeyman. The purpose of evaluation is to find ways to help the child realize his potential, to overcome impairments, or to compensate for incapacities. Without a good, solid diagnosis, no good, solid plan of remediation can be programmed.

Believe it or not, the results of a *good* evaluation can be quite positive and relieve a lot of parental anxiety. At least, the parents will know what they have to worry about rather than being beset by all kinds of nebulous fears. When parents realize that something is definitely wrong, but they don't know with whom or what, how serious it is, what they're doing wrong, or why the kid does what he does, then it's time to consider evaluation. When the parents run into problems with the child that they don't know how to solve, or when the child is involved in school-related problems that seem insoluble, then evaluation should be the next positive step.

It's a good feeling to know that remediation is possible, whether it's a learning disability, parental management techniques, or building the child's self-image that needs to be remedied. It's not a particularly good feeling to be overwhelmed with self-doubts and self-accusations as a parent.

The whole purpose of evaluation is to make specific remediation possible, not to classify the child and certainly not to limit him by means of the classification. Evaluation has to ascertain the degree of impairment, the level of functioning, and the possibilities and methods of improvement or remediation. If it does not, it's worthless.

When deciding whether or not to evaluate, parents should keep in mind what they expect such an evaluation to do for them and the child, and they should make this point very clear to the evaluators. The parents have a right to expect a therapeutic program plan as the result of an evaluation—true. But who or which evaluator, since often there are several different specialists involved in an evaluation, should have the final responsibility for prescribing remediation? Depending on the type of impairment and the degree of involvement, parents will have to depend on the recommendations of the *person whom they judge to have the most experience and expertise in the field,* whether this is the physician, the psychologist, or the educational specialist.

A good evaluation, then, should do several things for the parents: It should allay anxiety, first of all. It should accurately and meaningfully diagnose a specific deficit or problem area. It should assess the level or type of deficit. It should enumerate the specific remediation needed for improvement, estimating the amount of improvement that might be possible. And last, but certainly not least, it should be encouraging and help parents to see that, taken a step at a time, their problems with the child are, after all, not insurmountable.

6 Child-Oriented Therapy

What happens after the evaluation? Or what happens when you suspect that your child is really troubled by his behavior? Or you realize your relationship with him needs some repair? Well, you should look around for help in the specific areas in which you or your child need a little assistance: remediating a specific learning disability, overcoming your own frustration with the child, helping him learn to curb his impulsiveness—you name it.

There is a certain amount of resistance to the idea of therapy, and there really ought not to be, especially if therapy is taken to mean that one person attempts to help another who is simply having some kind of emotional, situational, or physical problem.

Unfortunately, when one thinks of therapy, one is inclined to think of a long-term, expensive, rather painful process. We've all heard stories about people who have spent six or seven traumatic years in analysis and occasionally wondered how effective therapy really could be. Fortunately, therapy need not be extended, painful, or crushingly costly. There are many types of therapy, even within the fields of psychology and psychiatry, and many of them are quite effective in relation to the hyperkinetic child, his parents, and his family relationships.

The precise definition of therapy, of course, rests almost entirely with each therapist's orientation. Some therapists follow a prescribed and inflexible systematized regime. Analysts, for example, accept a particular view of human personality and its constructs and adhere to certain methods for treating deviance. Most therapists, however, are eclectic in their approach, borrowing the best—and what works for them—from a number of theories and techniques. In other words, they are flexible in their approach and inclined to try new methods and techniques, which may or may not be based on a systematized theoretical base.

Parents need to know a little about the different types of therapy so that, when they need help for themselves or the child, they are able to clearly define the treatment goals, can decide if the approach is suitable, and are able to evaluate therapeutic effectiveness. For example, analysis would not be particularly suitable for the female child of a highly liberated couple; the goals might not complement the goals of the parents, and the effectiveness would be reduced by the home orientation.

Therapies are often viewed as polarized entities: individual or group therapy; brief, goal-defined therapy or long-term therapy; emotional or cognitive therapy (one dealing with emotional content or alleviation of fears and anxiety and the other with the more rational aspects of beliefs and assumptions); eclectic or specific-theory therapy; and directive or nondirective therapy. Most of this categorizing is artificial. I doubt that many therapists are confirmed in one direction or another but are more or less flexible as the situation requires.

Nondirective therapy requires that the therapist remain inactive, reflecting or restating the feelings, comments, assumptions, and/or states the client is relating. In directive therapy, the therapist can be more active, offering suggestions, making comments himself, and centering on specific areas he feels need attention. Goal-directed therapy limits itself to remedying specific situations, behaviors, and responses or intervening during crises; long-term, in-depth therapy is directed toward radical changes in the total personality structure.

I'm not at all sure it's realistic to believe therapy can critically alter the personality, and I'm pretty sure that, if it could, it wouldn't be moral to do so. Therapeutic goals should not be to make over the individual but to help him achieve maximum potential with what he already has. I most strongly believe that therapy can be beneficial; it can help the individual by altering improper responses, changing attitudes and behaviors, giving support and acceptance, prompting growth and alleviating the fears that inhibit growth, and, in general, being a beneficial and stimulating process.

No kind of therapy can benefit an unwilling subject. In other words, there are two essential components of successful therapy: a good therapist and a client who is willing to put a great deal of himself into the process. Most adults who seek therapy are willing to commit themselves to the therapeutic goals. That leaves a large, looming question about children and therapy. Most children neither understand the goals of therapy nor are they classifiable as willing victims. Children wind up in therapy because somebody sent them.

Does this mean that children are unwilling victims, or that therapy will not be beneficial? Probably not. Children have an overwhelming need or drive for self-actualization. I think that most children are more than willing to exchange improper behaviors and responses for more acceptable, positive actions which will in the long run lead to self-actualization. Given the choice, I think it highly probable that they will pick the more positive behaviors, responses, and methods of coping.

"Hyperactive children don't benefit from therapy." Translated, this probably means either that some therapists are not effective in handling hyperkinetic types and are therefore not able to promote positive changes, or that specific types of therapy are not effective in altering or changing the unacceptable behaviors or responses of hyperkinetic children. I can't imagine anything more devastating than for a child to go into therapy because he is failing—in interpersonal relationships with his parents, his peers, and his teachers, in his schoolwork, in controlling his behavior, in inhibiting his anger, in winning acceptance and approval—and then to fail in therapy. When you fail therapy, what else is there left?

BEHAVIOR MODIFICATION

Behavior modification, after a brief but happy period of popularity, has fallen into disrepute. Its proponents, by making extraordinary assertions about the efficacy of its application, managed to disenchant everybody else by making palpable the myth of mind control.

If the claims of radical behaviorists can be believed, they are capable of modifying all behavior, at all times, in all people, in all circumstances, etc., through the judicious application of the appropriate reinforcement. The chief proponent of behavior modification, B.F. Skinner, made himself extremely unpopular through the not uncommon mistake of generalizing the results of research further than was plausible. No matter what behaviorists claim, one can't really extrapolate from pigeons to people. Behavior modification techniques work perfectly with pigeons, imperfectly with children, and not too well with adults.

Many of the succeeding behaviorists who put the theories into practice in classrooms and other environments relied too heavily on tokens, chips, and other substitute rewards, creating a furor about the artificially contrived "token economy." It's far-fetched to assume that people will do anything to get a blue poker chip. Tokens are useful rewards in behavior modification because the rewardee sees some value beyond that which the token intrinsically possesses. Rewards the individual does not prize are not successful reinforcers of behavior.

Still, some adults feel there's something inherently

wrong in rewarding a child for acceptable behavior. This attitude is expressed by parents as, "I don't get rewards for doing what I should do. Why should the kid?" The answer, of course, is, "Why shouldn't the kid?" As a matter of fact, the parent is most definitely being rewarded for doing what he does, whether he is reinforced negatively or positively. Nobody does much of anything unless there is something in it for him and, without motivation, chances are most of us would do very little, and that includes getting up in the morning and going to work. Even the drive for self-actualization would be stifled by the absence of reinforcement. Without reinforcers to reward—or coerce—behavior, most people would lead pretty aimless lives.

There's a feeling that it's not quite sporting to attempt to influence the behavior of another person by bribery or coercion, especially if that person cannot adequately judge the situation and make a decision to act or not to act. This attitude strikes me as somewhat hypocritical, since adults generally do indeed attempt to influence, coerce, channel, and direct children's behavior into the patterns and routines they personally find acceptable and approvable. Apparently, it's all right to manage behavior providing the rewards aren't tangible, the goals are unspecified, and the process is unverbalized, but wrong when the rewards are evident and the goals and techniques are specific. A pat on the head is OK; candy is a no-no. Good grades are morally right; tokens are wrong.

Specifically in relation to hyperkinesis, behavior modification has been shown to increase attention or decrease distractibility, promote orderliness, decrease disruptive behavior, decrease aggressive behavior, increase socially acceptable interactions, decrease sibling fighting, and improve inhibitory processes and other observable behaviors. According to published data, even a factor such as impulsivity (as it relates to cognitive style: impulsivity versus reflectivity) is amenable to modification.

Used rationally, behavior modification techniques work well with hyperkinetic children in almost any setting and situation. The research is irrefutable. So why aren't modification programs more popular and why the reluctance to try them?

Perhaps the emphasis of the behaviorists has been a trifle misplaced. Perhaps they failed to recognize that other factors, besides the obvious reinforcing agent that is a visible or specific symbol of success, play an important part in modifying the responses of hyperkinetic children. There are the values the recipient attaches to the reinforcer, which can be quite subjective. There is the change, as positive interactions increase and negative ones decrease, from aversive or negative control to positive management. There are also the factors of acceptance, understanding, and approval—or maybe I should call it nonhostility—which are often brought into better focus and made more visible to the child as positive reinforcement and acceptable behavior continue to occur. (This may be a novel situation for some children.) Instead of a steady diet of parental criticism, correction, nagging, and screaming, the child begins to experience rewarding, pleasant contacts with parents. And then there is the matter of changed parental attitudes and expectations, which may be more realistic than those the child has been accustomed to and which bring relief from some of his frustrations and guilt. As the child begins to respond appropriately, parents are apt to view him with more approbation and to expect continuing appropriate responses which, if properly reinforced, are just as apt to increase.

Because of increased recognition of these other factors, many behaviorists have come to see the individual holistically (as a totality). They recognize that behavior modification is much more than a simple substitution of one behavior for another, which will automatically take place in the presence of an artificial reinforcer—the blue poker chip.

Behavior modification is also frequently criticized because the client is being "trained" as opposed to being "educated." I don't think children are, on the whole, trainable unless the trainer comes prepared with a whip and a gun and a whole set of extremely oppressive methods. I'm afraid the critics of behavior modification make the same mistake as radical behaviorists—assuming people behave like laboratory animals. They don't. The child can be shown appropriate behavior, and appropriate behavior can be elicited and maintained by proper reinforcement, but I think real learning (education) takes place when the child can substitute and change his responses. The differences between training and education, in this case, are somewhat contrived. What is education, after all, but a carefully arranged sequence of training segments, e.g., learning to read or learning math?

Operant Conditioning

Behavior modification relies on a technique called operant conditioning, which means, simply, maintaining approved behavior by providing an appropriate reward or reinforcer. There are four basic steps to consider: (1) the selection of an appropriate reinforcer, one that is of value to the recipient; (2) the immediacy of the reinforcement and the regularity with which it is to be received; (3) eliciting the acceptable or approved behavior; and (4) maintaining the behavior, both during the reinforcement period and afterward.

Selecting an appropriate reinforcer is sometimes difficult. Blue poker chips aren't always suitable, although they can acquire symbolic value. If the token has no meaning and cannot get the child something he wants, whether it's parental approval or a toy or special attention or recognition of success, it is worthless. Rewards or reinforcing agents can be almost anything or anyone: verbal acknowledgments, designated privileges, a favorite food, special events, free time, activities the child prefers, and many others.

Immediacy of reinforcement is important, as is the schedule on which the reinforcement is applied. As a rule, the more immediate the reinforcement, the more successful it will be, which is one of the reasons that tokens or points are used as reinforcers, particularly in group situations. They can be given immediately with a minimum of effort on the part of the reinforcer and without disrupting the group.

Generally, when one begins a modification program, acceptable behavior is reinforced every time it occurs. The schedule of reinforcement is later modified as the desired or acceptable behavior occurs more frequently. It has been found that a variable schedule of reinforcement is most efficacious (i.e., the desired behavior is rewarded unsystematically but frequently enough to maintain its appearance). The intervals between reinforcement are gradually extended until the time when the acceptable behavior has acquired some value of its own and hopefully reinforcement can be discontinued.

Eliciting the desired behavior can be a problem, too, especially if it is not in the behavioral repertoire (i.e., it does not occur spontaneously), or occurs very infrequently.

Unacceptable and acceptable behavior must be identified and specific behaviors distinguished, e.g., hitting or slapping siblings, resisting going to bed or going to sleep, not doing homework; helpful gestures toward siblings, attentive behavior (concentration on specific tasks), performing specific chores without argument or bickering.

If the desired behavior occurs, immediate reinforcement must be administered. If it does not occur, several techniques are useful, depending on the desired behavior and the age and capacities of the child. The child may simply be told what the proper behavior is. The instructions must be formalized and easily understood, and the correct performance should be demonstrated. Modeling is also a useful method. In some way, the child is shown the appropriate behavior—through demonstration, watching others, symbolic figures, or whatever. Role playing or practicing the desired behavior can be very effective. Once the behavior has been demonstrated, the child should be asked to reenact or practice the behavior and then be reinforced.

The reinforcing agent will supposedly maintain the behavior, but there are other methods that promote correct responses. The child can be taught to help regulate his actions by verbal commands to himself. This can be taken one step further by teaching him to use covert self-instructions that help him internalize directions. Self-reinforcing responses can then be modeled, so that the child is eventually able to self-reward acceptable behavior.

For example, given a child who is sensitive to belittling remarks and reacts explosively, one might demonstrate an acceptable method for reacting and then help the child reenact the proper sequence. When he is able to respond correctly to remarks, he is reinforced by some agent that has been specified, such as verbal recognition or a penny. He is then instructed to repeat to himself, when confronted by irritating remarks, a formula that will regulate his actions, such as "Stop! I will not hit this person. I will agree with him and make it into a joke." It is hoped that in due course the child will see that his responses defuse an explosive situation, that the other person's comments are not as antagonistic as they appeared, and that he can turn the situation around by not responding violently. Having mastered the proper response, the child can be taught to congratulate himself on his success.

Contingency contracting is another method for maintaining acceptable behavior if the child is old enough to understand the concept of reciprocal contracts. Of course, a contract can be as simple or as complex as both parties want to make it, so young children can make contracts.

Contingency contracting is a good example of the old maxim, "You scratch my back and I'll scratch yours." Basically, it implies that the parties of the contract will each perform certain goal-oriented actions which each of the parties has predetermined and agreed upon as fair. Generally, certain privileges or rewards are granted to the child, based on the performance of desired behaviors. The steps by which the contract can be fulfilled are specified, as well as the exact rewards or reinforcements, and the penalties for nonperformance are detailed. Contingency contracts should be written out in great detail and signed by both parties, indicating their acceptance of the contract terms.

Some systematic recording of the fulfillment of requirements and the granting of rewards and penalties should be part of the contract.

It's crucial that neither party infract the provisions of the contract, either by being lenient in enforcing penalties or by abusing the privileges granted. It is naturally a nuisance to enforce such contracts, but it's a bigger nuisance to live with the behaviors that contracts can help modify.

The behavioristic approach to eliminating unacceptable behavior and punishment is worthy of note. Extinction is the term applied to the elimination of behaviors. Behaviorists feel that unacceptable behavior can be eliminated by removing the reinforcing agents which the behavior normally produces. A concurrent theory is that negative reinforcement effectively maintains unacceptable behavior, so that, on the whole, aversive control (the absence of positive rewards) tend to perpetuate exactly those behaviors the parents want to eliminate.

Punishment is understood to mean either the occurrence of unpleasant consequences as the result of behavior or the removal or withdrawal of positive consequences. Behavioristically speaking, punishment as an aversive consequence does not effectively inhibit unacceptable behavior, and such punishment may be highly specific to a situation or person, so that the behavior can occur in other contexts. Behaviorists tend to use the elimination of chances for positive reinforcement as punishment, through isolation and time-out procedures and through a loss of positive reinforcement called the "response cost" procedure. That is, inappropriate behavior results in losing privileges, activities, treats, or some other event or object which is available to the child (e.g., watching TV, free play, attending planned special events).

The Parent as Therapist

The effectiveness of parents as behavior modification therapists has been proven. Parents can learn the techniques and adapt their responses to the child accordingly. Parents can also sabotage behavior modification programs by withholding earned privileges or not extracting penalties.

Most probably, parental effectiveness is contingent on parental attitudes and involvement with the child. If the parents see the child as essentially ungovernable and themselves as helpless victims, their effectiveness will be accordingly diminished. If the parents view the child as basically good and see his behaviors as independent aspects of his personality, their effectiveness will be relatively high.

It has occurred to me, reading the material on parental roles in behavior modification, that probably the single most important factor is the change brought about in parental management techniques. It's fairly obvious that a change from aversive methods to positive reinforcement methods would affect total management. This, in turn, would be reflected in changes in parental attitudes, which would elicit a more positive response from the child.

Behavior Mod in the School

Behavior modification techniques have been demonstrated to work well in the classroom situation, and many teachers will cooperate with a program of modification as long as it doesn't interfere with regular procedures and doesn't take any extraordinary effort on their part. Again, teacher effectiveness is predicated on the attitude toward the child. If the teacher's efforts are bent toward getting the kid out of the classroom because the teacher thinks he's a monster, it's not very likely he will expend much effort on changing the behaviors that would result in the child remaining in the classroom.

Whether or not the parents can modify their own responses, or make suggestions for classroom management, or need the services of a behavior analyst will depend upon individual circumstances. I have not come across any popular reference work that is primarily aimed at parents, showing them how to apply conditioning methods at home, although this may be an oversight on my part. I hesitate to recommend the professional texts to parents, since many of them are extremely technical. William Gardner's *Chil-*

dren with Learning and Behavior Problems is one of the better books for parents. It's readable, and suggested interventions and techniques are clearly detailed.

RELATIONSHIP THERAPY

Relationship therapy, referred to by some practitioners as play therapy, is a little hard to describe because it depends on the interelationship between the therapist and the child, and that precise relationship can differ from therapist to therapist. It is more an attitude than a theoretically based system. Relationship therapy attempts to provide an accepting and supportive environment in which the individual can experience himself as a complete whole, exactly as he is, without the confines and strictures placed on him by his environment. Within the context of the therapeutic relationship, the child is encouraged to come to terms with himself, his feelings, his fears, angers, and doubts, and his assumptions about his world, and eventually to reformulate his conceptions of himself and his universe in more appropriate and realistic patterns.

For the child, relationship therapy usually takes place within the framework of free play, although therapists with other orientations use play therapy techniques. (Even analysts make use of play therapy.)

The role of the therapist in relationship therapy is fairly nondirective; his primary function is to allow the child to express his feelings and to help clarify these expressions. The therapist may or may not be actively involved with the parents but generally attempts to bring them into the therapeutic process to some degree.

One of the most interesting things about relationship therapy is its nonjudgmental acceptance of the total personality of the child—good, bad or indifferent—similar to the client-centered therapy propounded by Carl Rogers. For the hyperkinetic child, such acceptance may be critical, especially if acceptance and approval are markedly lacking in his environment.

Relationship therapy is extremely beneficial for the hyperkinetic child whose original behavioral problems have been compounded by an overlay of frustration, fear, guilt, anxiety, and anger, and it certainly helps to promote a more positive self-image in cases where the image is extremely poor. However, it is usually a lengthy process, and how beneficial it can be in improving impulse control and attentive behavior and decreasing hyperactivity has not been made clear.

TRANSACTIONAL ANALYSIS

I mention transactional therapy here not only because I see it as a viable therapeutic process for children but because I believe it has some value in changing parental attitudes and responses. Unfortunately transactional analysis has been so popularized that the vocabulary has become bastardized while the concepts remain obscure. Probably, everybody has heard about "I'm O.K.," "winner," "losers," and "gamesmanship," but I wonder how many people understand Eric Berne's assumptions about ego states and scripting.

Berne postulates three ego states: the parent, the adult, and the child, which are further subdivided. He further postulates that our original "scripts" were written by our own parents, much of the scripting being done through nonverbal interactions. To these scripts were added innumerable counterscripts, which affect our attitudes, responses, and feelings, many of which are ambivalent.

It would be rather interesting to discover from which of these ego states our own responses and attitudes toward the hyperkinetic child arise: our own childhood sanctions, the dictates of our own parents, our own assumption of parental or societal values, or our rational adult state.

Scripting, of course, is an essential issue for hyperkinetics. According to Berne, scripts can be realistic and productive, or unrealistic and pathological. It would be good for parents to understand the concept of scripting to help them avoid writing nonproductive, or destructive scripts for their own children.

RELAXATION AND BIOFEEDBACK

There is evidence that the learning of deep muscle relaxation skills and electromyography (biofeedback) training reduce excessive activity, emotional lability, tension, and stress, and increase attentive behaviors.

While the techniques differ in application, the goals are similar—a reduction of tension. Research indicating that such reduction of muscular tension leads to improved behavior in the hyperkinetic child raises some interesting questions. How much learned behavior is present in the restless, acting-out behavior common to hyperkinetics? How much is the direct result of increased anxiety and tension created by the unacceptable behaviors? How much of the unacceptable behavior is caused by either the child's learned, improper methods of controlling behavior or the lability and frustration stemming from his awareness of lack of control?

Relaxation training, in essence, provides a viable alternative for the hyperkinetic child, a substitute for his impulsive ways of reacting. In this way, relaxation training is similar to behavior modification.

While researchers are hesitant to theorize on the basis of their evidence, I am not, and I believe that the evidence goes a long way to prove something I've noticed and observed in hyperkinetic children—they are totally and completely anxiety-ridden, scared to death of doing the wrong thing while convinced they can never do the right thing. They are often overwhelmed by fear, negative expectations, frustration, and guilt. The most minor occurrence can set off an explosion, which would not be hard to understand if we could change places with them for twenty-four hours and experience directly the totality of their anxiety. I have often wondered how such a child manages to survive without actually falling apart.

Interventive therapy that can modify any part of the anxiety–frustration–negativism–acting-out chain of response will probably affect the child's entire repertoire of reactions and responses. So, whether therapy's goal is to change a response or to alleviate the tension, intervention that modifies any part of the continuum will probably be effective.

Desensitization is a process that is often part of a relaxation therapy plan. Basically, the process attempts to modify or eliminate the emotions or anxious feelings elicited by specific situations. Eliminating highly charged emotional content from situations obviously allows the respondent to substitute more appropriate behavior for impulsive or compulsive responses. A good example of an inappropriate response is the fear generated in some children by the test-taking situation. Even if they are intelligent and know the subject, some children panic in testing and are quite unable to function adequately.

Relaxation, biofeedback, and desensitization therapies usually require the services of a specialist, although in specific situations parents may be able to use some of the techniques. For instance, parents might set up desensitization practice sessions with a child who reacts very aggressively and emotionally to namecalling.

FAMILY THERAPY

Family therapy is a special kind of group therapy, the goals of which are usually to modify the interactions and responses of the family group, to reduce interfamily conflicts, and to help the individual members gain insights into the mechanics of their problems. Family therapy can be based on any number of philosophies or theories. It's a particular technique, rather than a theoretical approach to therapy, although many therapists who specialize in the dynamics of family interactions tend to see problems as arising from bad or inadequate relationships within the family as opposed to stemming from outside or external situations.

To participate actively in this type of therapy, you have to be at least able to verbalize the problems, so family therapy is particularly appropriate for families whose children are at least able to express their feelings or talk about their actions. (This doesn't mean that parents separately, without the children, can't benefit from family therapy.)

There's quite a difference between group and individual therapy, so the skill of the therapist is of great importance. It takes a certain amount of expertise, tact, and sensitivity to keep family therapy moving along in the right direction. Family therapy, by providing some acceptable method for venting anger and frustration, can easily turn into weekly "bitch sessions," which are all right as far as that goes. If none of the faulty dynamics of family interaction are modified, however, the process is rather pointless. What may actually happen is that the therapy, by providing some relief, helps maintain what would otherwise become an intolerable situation.

SPECIALIZED THERAPIES

Many children are in need of specific remediation in areas such as speech, auditory, visual, motor, and academic treatment and therapy. Obviously, each of these fields is a specialty and therefore beyond the range of this book.

There is one thing I feel I must say, however. Every deficit, every disability, and every weakness is just one more strike against the child. He needs all the help he can get, and so every deficit, disability, and weakness needs treatment and remediation. No one person can provide all the services one child may need. He may need several kinds of therapy, either all at the same time, or at various times in his life. Finding good specialists in these fields is as difficult as finding a good therapist. But they are out there for the finding.

There are other forms of therapies, other techniques, which may be appropriate for the hyperkinetic child, some of which are not entirely conventional. The first thing that comes to my mind is dance therapy, which I thought was particularly suitable for a child with a high activity level or one who has psychomotor disabilities. However, skilled dance therapists are few and far between. What about formal dancing classes? I suspect the results would depend on the individual instructor. Dancing might not be therapy, but it might be therapeutic. I happen to think that hyperkinetic children need to learn as much as possible about controlling their own bodies. In a small group, with an understanding instructor, providing the child is able to inhibit his actions and listen to instructions, who knows what good things could happen?

Tumbling may also be another suitable pursuit for the highly active youngster.

Art therapy is a good approach for the child without good verbal skills but is so highly specialized an area that a therapist might be hard to locate.

Recently some articles have been published concerning music therapy and/or the use of music with hyperkinetic children, and the results have been positive. Music therapy has been quite beneficial, especially with children who have psychomotor dysfunctions.

For some children, yoga, transcendental meditation, or karate may be beneficial, besides being attractive pursuits for the child. All require a certain amount of discipline, which is something the child must acquire. (Karate is not necessarily limited to breaking arms and smashing skulls. There is a rather rigorous philosophy that goes along with the training, with emphasis on self-restraint, discipline, and preparedness.)

Any small-group activity (the group being limited to six or less and therefore manageable) in which the child can adequately function can be therapeutic for the hyperkinetic child. Cub Scouts, for instance, meet in small groups, and with the right den parent, this can be a positive, if not therapeutic, experience for the child. Small, supervised play groups, instructional classes of all kinds, and associations like the Scouts or 4H can provide an atmosphere in which the child can learn acceptable *group behaviors,* whereas his chances of learning to succeed in larger groups (like a classroom with twenty-five or more children), without an awful lot of help, are relatively slim.

SO WHAT IS THERAPY?

Therapy is anything that's therapeutic or beneficial. It can be a person, a place, or a thing. It can be an attitude, a technique, a theoretic process, or just a chance to get away from it all once in a while.

I urge parents to keep an open mind and an eye open for opportunities for the child. All children have abilities which ought to be encouraged, but for no child is such encouragement more necessary than for the hyperkinetic. He should have as many opportunities as can be provided to help him discover his potential, strengthen his capabilities, and overcome his deficits, whether through conventional therapy, behavior modification techniques, remedial reading classes, small-group interactions, or training in a special skill or ability.

In terms of the hyperkinetic child, therapy must be aimed at increasing competence, socially, emotionally, and/or educationally, while alleviating the tensions created by his behavior—or lack of behavior. Any thing, place, or person that can do either or both of those things is therapeutic. Therapy aimed at any other goal is not likely to produce positive results.

7 Drug Therapy or Speeding

After collecting a quantity of data on the subject of drug therapy, my attitude toward drugs hasn't changed and can be condensed into one short paragraph: Don't use them, unless all else has failed and you're at the end of your rope with nowhere else to go except straight down. Even as a last resort, drug therapy alone is not effective, and other intervention techniques must be used concurrently. Furthermore, drug therapy must be carefully monitored, regularly and periodically, to ensure safety.

I would like to end this chapter right here, because drug therapy is a subject that tends to make me angry. But my purpose is to give parents information, and there are some parents who need information on drug therapy.

Nobody knows how many children are now receiving medication to alleviate hyperkinetic symptoms. Most estimates run to about 2 percent of school-age children but, since there is really no way of establishing such numbers, this estimate could be quite low. The majority of these children receive psychoactive or stimulant drugs—amphetamines, commonly known as "speed."

DRUGS AND DOSAGE

Psychoactive Drugs

The most popular of these is methylphenidate (marketed by Ciba Pharmaceuticals as Ritalin). It has been in use for about twenty years, and its major advantage is that it doesn't suppress the appetite as much as some other psychoactive drugs. The usual dosage is twenty milligrams in one or two doses daily, although dosages can be as high as sixty milligrams.

Dextroamphetamine (sold by Smith Kline French as Dexedrine) is the second most popular. It's been around for close to forty years. The usual dosage is ten to twenty milligrams with one five- or ten-milligram tablet in the morning and another smaller dose at noon. It comes in capsules and in liquid form.

Pemoline (marketed as Cylert, by Abbott Laboratories) was introduced in 1975 after quite a controversy with the Food and Drug Administration over research methodology. The usual dosage is 37.5 or 75 milligrams in the morning but can be as high as 112.5 milligrams. It purportedly suppresses the appetite less and has a longer-acting effect than the other psychoactive drugs.

Amphetamine (Benzedrine) and deanol acetamidobenzoate (Deaner) are rarely used in the treatment of hyperkinesis.

Nonstimulant Drugs

Nonstimulant drugs are considered less effective than stimulants and are used far less frequently. Tranquilizing phenothiazines (chlorpromazine marketed as Thorazine and thioridazine marketed as Mellaril) are used in only about 5 percent of cases treated with drugs. There is little evidence that they are effective, and they do have side effects, such as drowsiness, listlessness, and other symptoms, as they often do in adults.

Antidepressants are rarely used. Imipramine (Tofranil) is the only antidepressant officially recommended for use with children under twelve. Side effects include suppression of appetite, weight loss, nausea, tremor, and sleepiness. Antidepressants are used so infrequently that there is little research on their safety.

Minor tranquilizers such as diphenhydramine (Benadryl) and hydroxyzine (Atarax) are sometimes used. They also can produce drowsiness, although there is little documentation of serious side effects.

Anticonvulsants, such as phenytoin (Dilantin) and phenobarbital, are felt to not be effective or to aggravate the symptoms of hyperkinesis, so it's apparent that the child who must take anticonvulsants and is also hyperkinetic should be carefully watched.

Psychotropic drugs, such as phenytoin and lithium, are sometimes used in medicating aggressive and impulsive teenagers. However, there is not enough research available to form conclusions about actual results.

Caffeine is sometimes used, but the results of research tend to be conflicting, so I suppose it's a matter of trying and finding out if it has beneficial effects.

SIDE EFFECTS

The subject of drug therapy, particularly medicating with stimulants, is highly controversial, to say the least. The dangers of prolonged use of pharmacological therapy are now being pointed out, and the long-term consequences are being questioned.

Perhaps the most serious side effects produced by stimulants are increased heart rate and other cardiovascular changes, such as increased blood pressure. Despite all the research, nobody has documented what happens to the patient fifty years after he stops taking medication. Or forty years. Or thirty years.

Among other side effects, there is what one author calls a "minor" suppression of growth rate, although growth may be inhibited 25 to 40 percent during the period of medication. When drug use is discontinued, children purportedly make great advances in growth gains that are considered to make up for the suppression, although there is research that contradicts this notion.

Other side effects, most of which are common during the early weeks of treatment, include insomnia, anorexia, sadness, nausea, headache, vomiting, abdominal cramps, irritability, rashes, twitching, weight loss, and nervousness. Infrequently, serious mental disturbances and personality disorders occur.

These side effects are thought to be transitory and are not considered serious if they do, in fact, disappear. However, research indicates that many of these symptoms persist to some degree and are not commonly reported by parents if minor.

Although it is not mentioned often, some stimulant drugs can cause serious side effects when used in combination with other drugs such as phenobarbital, phenytoin, imipramine, and mysoline.

Even partisans of medication point out the poor quality of the research that's been done to establish the effectiveness and safety of prolonged drug use. Of the studies that were not so seriously defective as to invalidate their results, very few support the claims made by the drug companies.

Despite recognition of the effects of long-term use of stimulant drugs on adults, a lot of people say that psychoactive drugs are just fine and dandy for children. Many advocates of stimulant medication base their arguments on the hypothetical "paradoxical" effect of these drugs. (They presumably stimulate adults and paradoxically calm children.) But since we are not speaking of two distinct species, this argument is slightly specious.

DOES POPPING A PILL REALLY HELP?

In some cases, drug therapy might be worth the risk of possible side effects if it were an effective remedy. There's a lot of written material out there that says that stimulant drugs decrease hyperactivity. Most of the research is unsophisticated, inadequately controlled, and poorly structured, thereby introducing an element of suspicion as to the validity of the results. (When one discounts the tremendous bulk of drug company-sponsored or researched studies, the evidence for positive response is not impressive.)

Hyperactivity, attentional or concentration defects, and aggression or acting-out behavior seem to be reduced somewhat by stimulant medication. Because the child is more subdued in the educational setting, it has been theorized that stimulants promote learning. There is no evidence that this is at all true. In fact, the preponderance of evidence points to the contrary: Stimulant drugs have no effect on intellectual abilities, do not accelerate academic achievement, or facilitate retention of material. Nor do they make the child more tractable in situations that do not require strict conformity or more amenable to therapeutic processes. Many of the measurable differences have been recorded in artificial, laboratory-type atmospheres and involve monotonous and/or repetitive tasks in areas in which great compliance is required—hardly real-life, everyday situations.

Medication does not improve the possibility of a positive long-term outcome. The child may be less active, more attentive, less distractible, and less aggressive in his interactions, but discontinuance of the drug almost automatically eradicates improvement unless other therapeutic processes have modified or corrected deficits or behaviors. So, a hyperactive child who is treated with stimulant drugs, and stimulant drugs only, really make few gains no matter how long the therapy is maintained. What may happen is that the parents trade a five-year-old hyperkinetic and ten years of drug therapy for a fifteen-year-old hyperkinetic.

Children who respond best to drug therapy are those whose clinical symptoms are the most severe: They are more hyperactive, show soft neurological signs, have abnormal EEG's, and show evidence of learning disabilities. Some authorities believe they can predict the response to stimulant drug therapy based on the severity of involvement in the child. This has led to the most pernicious kind of diagnostic procedure: making the diagnosis of hyperkinesis contingent upon the level of response to psychoactive drugs. If the patient responds properly to drug therapy, diagnosis is automatic. In other words, if I respond adequately to insulin therapy, I am automatically a diabetic, and if I were to respond appropriately to medication with quinine, I guess the diagnosis would be malaria.

Some children do respond to drug therapy. About 35 to 50 percent of *acutely* hyperactive children benefit "dramatically," another 30 to 35 percent benefit "moderately," and 15 to 20 percent do not improve or get worse. However, estimates of positive effects range from a high of 70 percent (research data) to a low of 30 percent (clinical data). About 10 percent of the total treated show a definite negative response, including prolonged side effects, emotional disorders, etc.

Obviously, nobody knows just how many children respond to drugs. It's more than likely that the high percentage improvement rates were derived from samples of extremely hyperkinetic children, while the low estimates may have been taken from a more cross-sectional sample involving severe, moderate, and mild cases of hyperkinesis. Until definitions are refined, testing procedures and measurements are regularized, and conditions are controlled, I don't think anybody is going to be able to come up with precise numbers.

One of the more interesting things to come out of the better studies on drug effectiveness is material on the placebo effect. A placebo is no more than a sugar pill, an inert or ineffective substance given to a control group to measure the possibilities of undue favorable or unfavorable reactions or expectations resulting from the actual administration of the drug to be tested.

While it is felt that the effect of placebos is not as drastic as the effects of medication, there does indeed exist a measurable, positive response to the administration of placebos, which certainly says something about the effects of expectations, doesn't it? Changes classified as at least "moderate" have been reported.

Drug therapy is a course of treatment for which the long-term side effects are not known, immediate effectiveness is questionable, and long-range effect is being disputed. But never fear, there are many authorities who will tell us that prolonged use of stimulant drugs does not lead to drug dependency.

While I'm willing to concede that there may not be a problem of physical addiction, my concern is the possibility of emotional dependency on stimulants or other medication. Most drug users and abusers are not using drugs because a physical addiction exists; many are using drugs because of a *emotional* addiction. Drugs, like alcohol, are a crutch, and a very poor crutch at that. Is it either right or proper or necessary to teach the child that the little pill is the controller of his behavior, that he is really not capable of control, but not to worry, because the little pill will take care of everything for him? The seriousness of "closet" drug addiction, often involving prescription drugs such as tranquilizers, is a problem that has finally been acknowledged. Like alcoholism, this problem has reached the proportions of a national disaster. Parents therefore should consider very seriously and rationally the possible consequences of relying on drugs to control the child's behavior.

WHO MANAGES DRUG THERAPY?

A great deal has been written about the proper management of medication therapy. A great deal has also been written about the fact that drug therapy is hardly ever managed safely, adequately, comprehensively, or beneficially. The official guidelines for the administration of drugs, such as stimulants, to children are followed by only a minority of physicians. Many pediatricians and general practitioners are simply not aware of the dangers, the consequences, the actual effectiveness, and the precautions that should be exercised when prescribing such drugs.

I should note here that the drug companies have done a lot to promote their individual and collective drugs as being safe, sure, effective, and beneficial. Ciba promoted Ritalin at meetings with PTAs and other organizations.

They invited authorities and local physicians to their presentation, which was inclined to be biased and sales-oriented. Several drug companies send handbooks to physicians that offer to teach them about hyperkinesis (its symptoms, diagnosis, treatment, and outcome) in one quick, easy lesson. (It takes about an hour to read the handbook.)

The more rational authorities who regard drug treatment as an alternative, specify care and caution in prescribing, frequent or continuous monitoring, and the inclusion of other appropriate types of therapy. Many of them, like Daniel Safer whose approach is quite pragmatic, advocate the combination therapy approach as the only one likely to lead to a successful outcome.

Safer and others like him admit that what often happens is that, once on medication, children receive no other form of therapy, so that no positive changes or improvements are noted on the discontinuance of medication. Many children remain on drugs, even after they have no more need of them to modify their behavior, simply because no one has bothered to find out if they still need medication.

Many authorities see the physician as the appropriate manager of therapy, particularly when the child is on medication. I think that's ironic, considering the kind of management many physicians give to such cases—little, if any. (I read a rather informative book by an advocate of drug therapy, who made a great point of proving how much valuable time could be saved by drug therapy as opposed to the use of psychological or psychiatric therapy. I couldn't quite understand why it was so important that we all cooperate to save this man's time. I would prefer to save the child no matter how much time was required.)

Theoretically, then, the physician is the one who has the training, expertise, and ability to manage the total therapeutic process, including evaluation, diagnosis, recommendations for psychoeducational procedures or special therapies, and whatever else the child may need. I do not believe that many physicians have such a grasp of the subject or are willing to spend the amount of time good management would require. Who does that leave? Guess.

A number of physicians report that considerable pressure is exerted on them to prescribe psychoactive drugs: pressure from the parents directly, who insist upon medication to decrease the most disturbing and inconvenient symptomatic behavior, or pressure from the school, indirectly relayed by the parents, for alleviation of the problems so that the child can remain in school or in the regular classroom. I have heard of parents and educators who were insistent in their attempts to have children medicated, but somehow, I can't quite imagine a physician prescribing psychoactive drugs against his better judgment.

The best possible practice of medicine tends to the conservative, and parents should look askance at superficial diagnostic procedures and abbreviated evaluations. I have been fortunate in my physicians, who have always been quite conservative, good diagnosticians, and nice people. I asked our family doctor, who's a very relaxed and moderate kind of fellow, what he knew about hyperkinesis, to which he replied, "Nothing." I asked if he would prescribe psychoactive drugs such as Ritalin for children. He replied, "No, I don't know anything about them." When asked what he would do with a hyperkinetic child, he informed me he would have to send the child to a specialist who had some knowledge of the problem, which did not please me. So, I asked him how many hyperkinetic children he had ever referred, to which he replied, "Oh, I've never seen one," which pleased me immeasurably. Now, there's a grand, grand conservative doctor.

Part Two

8 The Hard-to-Manage Infant

The hard-to-manage infant is either a recently developed phenomenon, or parents have chronically denied the existence of troublesome and negative babies. There have always been a few colicky, inconsolable infants. They were never talked about, except in retrospect, when grandma was delighted to tell about the three-month period when *you* cried and screamed, night and day, and refused to be placated no matter what she did.

Perhaps, keeping in step with the times, mothers who were reluctant to admit they were having problems handling their babies (maternal instincts are supposed to confer automatically instantaneous wisdom and ability and make mothers perfect caretakers for their infants) have come out of the closet and asked for help.

There are a number of studies indicating that the hard-to-manage infant is decidedly an infant "at risk," meaning that he is likely to persist in his inadequate and negative responses to situations and stimuli, or lack of stimuli. Certain behaviors are supposedly indicative of a presumed hyperkinetic predisposition or precondition, the symptoms of which, in the infant, are quite generalized but become more easily diagnosable with age.

My personal experience, which is, I understand, quite common, is that the two children who were later to be called hyperkinetic were model infants. My first child, who is reportedly normal, was my difficult child, because I didn't know a darn thing about babies. My approach to motherhood was highly romanticized and not very practical. Beyond knowing which end of the baby to diaper, my ideas of infant care were not very precise. I naturally relied on my relatives and my pediatrician, all of whom dropped pearls of wisdom into my lap, all of which was contradictory, nonsensical, unrealistic, morbid, ineffectual, inefficient, some combination of all of these, and/or too late to do any good.

As I said, the reputed hyperkinetics were both exemplary babies: healthy, happy, cheerful, easy to schedule, sound sleepers (when they felt like it), extremely strong and active, well developed in motor ability and intelligence, easy to nurse and feed, and in every other way pleasurable and appealing.

It has occurred to me, long since their infancies, that we are the fortunate beneficiaries of blind chance: an accident of birth produced a highly active, somewhat demanding baby, whose overall personality, by some unique and equally fortunate combinations of circumstances, I was personally biased to approve. My response was, therefore, approbative. The initial relationship having been established on the basis of mutual affection and acceptance, not all the problems we jointly faced—and will face—nor our negative interactions, nor much of anything else, can entirely erode that primary relationship.

I have occasionally imagined the outcome had one or both of these children been more active, more demanding, or more difficult to handle. Since I am reasonably aware of my limitations—and if I'm not, someone is always handy to point them out to me—I'm not at all sure the results would have been positive or happy. I don't think I handled the first hyperactive child well. It's quite miraculous that I handled her at all, since I hadn't the vaguest idea of what was going on, what the problem was, what I should be doing, or how to do it. I believe that I have been more effective with the second child, but there are many, many times when he irritates me beyond belief and I irritate him. Calamities, disasters, and adversities rain on our heads, everything is wrong, and we both wish we were somewhere else far away.

Whatever happens between parent and child during this short first year, good or bad, comes back to haunt them or sustain them later. Although negative interactions and patterns of behavior can be changed and improved, it's a lot harder to change them than it is to establish good, solid relationships in the first place.

PLACID, HE AIN'T

The word most frequently used to describe the soon-to-be-hyperkinetic child is "difficult," though exactly what is meant is left to the imagination. Does it mean difficult to control, difficult to establish rapport with, difficult to like, or difficult to adapt to, or does it mean that the infant creates difficulty for his caretakers?

When one speaks of an adult being difficult, one implies that the adult is not compliant, that he is not cooperating by being agreeable, as in the phrase, "You're just being difficult!" The infant is characterized as difficult because, I suspect, we really don't know or understand what is going on. We simply know that he does things that don't suit us. Understanding why or how he behaves as he does, we would not be given to such oversimplifications and overgeneralizations.

The difficult infant is extremely active—turning, twisting, pushing with his feet, and wriggling. All this early activity soon turns to a superabundance of more directed, but still extreme, activity—trying to crawl, rocking on his hands and knees, pulling himself into a sitting position. He is quite mobile, even at a very early age, propelling himself around with tremendous exertion—off the bed, around the crib, under the bath water.

The infant's physiological functions may be irregular. His needs fluctuate widely and are never the same on two consecutive days. Irregularity makes demand scheduling pretty impossible. It also makes trying to figure out what he needs at any given moment very difficult.

This baby often seems to be hypertonic, overreflexive, and in a state of hyperarousal and overstimulation. He is inclined to overact with fierce bursts of rage. Crying quickly turns to screaming—prolonged, strident screaming. When aroused, he cannot be placated or soothed.

His sleep is disturbed. He may not establish regular sleeping and waking patterns. He may sleep lightly and be easily awakened, so that his parents tiptoe around the house for fear of waking him during brief cat naps. He does not fall asleep quickly or easily. He may seem to fight sleep. His sleep is often disturbed by excessive movement and he wakes himself suddenly and explosively.

He is very demanding and becomes enraged at delays in the gratification of his needs. When hungry, he progresses from whimpering to crying to screaming in three minutes flat.

He is often advanced in motor development and quite strong. Some researchers have characterized his motions as jerky, rather than rhythmic, although how one distinguishes jerky movement in a small baby, when all movements are uncoordinated, is a little hard to tell.

He is inclined to a pronounced startle reflex in the presence of strong or unexpected stimuli, such as a sudden noise or bright light. He also tends to overrespond to modulated stimuli, although he appears to be somewhat selective in his responses. Light or noise may not startle him, while a quick movement in handling may set him off.

He may be irritable and fretful. He may look perpetually displeased and smile infrequently. Some way or another, he generally lets his parents know he's dissatisfied with the service.

The infant is difficult to handle physically. In the bath, he's eellike and hard to hold onto. He grumbles, squirms, and twists away from the bottle or breast at feedings. Later, he is difficult to spoon-feed—wriggling, sliding down in the seat, crawling out of the seat, grabbing the spoon, and generally making a mess of himself and his caretaker. It isn't that he's not hungry, he's just too busy doing something else to cooperate.

He's difficult to dress, either becoming as rigid as a board or wiggling and jiggling. When he's angry, his body is rigid and he fights help and comfort. He may strain away from being cuddled and soothed.

His responses are inclined to be unpredictable: Something that pleased or soothed him at one time will drive him into hysterics at another. His reactions to unusual or new stimuli are even more unforeseeable. A strange face or object may delight him or send him into paroxysms.

Any digestive upsets are probably the direct effect of his fussing and fighting in the feeding situation. He doesn't get enough in his stomach to hold him over for a reasonable length of time, or he ingests too much air, causing gastric distress (bubbles or spitting up).

This child may seem to be preoccupied with his own physiological functioning and is easily preturbed by minor occurrences. The physical sensations that immediately precede a bowel movement or urination may disturb him, as may any slightly uncomfortable digestive state.

The infant is awake longer than anybody would think possible. He may sleep as little as ten to twelve hours a day. While awake, he demands stimulation in one form or another. He is rarely content to sit or lie quietly without something on which to affix his attention. His parents are apt to regard his demands for stimulation as demands on their time and attention, which is not always true, although he probably commands more parental attention than do more placid, less active, less wakeful babies.

He demonstrates quite early he has a mind of his own. He will, for example, choose a favorite sleeping position and will not go to sleep unless placed in that position. He will work like the very devil to get to something that he wants if it's not within easy reach.

As he gets older, he wants to be where the action is.

He wants to be in the middle of whatever is going on, although his participation can often result in a state of hyperarousal.

Many authorities feel that this infant cries excessively. This has not been my experience, but I will concede the possibility. Whether or not this kind of crying is, has been or will be mistaken for colic is a matter open to speculation.

PARENTAL RESPONSE

The first thing that needs to be examined is the parental response to the difficult infant. It wasn't so long ago that any behavior or personality disorders the child developed were ascribed to his parents, particularly his mother who was chief caretaker and prime target when somebody was hunting around for a plausible scapegoat. This lopsided view of the developing personality has been modified, recognizing the infant reacts to and initiates actions with his parents at least as often as the parents do.

Children are not defenseless, nor do they consider themselves to be. They are dependent upon their parents, but not helpless and *not* defenseless. They very quickly develop a repertoire of defenses against their parents. They are undoubtedly aware of the methods by which they interact with adults, although they lack the vocabulary and the ability to conceptualize and express them. It is a serious mistake to equate the inability to conceptualize or express abstractions with the notion that awareness of the methods or mechanics of the concept does not exist.

So, theoretically here is an infant who's endowed with a prepackaged personality, a level of awareness that can't be measured, many needs, and no means to fulfill his needs except through a process of parental interaction. The personality is not placid, it's difficult. His caretakers find him exceedingly troublesome, especially since no printed instruction sheet came with the child explaining the mechanics of his special personality.

The most common, and quickest, parental reaction is

anxiety, which usually comes off as irritation or avoidance. The parents know that something is wrong—with the infant, with the parents, or with all three. But what? Fatigue compounds the problem, so that the parents can't really focus their attention and think clearly.

Parental response to the difficult child is a natural, honest response. Unfortunately, it's not considered nice to dislike or loathe your own children—or at least, you're not supposed to admit you do. There's admittedly not much to like about a screaming, cantankerous infant, and the parental response is something like: "My God, doesn't that kid ever sleep?" "He's been screaming for two months and I can't stand it any more." "That kid is driving me crazy." "I can't take any more of it."

The tension escalates as the parents' attempts to modify either their handling procedures or the child's behavior do not succeed. No matter what the parents do, the child becomes more reactive and less compliant.

Before too long, the child and the parents have become enmeshed in a transactional morass, which will result in more and worse inappropriate behavior on the child's part and intensified anxiety, irritation, and/or avoidance on the part of the parents. And, of course, there's that little thing called guilt. The parents know they shouldn't feel hostile toward their child—but they do.

Whatever has happened, the child is impossible; and it's really nobody's fault.

INTERVENTION

It's not a pretty picture, is it? Fortunately, there are intervention techniques that will at least reduce, if not eliminate, some of the difficulties. These techniques fall roughly into two categories: what to do for the infant, and what to do for the parents, particularly for the chief caretaker. The benefits of intervention accrue to both parents and child. Sometimes, the "avalanche" effect takes over, and a small improvement in one particular area affects the total range of behaviors and responses on both sides, ultimately improving each and every interaction.

The first step is to accept the situation for what it is. The child is difficult and creates difficulties for his parents. He also makes difficulties for himself. The parents, after a realistic appraisal of the situation, must take steps to remedy the problem before too much time has gone by and they are exhausted and without resources.

The child is what he is and, at this stage of the game, there's really not much he can do about it. The parents are far better prepared to make changes in their own attitudes and expectations, modifications in their handling and coping mechanisms, and improvements in their responses. In other words, having accepted the situation as it exists, with the understanding that there are many positive aspects of the child's personality that will become more evident as he matures, there are many things the parents can do to help themselves and help the infant. The sooner they begin to help the child behave in an appropriate manner, the sooner the parents will like him better.

Since the infant makes excessive demands on his caretakers, the parents will have to face to the fact that they must make arrangements to devote extra time to his care. This means that other tasks must be delegated, relegated, or dispensed with entirely.

The chief caretaker, usually the mother, must take precautions to ensure that she is not overextended and likely to become exhausted during the first few months of the struggle. This sounds very simple, but it's very hard to do if there are other children to care for, a house to run, and a lot of other everyday complications.

When the parents realize that the child will require excessive time and attention, draining their resources at least initially, they should try to recruit outside help to handle extraneous duties—cooking, cleaning, shopping, chauffeuring other children, and what not—at least until a fairly comprehensive schedule has been established. It's very important to rate priorities—in this case, the needs of the infant and the chief caretaker. If turning to your friends and relatives for help—or hiring some help—will enable you to minimize difficulties and establish a working basis between child and parents, then outside help is a dire necessity.

Hiring help can often pose a financial problem, but it is frequently well worth the investment. It's not at all surprising that this child is often much more appealing when his caretakers have had some respite from caring for him. Nobody, and I really mean *nobody,* can cope with a difficult infant all day, every day, without relief, and keep their sanity.

The parents should, naturally, be supportive of each other and try to understand each other's responses and feelings in relation to the child and his behavior. Since human nature is not a remarkably stable commodity, it frequently happens that one parent tends to blame the other for mishandling the infant, or one parent minimizes the difficulties and tensions produced by the child's behavior. (People who do not have to care for the child usually make half-witted statements because they feel they ought to reassure anxious parents that the child is all right. It's not all right, if the kid is driving everybody bananas, even if he is medically sound.) Both of these approaches tend to perpetuate the situation, either because the parent feels he is personally inadequate and can't do anything constructive or because he feels that, since the infant is fine, there must be something wrong with him—and he's not going to talk about it for fear that talking will make it true.

THE NEED FOR STRUCTURE

The single most important word in this book, and the most important word that can be used in relation to the hyperkinetic child, is "structure." The first, and only, commandment for parents of hyperkinetic children is: "Thou shall provide structure—or else!" Over the next few chapters, you'll find liberal use of the word "structure," because any program designed for the child must have structure. Without a structured environment, the child will have difficulties functioning in appropriate and approvable ways.

What is structure? Basically, it's a stable, durable construction. It has form, solidity and permanence. It may have fluidity and mobility, but it must be elemental, deep-rooted, firm, and steady.

If I had to reduce the problems of hyperkinesis to a single sentence, I would have to say that the child seems bereft of an ability to create environmental structure. He doesn't seem able to initiate, or establish for himself, the boundaries in which he can function adequately. Without structure, hyperkinetic children of all ages tend to fall into a state that resembles panic, and I would hypothesize that the absence of structure produces terrible anxiety and apprehension for the child, which feeds the symptoms of hyperkinesis; these symptoms in turn are exacerbated by rising fears and anxiety.

The parents must respond, in infancy and early childhood, by creating structure for the child and, as he matures, help him to learn to create new structures for himself. The first structure that needs to be constructed is a practical and workable schedule.

ESTABLISHING A SCHEDULE

I recently talked with the mother of a difficult infant, who had an exhausting and pretty dreadful experience during the first two and a half months of her child's life. He woke and screamed every hour, night and day, until she literally did not know what to do with him or herself. She occasionally hid in the basement laundry room and cried. Getting no concrete advice from the pediatrician, she changed doctors and was finally advised to schedule the child rigidly, responding to him only at definite intervals.

Ordinarily, rigid scheduling is not my cup of tea, but I have to admit that, the more difficult the child, the firmer and tighter the schedule must be. Scheduling should not have to be a rigid, inflexible punching of a time clock: The day is divided into four-hour segments, feeding occurs at precisely 10, 2, and 6 o'clock, and the child is not handled at any other time. But in dire circumstances, perhaps stringent methods are necessary.

Depending on a lot of other factors, such as the child's weight and size, the amount of nourishment taken at feedings, the occurrence of suitable uneventful pauses in the day, etc., the parents must determine a proper and practical schedule for the individual child.

Categorically, the infant should not be awake every hour, and he should not be fed or handled every hour. A practicable and reasonable interval of time must be established, and that interval should be maintained as closely as possible. Fifteen minutes early or a half-hour late probably won't destroy the effectiveness of the schedule.

Every day must resemble every other day: Bathing takes place at a certain time, playtime is established during a time convenient for the parents, outings take place in the afternoon at a certain time, the child is put to bed for the night at a certain time.

Putting a scheduling procedure into effect by not responding to the child's crying at other times is similar to traversing hell without an asbestos overcoat. Parents must be firmly committed to the idea of structure because, every time they depart from the schedule, the structure is weakened. I don't mean to make parents into timekeepers, with a stopwatch in hand, who are unresponsive to the child's needs. Quite the contrary. The child most likely needs a great deal of stimulation and should be handled, cuddled, and played with as long as most of the parental response takes place as part of a normal, everyday routine.

Let me elaborate on a typical schedule for a two- to four-month-old infant. He wakes between 6:30 and 7:00 A.M. He is changed and fed. Since this is not a particularly good time for interaction, he is put back to bed, where he is expected to play quietly. He wakes again between 10:30 and 11:00 A.M. which is a particularly convenient time for his parent to spend some time with him. He is fed, bathed, dressed, and played with, all of which takes an hour or a little more. He is then placed in his crib with appropriate gadgets and amusements and, after another half-hour or so, when he begins to show signs of irritability or tiredness, the parent follows a routine usually used to help him get to sleep. He wakes at about 4:00 P.M. He is fed, and since an older child is home from school, he is allowed to participate, by observing, in the older child's play. Or his mother decides that this is the time for an outing, if there is to be one, or she puts him in an appropriate infant seat and move him around with her. (The idea is to encourage the child to participate but not to allow him to be the center of attention, as he was earlier.) He may or may not be placed in his crib for a while, depending on his sleep needs. Eventually, he is urged to go back to sleep. He wakes again at about 8:00 P.M. If the mother is the chief caretaker during the day, this is an excellent time for someone to relieve her and assume the role of caretaker. The child is fed, handled, amused, and played with. Eventually, depending on the situation, he is prepared for the night; he is fed again if necessary, and bedtime procedures are initiated, which might include rocking, talking soothingly, or gently patting him. He is put in bed, hopefully for a decent interval. If he wakes during the night, he is changed, fed, and put back in his crib without much ado.

If the child does not awake at regular intervals, he may have to be awakened. The temptation to get some peace and quiet can be overwhelming, but deviating from the normal routine can be pretty traumatic. If the child wakes between intervals or much too early, the parental response must be predicated on the reactions of the child. If the appearance of the parent excites the child and makes him redouble his efforts for attention, then the parent should not intervene. On the other hand, if the parent can quiet the child and encourage him to amuse himself by giving him a toy or turning him over or some rather simple device, then no harm is done.

THE WRONG APPROACH

Two suggestions are frequently offered for management of the difficult infant, both of which are unlikely to produce success unless parents understand what is really going on. First, they are frequently advised to turn a deaf ear to the child and allow him to work out his problems on his own, chiefly by crying a lot. Crying a lot does not improve the child's disposition, and it may in effect teach him that, if he cries enough, eventually his parents will respond. In this context, parents are advised not to spoil the child by reacting to his demands and that he should learn to handle frustration, since his behavior is frequently translated as an infant temper tantrum. Parents are urged not to coddle the child by picking him up and handling him. It's too easy to mistake the genuine needs of the child for his learned-from-experience demands for attention. Advice to not spoil the child seems to be based on the theory that all infants require a certain minimal amount of care and that going beyond the minimum is spoiling him. This is not true. Infants require individualized amounts of care and attention. An active, vigorous infant will definitely require more time and care than a less active, placid baby. As for frustration, it is better to learn to cope with frustrating experiences after one has mastered a few of the mechanics that enable one to modify or act upon the source of frustration. Any psychologist can tell you that enduring prolonged frustration, when one is powerless to act upon its source, is not a particularly positive situation. Frustration piled on frustration leads to more frustration, not resolution. If the infant does overreact to frustration, allowing him to be frustrated needlessly will not help him develop new techniques for dealing with his feelings. On the contrary, it may intensify his feelings and his response to frustration, so that he eventually acquires the habitual behavior of overreacting, since in actual practice overreaction is the only behavior that produces the desired effect for him.

The second misguided suggestion is to reduce stimulation in the child's environment by lowering light levels, eliminating sounds, keeping personal interactions at a minimum and, in general, "protecting" the child from his environment. If the hypothesis of optimal levels of stimulation is accepted, reducing stimuli would tend to increase the infant's efforts to reach a satisfactory level of stimulation.

Besides which, it tends to inhibit normal interactional development between parents and child.

ENVIRONMENTAL STIMULATION

There's a good bit of research that indicates that *adding* modulated stimulation to the environment is an effective means of preventing hyperarousal or hypereaction. The kinds, amounts, and levels have to be determined individually, through a process of trial and error. But there are some rather quick and easy devices that seem to be helpful. The following suggestions are by no means comprehensive. They are intended to give you some ideas or clues as to what you can do and what's available.

For the very young infant with sleep problems, a mechanical device for setting his crib or cradle in motion may prove satisfactory. Placing an electronic gadget in or near the crib that simulates a heartbeat has also proved useful. Something as readily accessible as a metronome placed near the crib may be a satisfactory source of stimulation. Soft and gentle music such as lullabies may help. Sometimes gently rubbing or touching the infant's back or legs can help him get to sleep.

When the infant is awake, many different types of stimulation can be added to his immediate environment:

Visual stimulation. Mobiles, shifting lights, pictures, and all sorts of gadgets can be attached to the crib. Several years ago, there was available a plastic pouch arrangement into which one put water and a fish; it was a great eye-catching, eye-tracking device. A parent who finds that visual stimulation appeals to his infant will undoubtedly be able to find a lot of displayable objects which do not have to be either esoteric or expensive. Test anything bright, mobile, or both that's safe to attach to a crib.

Auditory stimulation. Talking, singing, and soothing music are useful. (Children very quickly develop preferences for different kinds of music: vocal, instrumental, classical, popular, etc. Do not use rock music, since it tends to overstimulate.) Pleasant sounds such as recordings of the ocean, bird songs, and the like are also suitable.

Tactile stimulation. This can involve touching and holding, and a variety of textures and materials to hold, feel, and examine. Swaddling seems to have a very calming effect on extremely hyperactive infants, but it must be done with great care. It should immobilize the infant, not restrict his movements, which tends to increase, frustrate and irritate.

There are devices that combine several types of stimulation. We had a plastic gadget that was tied into the crib, which the child could kick or push against with his feet and which "rewarded" the kicking or pushing with jingling sounds. Some crib attachments can be observed, felt, manipulated, and tasted, which is a good combination.

Changing the scenery by moving the infant from room to room with you may be helpful, especially if you keep up a steady stream of conversation. Talking in a modulated tone is a good way to maintain contact, establish rapport, and keep him occupied all at the same time. For some reason, parents tend to talk to infants only when handling them and then only in baby talk. Even if you feel a little foolish, tell the infant nursery stories, tell him about your own childhood, or tell him about the history of Western civilization. Just keep talking.

A bright, sunny window where there's little danger of sudden or unexpected noise is a good place for the baby, especially if there's a little breeze to tickle the skin and a few flowers or leaves outside to move in the breeze.

Playing with the infant is a good interaction to initiate and habituate. It's difficult, I know, to think of *modulated* games to play with an infant who can't respond yet. Never mind, it doesn't much matter what you do, as long as the child knows it's play. Count toes and fingers, clap his hands, pretend your fingers are a spider and walk all over him, sing nursery rhymes and gently pat him, and do other silly things. A note of caution—since the child tends to overreact, tickling and other forms of overstimulation should be avoided. If dear old auntie has a bad habit of tickling babies, tell her emphatically not to tickle this one. If she does anyway, take the baby away from her and tell her better luck next time. It's better to have auntie miffed than to have a screaming baby to cope with.

Older children are a particularly pleasant, interesting form of stimulation for the infant. Again, the parents must be sure to avoid overstimulation, but babies are not particularly fragile creatures so, if the infant will submit to his sibling's handling with good grace, the parents can assume that all is well.

When the infant tends to hypereact, parents tend to prohibit older children from interacting to the point where the baby is no fun for them, which makes them quickly resentful and antagonistic. Clearly defined rules for handling and playing with the baby should be outlined and demonstrated if possible. The infant may be in need of a "cooling off" period after such a play time but, unless he becomes hyperaroused, parents should allow free interaction periods.

RESPONDING APPROPRIATELY

As a rule, when the child wakes on schedule, prompt attention is a good idea. If the child has slept for four hours and wakes, and you know he's probably starving, there's no point in making him wait. After all, he has behaved properly—he has slept for four hours. He should be rewarded immediately. It's reasonable to assume that the learning process will eventually teach him that his needs will be cared for in a moderate length of time, and he will learn to temper his immediate, forceful reaction accordingly.

In dealing with the difficult infant, what the parent needs to do is to establish structure in the form of a steady routine. Having scheduled the infant, the parent proceeds to reward or punish him for acceptable or unacceptable behavior: rewarding by his presence and care, punishing by his absence and inattention. Responding negatively—irritably or with anger—should not be equated with punishment and only confuses everybody. A young child doesn't perceive the differences between positive and negative responses from his parents. As a matter of fact, if the only responses he gets are negative, the child won't know that there can be positive responses. It is far more effective to teach the child that the parents *will not respond* to inappropriate or unacceptable behavior than to wait for him to learn that a negative response is essentially punitive and unhealthy, which he may or may not learn by the time he's fifteen.

No matter how conscientious the parents and how good their management, there are no foolproof methods for handling the infant, and some days are just going to be awful. The reasons no one has been able to devise a comprehensive management system are pretty obvious: Each child *is* unique, each reacts differently to different stimuli and situations, the optimal levels of stimulation can fluctuate widely on any given day, and incidentally, all parents are unique, too.

The only way to make prediction possible or to arrive at the best possible management techniques is through close observation of a particular infant while the parents experiment with techniques and devices. It takes time, interest, attention, and involvement, just like getting to know any other person. Parents have to learn to pick up clues, subtle or obvious, as to what is happening or what is going to happen in the next ten minutes. For instance, a certain kind of irritable crying may indicate boredom or the onset of fatigue. Particular twistings or squirmings may indicate boredom and a need for change.

DECIDING HOW TO RESPOND

Parents should formulate concrete and exact decisions as to how they should and should not handle difficult and/or disruptive behavior. It's too late to make these decisions in the middle of a crisis. Sometimes the major problem isn't bad management on the part of the parents. It's lack of management.

Deciding on policy is related to deciding to schedule or structure. It's a very necessary ingredient in the structuring plan. Managing the difficult infant without a formulated decision on how to respond is like trying to build a house without blueprints. Having pinpointed specific behaviors that upset them or cause anxiety, the parents should evaluate their own responses to the behavior, looking at the possible consequences of those responses, and then decide how they should respond and what they think the outcome should be.

Let's take a hypothetical infant who wakes frequently, day and night, and screams lustily until his parents respond—by picking him up, trying to soothe him, feeding him, etc. What is it that the parents want to do? What is the goal? Obviously, they don't want the child up every hour or so, and they don't want him screaming. Well, how do the parents respond? Do they always respond? In the same way? Or in forty-three different ways? Should they attempt to ignore the screaming? Should they respond with soothing behavior? Can they find a method that quiets the child and allows him to sleep longer? Do they want to try to ignore the child's crying except at specific times? How do they really feel about letting the child scream without intervening?

Now comes the hard part. Having decided *how* they should react, the parents must stick to it. Or at least until it proves unsatisfactory or futile. If the child wakes and screams on two successive nights and the parents do nothing, but on the third night, pushed beyond endurance, jump up in irritation and run in, grab him, and attempt to placate him, cursing and swearing all the time, the child will learn that, if his behavior continues, eventually he will be rewarded. Not every time, but often enough to reinforce the behavior. The parents should grit their collective teeth and let the infant cry for five or six days. Any appreciable decrease in waking-and-crying episodes indicates partial success. However, if the child continues to behave in such a manner for two or three weeks, the parents had better look for a more appropriate, and successful, response.

Deciding upon an appropriate response to the infant is not the same as maintaining total consistency of response, which is *not* a reasonable expectation. There are just too many outside uncontrollable variables that affect parental response to expect complete consistency. However, a decision to verbalize and systematize their management of the infant will help parents maintain moderate consistency—and this is all important.

HELP FOR PARENTS

Denial of parental feelings toward the child sometimes hinders the ability to change and modify response. The impact of the parent's feelings of guilt, hostility, and indifference, and their concern about their apparent powerlessness or inability to cope with the child, prevent positive change. But there really should be no guilt involved in admitting that caring for the difficult infant twenty-four hours a day, seven days a week, is too much to ask of anybody. The parents must have some breathing space, apart from the infant. How you work out a schedule for time away from the burden of caring for the child depends on circumstances, availability of substitute caretakers, finances and other factors. The parents should find means of providing relief, regularly and as frequently as possible, whether it's for a few hours each day, or for several longer intervals each week.

Providing substitute caretakers is not easy, since it's difficult to find anyone capable of taking over and managing the child, or who is willing to expend the kind of attention and energy the child demands, for either love or money. Others are willing to expend the energy, but their management techniques leave a lot to be desired. (Disrupting the parent's hard-won schedule is not my definition of desirable management.) And there will always be a few substitutes who have no notion how to cope with the child and blindly panic, which is a big help.

There are a few programs, generally run by local mental health agencies, that are now providing short-term care for handicapped and retarded children, so that parents have some relief. The programs are far and few between, and getting into such a program is probably difficult. However, unless you get out there and find out what's available and possible, you can be sure that nobody is going to come knocking on your door offering assistance.

There are a number of other things parents can do for themselves that will help alleviate the tensions, improve interactions, and make the handling of the child less exasperating.

The first step is to get psychological support for the parents. There are existent groups of parents of hard-to-manage infants, which not only offer support but also share constructive advice and criticism. Supportive therapy (which has a variety of names, including "crisis intervention") can be extremely beneficial, especially while the parents are working out a system of management procedures and responses.

Associations, such as the Childbirth Education Association, offer instructions and courses in infant management. There are a large number of how-to-do-it-type books on the market that detail how to change or improve your interactions, physical routines, expectations, and child care practices. (Sometimes a small change in routine can make a great deal of difference. As an example, suppose the infant reacts strongly to being dressed or undressed. There are simplified methods of dressing and alternative articles of clothing that can be substituted so that the routine can be modified and made easier.) There are usually university-affiliated services and clinics that provide courses, lectures, and training in a variety of areas, such as physical routine, breast-feeding, behavior modification techniques, and much more that may help parents. There are also courses, instruction booklets, and handbooks aimed at helping parents understand and cope with their own reactions to the child.

Finding the services you need is the hard part. Generally, the closer you live to a large urban area, the better your chances of finding a service to fit your immediate needs. The most effective way to find out what's available is to call local mental health or mental retardation centers, local university child-oriented programs and facilities, local private clinics, and practitioners in the fields of pediatrics, psychology, and psychiatry and ask a lot of dumb questions. Feel free to use my "dumb person" approach. It's effective when I'm at a dead loss and I don't know who to talk to. Try to sound slightly hysterical.

"My name is Rogers and I have a problem. I do hope you'll be kind enough to help me, because I really don't know who else to call. My problem is . . . (detail the problem briefly—ten words is about right.) Now, by any chance, do you happen to know whom I should talk to or what department (program) is available or how I can get any information at all?"

People will normally respond with kindness and do their best to be helpful. Even if they can't help you with concrete information, they may be able to refer you to someone who can. It may take ten phone calls to find the kind of services you feel you need but, if nothing else, you've had a chance to talk to some very nice people.

IT'S REALLY NOT SO BAD AFTER ALL

With proper handling, after the first few weeks or months, the parents may actually find themselves possessed of a very gratifying baby. If they can concentrate on the child's positive aspects and minimize the negative ones, they can put their interrelationship on a solid footing.

Although somebody is sure to find something wrong with my attitude, I have always found active infants to be very rewarding. I thought they were much more fun and more interesting, especially as they became mobile and responded with purposeful behavior. Certainly they made more demands, had to be watched more carefully, and needed more time and attention, but they were never boring.

I suspect I did a lot of things that might be considered a little unusual. My daughter Gerry was fascinated by the Christmas tree the year she was born, so I left it up for months and months. To keep her amused for a long time, all I had to do was put her in front of the tree and plug it in. But people kept nagging me about the tree, so I finally took it down. I was sorry. I never found a substitute for the Christmas tree.

I had a large collection of infant seats, jumpers, swings, and other devices that were scattered everywhere, and I just moved the baby around with me, wherever I went, and never thought too much about it. I tied a lot of toys onto these seats, and when the child had thrown them all away, I just picked them all up and started over again.

Both children spent a lot of time on the floor on a very large blanket, their occupation being to crawl off of it. Every once in a while, I put them back in the middle and let them squirm off again.

My son Ben was the most delightful baby I've ever seen. Despite the fact that he was awake a lot, there were no other indications that he might be prone to hyperkinetic symptoms. He was a cheerful, vigorous little beast. He was strong and active (which we admired unreasonably), intelligent and perceptive (which we adored), he was responsive and loved to cuddle, he was a sound sleeper and easily established sleep patterns, including a long stretch between midnight and 7:00A.M., in his second month, he learned to amuse himself with toys and loved to "follow" me around, he was easy to feed (he was always what is called an "eager eater"), and he certainly didn't cry very much. The rare times he screamed, the problems were obvious and easy to solve—he was tangled up in something, he was stuck somewhere, he had diaper rash, and once he was actually being jabbed by an open diaper pin.

By the time he could walk, he was considered a very advanced, captivating little boy. What happened to that captivating little boy is another story.

9 The Hyperactive Toddler

The hyperactive infant reaches what is known as "the terrible twos" about a year early, which tends to intensify and prolong the frustration, irritation, and negativism involved in efforts to control him that parents normally encounter at a later age. I don't mean that the hyperactive child is advanced a whole year in motor or intellectual development, although he may be quite advanced for his age; I mean that he begins to do things, behave in particular ways, and learn coping mechanisms and techniques normally expected at a later age, when it's easier to modify and manage his behavior.

Toddlers are, on the whole, very difficult people to have to live with. There's so much that has to be learned—and the amount of learning that's accomplished in this brief period is incredible—and so much that has to be taught, that it's a trying time for everybody.

Toddlerhood, for my purposes, is defined as the period of time beginning when the child begins to walk and ending when he is (1) intellectually advanced enough to be expected to be somewhat reasonable, cooperative, flexible, and integrated enough to require less direct attention and manipulation; (2) when he is totally mobile; and (3) and when he has achieved some measure of independence and self-motivation. These three conditions do not occur simultaneously, and one can precede the others by quite some time. The hyperkinetic toddler becomes mobile long before he requires less attention and has acquired independence. Chronologically, this takes place at about two and a half to four years of age, depending on the severity of the hyperkinesis.

WHO MANAGES WHOM?

This question is open to a great deal of speculation. It's plausible that sometimes parents manage, sometimes the child manages, and sometimes nobody manages, in which case it is hoped that someone will come along who can manage everyone else. I very specifically use the word "management," as opposed to the word "control," to indicate what I think the proper function of parents is: to direct, guide, conduct, and work toward specific goals. "Control" suggests both more power to direct and more influence over the outcome than one person is able to exert over another, whether parent or child.

On the occasions when I've been asked to control one of my children, I have gone to some length to explain that I was not able to control anyone other than myself (which sometimes I didn't do too well), that my techniques of control were extremely limited, and that I thought it was highly unethical, anyway. Now, if what was requested was management. . . .

While refuting the idea of control, I am perfectly well aware of the existence of controlling behavior (e.g., one person attempting to control the behavior of another). Controlling behavior may work situationally and occasionally, but over the long haul it has limited practicality and effectiveness simply because, once the other person recognizes what is happening, he can begin to play games of his own, which will counteract the original controlling behavior.

Parental management of the hyperactive child is an area in which there is a lot of confusion as to the roles, responsibility, effectiveness, and detrimental effects of the parents in relation to their individual child.

In the course of my research, I came across, again and again, two seemingly rational dicta: First, parental management is a very important factor—some authorities feel it may be the most important in the eventual outcome. Second, and this is where the situation becomes somewhat muddled, while parents are exonerated as the cause of their child's hyperkinesis, it is most forcefully pointed out that poor, inconsistent, or aversive parental management greatly aggravates the condition. It seems to me to be a little simple-minded to remove the onus from the parents only to reinstate it—in different terms—and without taking into account several other factors.

True, a chaotic home situation, a lack of consistent, firm, patient management, open anger and hostility directed toward the child, or parental indifference can exacerbate the symptoms of hyperkinesis. Why is it though, that many authorities fail to notice that it is often the child who creates the chaos? How can parents perform superhumanly: provide total, twenty-four-hour-a-day consistency, patience, firmness, and loving attention? Having told us we ought to be superlative parents, is anyone going to tell us how?

Why don't authorities tell us what to do about our home management techniques in order to improve them, to eliminate our own incorrect responses, and to enhance the relationship? Probably because they lack what's known as "hands-on" experience. Raising a hyperkinetic child is a good bit different than dealing with hyperkinetics in a clinical atmosphere. It may not be the easiest thing in the world to be the child's physician or therapist, but it's a lot easier than being his parent.

So, while we're counseled to desist from screaming and yelling at the child, to stop responding punitively, to regularize our households, and to stop being nervous wrecks, much of this advice is useless. Certainly, we're all willing to try to be better parents. The problem is how.

THE WILD CHILD

"Wild child" is no misnomer for the hyperkinetic toddler. He is constantly on the move, exploring, examining, investigating, inquiring, touching, feeling, grabbing, handling, manipulating, mouthing, biting, tasting (sometimes swallowing), crumpling, tearing, masticating, smearing, rubbing, picking, and more. Anything that can be done with one pair of hands and one pair of feet, this child does twice over in one day.

Unfortunately, his response to being mobile in his universe, a response of highly active investigation prompted by acute curiosity, is not always looked on favorably by parents. So much of his waking life is spent in highly mobile activity that it would take a crew of clean-up people to keep the place neat and tidy. Besides which, he requires constant supervision because he gets into so many unacceptable—and downright dangerous—situations. He is headlong, impetuous, determined, and *fast.*

During the day his parents become exhausted keeping up with him. Very often his sleep requirements are minimal, so that the caretaker doesn't get a breather during the day while the child naps.

He may actively resist parental control, so that he cannot be deflected from an object or activity he desires. The parents often become exasperated by his persistent efforts to do or get something they have denied him.

If the child was difficult in infancy, the difficulties are often carried over into toddlerhood. They are compounded by the emergence of new behaviors, new adaptations, and new abilities. If the child was difficult to feed in infancy, he is much more capable of irritating behaviors now. If he demanded excessive attention as an infant, he can now actively seek out his parents and insist upon attention.

Unfortunately, a great deal of *normal* toddler behavior runs contrary to parental expectations and acceptableness.

The highly active child is apt to run into parental sanctions at every turn.

I always thought that a good course in child development should be required of all about-to-be parents. I still think a developmental course would be extremely helpful—and reassuring—to most parents, especially to those with active children. It would help explain some of the "inexplicable" behavior and also give parents some rational basis on which to base sanctions.

The difficult infant's symptoms can be cataloged, because infant behavior is relatively simple and uncomplicated. The toddler's symptomatic behaviors are so diffuse and complicated that it's impossible to describe a typical hyperkinetic child. He may be so hyperactive that he literally ricochets around the house, or he may be just a highly active youngster, or he may be anywhere in between. He may or may not show evidence of mood swings, irritability, distractibility, a short attention span, impulsiveness, or explosiveness. He may or may not demonstrate psychomotor or other dysfunctions. He may or may not indulge in aggressive, acting-out behaviors.

The only thing universal about hyperkinetic toddlers is the kind of response they are likely to elicit from parents and other adults, a very negative, aversive, hostile reaction.

Is it possible to avoid responding negatively, aversively, or with hostility? Probably not. At least, not always. Let's put it this way. On the average, the parents of average-activity toddlers probably say "No!" about 100 times a day. The parents of a hyperactive child probably say "No!" 300 times a day. Saying "No!" 300 times a day wouldn't be so bad if there were a total of 300 positive interactions to counteract the negative ones. But gradually, all interactions tend to become negative or aversive, leaving no time or space for a positive, healthy response. While all this is happening, the child is learning that a negative response is the only one he's going to get, and the parents are learning they don't much like this kid. And that's trouble.

The most important thing parents can do is to avoid

telegraphing the decidedly harmful message that the hyperactive toddler can't do anything right or acceptable. There are two ways to avoid sending this message: Never send the message to begin with or, if you do send it, modify the message you're sending.

It should be understood that I'm not talking about periodic lapses, even if they occur ten times a day. I'm talking about a steady, consistent, unvarying diet of negativism. Everybody sends negative messages to everybody else periodically: I send them, you send them, my parents sent them, your parents sent them, all the way back to Neanderthal. As long as the majority of messages and responses are positive, periodic mistakes probably won't kill anybody. They never have.

GOAL-DIRECTED MANAGEMENT

Bruno Bettleheim made an interesting observation (in *Conversations with Mothers*), when he suggested that parents have to make an investment in the child if they expect the child to be what they want him to be and have the attributes and abilities they want him to have.

Any businessperson knows that, while the primary goal of business is to make money, immediate goals have to be more precisely defined in order to attain financial success. Short- and long-range plans must be worked out for reaching one's goal—showing a profit.

Why we don't think of children in terms of short- and long-range goals is beyond me. Often, we have nebulous ideals and expectations that are, on the whole, pretty remote and undefined. But how many parents could make a list of short- and long-term goals if they were asked to do so? (By goals, I don't mean vague aspirations such as "I want him to be happy" or "I want him to be a pianist." Wishful thinking is not goal setting.) Would parents be able to enumerate goals for the next year, or the next five years, along with their plans and methods for attaining projected outcomes? It is doubtful.

By and large, parents don't formalize and organize a step-by-step procedure for reaching desired goals for their children. Things usually turn out pretty well without such careful organization. However, since the parents of the hyperkinetic child bear the responsibility for creating structure and purpose for him, goal-setting is not only helpful, it's required. It's imperative to know, when attempting to structure an environment, the real purpose of the structures and limits. Just what are the parents trying to do, and what do they expect the outcome to be?

Goal-setting is a three-part operation: it must include consideration of the child, the parents, and the objectives. The welfare of the child is paramount, but the welfare of the parents is secondary only by a very small margin. The goal or objective must be precisely defined, although it may not at first be readily apparent. For example, the parents may know they want to reduce conflicts between themselves and the child, which is mutually beneficial, but exactly where and how these conflicts arise is not clear. Closely examining conflict situations, the parents may be able to pinpoint the kind of interaction that normally results in an antagonistic confrontation.

The following are goals (precise and otherwise) that parents might consider:

Goals for the child:

Cry less
Be less destructive
Be happier
Learn to control himself
Be ready to enter kindergarten at the usual age
Understand the boundaries of acceptable behavior
Respond positively
Be less aggressive
Be less difficult to control
Be less negativistic
Not fight with his siblings
Be less demanding
Challenge my authority less frequently

Not need constant supervision
Not look for trouble (punitive intervention)
Be well-liked by other children and adults

Goals for the parent:
Be less angry
Be upset less often
Not have to watch him every minute of the day
Be less punitive (mete out fewer punishments)
Be calmer in handling him
Holler at him less
Be more understanding
Have some time of my own
Be more positive
Be more direct in handling him
Give him less attention
Not ignore him when he's being good
Be stricter
Demand better behavior
Not expect him to be perfect

Obviously, child- and parent-oriented goals are closely related. If the child weren't difficult, the parents would not be upset or angry or yelling a lot. But there's really no good solution to the problem of being angry or yelling too much. Efforts to reduce undesirable interactions, based on imprecise evaluation of the mechanics that produce them, are not very effective. In other words, the parent cannot prevent himself from becoming angry unless he does something to modify or eliminate the reason he gets angry.

Defining a precise objective is the next step. Let's assume the parents choose two goals: They want the child to be less demanding of their time and attention, and they want to be less angry when he makes excessive demands. They would earnestly like to behave more rationally and less punitively toward the child, especially since they realize there must be some reason for his excessively demanding behavior.

Human behavior is difficult to analyze and dissect, but with a little effort and perseverance, the parents should be able to isolate particular incidents in which the child was extremely demanding and they were irrationally angry. Having isolated such incidents and situations, they must try to discover the typical mechanics that resulted, first, in the child's excessive behavior, and second, in their excessive reaction.

The parents may decide, depending on their evaluation of the specific situation, that the child must learn to amuse himself at times and that he demands attention when he feels he is not getting enough positive attention, or they may decide that, because of his excessive demands, they are not, in fact, initiating positive, rewarding interactions between the child and themselves. They may decide that the demands are indeed excessive and that they have made a serious mistake in responding to them, hence many demands should be ignored. There may be more than one operant working, so that the undesirable interaction is the result of several factors.

Goals can be multidimensional and include more than one factor, but it's better to limit them to *workable* objectives. Goals are only as good as their usefulness, so they must be practical and practicable. If the parents can't implement the goal, it's worthless, which is why the goal should be refined and made as self-contained as possible. I suggest you set up a chart like the one on the next page because it will help you evaluate the possibilities, especially for the next step in goal-oriented management, which is implementing the objective or figuring out how to accomplish what you want.

My hypothetical parents realize they have a problem which they have helped create. The child is excessively demanding of parental attention. Because of his demands, they have attempted to ignore him, resulting in their withdrawal from interactions with him. This withdrawal, of course, has resulted in more drastic attempts on the child's part to get their attention. Somewhere along the way, they have fallen into the pattern of ignoring the child's moder-

Goal for the child: Reduce his attention-getting behavior
Goal for the parents: Don't get so angry when he's demanding

Objective	*Ways to achieve objectives*
1. Initiate more positive interactions	1. Spend ½ hour with him before other children return from school
2. Don't respond to demands	2. Spend ½ hour with him before bedtime
3. Isolate him when he acts out because he doesn't get attention	3. Ignore him after parent has replied verbally
	4. Walk away when child makes persistent demands
	5. Send him to his room for 10 minutes when he gets belligerent
	6. Etc.

ate bids for attention and are irritated at and respond angrily to his excessive and rather aggressive attention-getting mechanisms. Very few positive interactions now take place between them. The parents realize that, by responding with anger, they are prompting the child to continue his successful, if negative, bids for attention, and they are becoming progressively more angry and hostile toward him.

The parents decide that they will have to set up situations in which pleasant transactions can occur, that they won't respond to excessive demands, and that, if the child really acts up, they will put him in his room by himself for brief periods. How will the parents implement their program? The mother decides she will set aside periods of time when she will give the child her exclusive attention. She will spend at least a half-hour with the child right before the other children come home from school, because this is a time when he is extremely demanding. She will set aside a "quiet time" for reading and talking with the child before his naptime. The father will give the child a brief period of concentrated attention immediately upon his homecoming. He will also spend at least a half-hour with the child immediately before bedtime. Both parents will make an effort to respond to moderate, reasonable requests for attention and do their best to be unresponsive to frequent and excessive bids. The parents will try to avoid angry responses to unacceptable behavior by briefly commenting on its unacceptability and then walking away. When the child becomes actively abusive or aggressive, he will be immediately confined to his room for ten minutes.

The parents know that it's going to be awfully hard to stick to their decision and change their responses and that it will take some time for the child's behavior to begin to improve. Keeping a record of improvement—both the child's and the parents'—is often an appropriate kind of encouragement. The record might look something like the following. (Use a check mark for each occurrence, and leave plenty of space for lots of checks.)

DAY	*CHILD*			*PARENTS*		
	Acts aggres-sively	*Acts moder-ately*	*Responds appropriately to positive approaches*	*Respond angrily to bids for attention*	*Maintain positive schedule*	*Ignore excessive behavior*
1						
2						
3						
etc.						

When the majority of check marks fall on the positive side of the ledger, the parents may want to modify further or add to their program. For instance, they might initiate a reward system when the child initiates positive interactions instead of using irritating tactics. They might decide to make an effort to help the child learn to play by himself. As long as the child and parent goals remain the same—the reduction of excessive attention-seeking behavior and the reduction of negative parental response—they can add any number of factors to their program.

When one particular behavior has been modified, it's time to move on to another. I do not recommend that parents initiate several programs to begin with. It's a lot simpler to isolate one factor at a time and work on it than to try to manage three or four, although modification of behavior in any area may bring about improvement in others automatically.

A COMMITMENT TO STRUCTURE

If you were fortunate, as I was, and slid through your child's infancy with a minimum of toil and trouble, structure has not been an important factor in your life. Well, times change, and so do situations. (If you haven't read the section on structure in Chapter 8 please read it now, or you won't know what I'm talking about.)

Structuring the environment is a critical step in parenting the hyperkinetic child, and this cannot be said often enough. Without structure, the child's world becomes such a haphazard place that neither the child nor the parents can abide it.

Limits must be established and maintained, firmly and inflexibly. They must be well defined, so that the child can understand them, and they must be consistent. What's wrong today is either always wrong or it's not ever wrong, including today. What's permissible today is always permissible.

Penalties for exceeding limits should be predetermined and should fit the crime. They should be enforced as firmly, patiently, and kindly as is humanly possible. It only confuses the child when the parent enforces penalties according to whim—sometimes mildly, sometimes not at all, and sometimes harshly punishing the child far in excess of the seriousness of the breech. Horrendous crimes should be distinguished from minor infractions of the rules, and penalties meted out accordingly. (By the way, there are few horrendous crimes that toddlers can commit. The few that are possible (e.g., running into the street or sticking things into wall sockets) usually involve direct and immediate danger to the child himself.)

All children, including toddlers, inevitably break rules and regulations and challenge limits. This is, I believe, a very natural function of childhood and is hardly ever meant as a challenge to adult authority. (Children do challenge authority, but not as often as they just kind of slide over the edges and breach limits. This is often described as "testing the limits," but I'm not sure that's an adequate description either. Children appear to test the limits to see if they are actually there, if they can be manipulated, or if it's possible to broaden them. But I suspect that, in most instances, infracting the rules just happens, with no particular motive and certainly not an ulterior one.)

Scheduling is still an important factor. While the schedule changes with maturity, the regularity of occurrences and events is still vital. Each day must assume a definite pattern that makes it resemble each other day. I'm well aware that sticking to a precise routine is a pain in the neck and impossible at times, but generally abiding by a schedule permits more flexibility than inconsistency does. That may sound like a contradiction, but it's not. If the toddler is maintained on a relatively precise schedule, he will be more likely to respond appropriately to occasional variations, he will behave more acceptably in response to modifications of the schedule, and he will probably meet new situations or stimuli more equitably than the child whose parents seesaw back and forth and fight with him all day.

TODDLER PROOFING

There is a deplorable tendency, deeply rooted in our child-raising practices, which for lack of a better name I'll call, "My grandmother's priceless heirloom was on that table before you got here and it's going to stay there or else!" Parents typically resist child-proofing their homes, which I can't understand. What's the point of leaving grandma's priceless heirloom on the table, when you know darn well it's going to get broken? For your own sake, if not for the child's, put grandma's heirloom away carefully until a more practical time, and plan a party to celebrate it's reunveiling.

Several years ago, I was appalled to see a mother smack her one-year-old daughter who reached into the kitchen trash can. It seemed to me like a very natural thing for the child to do, and if the mother didn't want the child reaching into the trash can, why didn't she buy one with a lid?

Child-proofing the premises means putting away breakables, installing baby gates on stairways, arranging special play areas where everything is safe, moving dangerous objects and substances out of reach or locking them up, being careful to put away items such as tools, paints, or other things the child could get into trouble with, and doing a lot of other things to make the environment relatively safe.

If there are other children, especially older children, keeping things out of the child's clutches can be a serious problem. When I suggested to my older children that they lock their rooms upon leaving, they thought it was a terrible idea so, when Benjamin got into their things, I was not unduly concerned.

The hyperactive toddler needs some space in which to work off his excessive energy, both inside and outdoors, and this space should be as safe and childproof as possible. He should not be expected to play in the livingroom and keep it clean, tidy, and intact. He needs to be supplied with playthings and toys that suit his activity level and abilities. He may or may not like large wooden puzzles, but he will love a tricycle.

MANAGEMENT VERSUS CONTROL

Problems of parental management of hyperkinetics are probably caused by several factors. The child may be having real problems bringing his behavior up to parental expectations, and parental management techniques may not be anything to write home about. If the child tends to impulsiveness, he is already experiencing conflict between his impulsiveness and the rules and regulations. If he's very active and distractible, he has already been deluged with parental sanctions.

Commonly, when we think of discipline, some sort of punishment comes to mind. I think it's time to draw a distinction between discipline and punishment, between management and aversive control.

Aversive control is an extremely powerful and efficient method for reinforcing negative (unacceptable) behavior, which may not be exactly what the parents had in mind. I'm sure all of us can think of instances in which a child, having been punished for a particular action, performed the same action a half-hour later, astonishing and enraging the adult who had already punished him and warned him, "never do that again!"

Aversive control, in the absence of positive reinforcement and with withdrawal of opportunities for positive interaction, emphasizes the prevention of unacceptable behavior through punitive measures. It does not encourage or enhance the possibility of acceptable behavior occurring.

Punishment per se is used to eliminate unacceptable behavior. Not only does it have unpleasant repercussions (it can teach the child to fear, if not hate, the punisher), but it also isn't really very effective except in inhibiting extremely situational-specific behaviors. It's not uncommon for a child to learn, through punishment, to inhibit a particular behavior when his parents are around, but that it's perfectly safe to indulge in that behavior when his parents are absent.

Discipline, on the other hand, is more rationally oriented. It relies more heavily on the loss or withdrawal of privileges than on punishment as a deterrent, and it recognizes and encourages acceptable behaviors.

To simplify the differences between discipline and

punishment, punishment says, "If you don't pick up your toys and put them away, I'll spank you." Discipline says, "If you don't pick up your toys, I'll have to pick them up and put them up in the closet for today, and you won't be able to play with them." Discipline also says, "You really did a good job picking up your toys. Your room looks very nice now."

I think parents need to take an honest look at their management techniques and appraise the consequences of their methods. What do parents do when unacceptable behaviors appear? What methods do they use to inhibit these behaviors? What do they do when acceptable or approved behaviors occur? Do they reward or show their approval for acceptable behavior? How much of their parent-child interaction is basically punitive? How much is really positive? Are their methods for inhibiting unacceptable behavior effective? Are there better ways to react to unacceptable behaviors? What can they do specifically to encourage the occurrence of acceptable behaviors?

Putting ideas down on paper is always a good approach to problem solving, so you might want to try a list of target areas like the one on the next page.

I have used the feeding situation as an illustration because I recently talked to the mother of a child who has turned the feeding situation into a three-ring circus. He has developed a marvelous repertoire for entertainment at mealtime, although his parents are not particularly amused. Since the child is still so young that his parents have to feed him, I suggested that they remind him once or twice that it was mealtime and that he was expected to cooperate. If he did not they should get up and walk away—with the food, of course—and say, "Well, that's it. Better luck next time!" The mother objected to my suggestion, because the child would naturally be hungry. I rather thought that the point the parent was trying to make was: "If you are hungry, dear child, now is the time to eat. It is not the time for me to amuse you. If you are not hungry, we will both go somewhere else and do something else." Period.

If my approach to ironing out problems in the feeding

Unacceptable behavior: Highly distractible when eating, prolonging meals indefinitely
Desired behavior: Eating quickly and completing meal on time (in thirty minutes)

How we normally react	*How we should react*
1. Irritably	1. Calmly
2. Repeatedly calling his attention to food	2. Reducing distraction
3. Feeding him	3. Reminding him to eat once or twice
4. Waiting for him to make up his mind to eat	4. Ignoring his getting out of his chair
5. Making him sit back down often	5. Leaving the meal on the table for thirty minutes and then removing it
6. Forcibly keeping him in his chair	6. Not giving snacks between meals if he doesn't eat
7. Giving him toys to amuse him while we feed him	7. Not playing or arguing with him
8. Getting angry and shouting	

situation sounds a little hard-hearted, remember that it's still a lot better than shouting, making the child sit in the chair, forcing him to eat, hitting him, getting angry and upset, and a whole lot of other possibilities. The child will not starve to death if he misses a couple of meals and, in a very short time, hunger being the impetus, he should begin to understand that he must eat first and then play.

Withdrawal of opportunities for positive reinforcement is not a bad method of discipline. It can be deleterious when too much positive interaction is withdrawn, leaving only negative responses. Isolation for fixed, brief periods of time, loss of privileges available to the child, ignoring inappropriate or unacceptable behaviors (which is very hard to do but has a positive payoff), and expressions of disapproval are good methods for reducing the appearance of the behaviors parents are trying to eliminate. I have been known to say to my children on occasion, "I refuse to get mad, if it kills me. I am going to my room and I'm going to stay there until I'm sure I'm not mad. I will not do anything to you, for you, against you, or any other way, until I decide I'm ready to do so. Good luck!" This may not exactly be the approach the behaviorists had in mind, but it was the best I could do under duress.

APPROVAL AND OTHER REWARDS

It is commonly accepted that most children respond with appropriate behavior because they seek parental approval. That's probably true of hyperkinetic children, too. Why, then, is it so common to hear that hyperkinetics don't seem to respond to the traditional rewards, such as parental approval? Probably because they're a little confused and their self-esteem, even at a very early age, is a trifle shaky. The frequency of negative and aversive methods, mixed with positive reinforcement would tend to confuse anybody. If their expectations are negative, it will be hard for them to recognize and accept positive reinforcement, especially an intangible, insubstantial reward like approval.

Approval is *not* the absence of criticism, although I have tried to make my children believe that for some time now, without much success. Approval, as a reinforcing agent, is necessary for the hyperkinetic child. It may be that this child has more need of verbalized, specific expressions of approval than a child who runs into fewer parent-child conflicts. The question remains, Are verbal expressions of approval enough to elicit and maintain acceptable behavior? Not for all children. Some children seem to need more direct, concrete rewards—and not all these children are hyperkinetic.

Tangible rewards effectively reinforce behavior, especially in young children. They are particularly effective when coupled with expressions of approval for the specific behavior: "You did a good job." "You played very quietly. I never heard a sound."

Choosing appropriate "carrots" is a matter of picking

something desirable to the child. The age of the child, his ability to recognize the relationship between the behavior and the reward, the immediacy of the reinforcer, and the frequency of reinforcement are matters that must be decided individually. Edibles like raisins, fruits, and nuts, and tokens, pennies, and gold stars might be adequate reinforcers for a toddler.

Handing a child a token for acceptable behavior will not modify his behavior. The token or reward serves a threefold purpose. It enhances the value of the behavior, it solidly signifies success, and it also prompts to parents to respond in an approving manner. Tangible rewards are probably symbolic of many things, so parents should not make the mistake of thinking of rewards as bribery. Parents can think of a system of rewards as a cueing device to remind them to verbalize approval, appreciation, and acceptance.

IMITATION AND MODELING

A child between birth and five has to learn an incredible amount of information and numerous skills, behaviors, attitudes, and crafts. He acquires a large part of his lifetime vocabulary. He acquires tremendous skill in controlling and managing a very complicated system of muscles, bones, tendons, and nerves. He achieves a large measure of his independence. He acquires a great deal of cognitive skill in interpreting, and integrating facts, and he develops his individual outlook on life and acquires a vast repertoire of behaviors, attitudes, and responses, many of which he learns by observing the important adults in his life.

The hyperkinetic child is one who is, because of adult attitudes and responses to him, inclined to include some very obnoxious and totally unacceptable attitudes and behaviors in his repertoire: being aggressive, abusive, and sometimes violent; adamantly and openly venting frustration on the nearest object or person; hitting, slapping, and punching rather than settling disputes verbally; initiating hostile or aggressive interactions; seeking negative or punitive responses from adults; engaging in provocative and irritating behavior; and responding to friendly or positive gestures with rejection or abuse. It is imperative that a child, particularly one who will encounter negative and abrasive situations, learn something about appropriate responses. From whom other than his parents, whose responses, characteristics, and mannerisms he initially imitates, will he begin to learn about patience, kindness, friendliness, cooperation, and tolerance?

What's the best way to teach the child how to behave? To show him, explicitly and directly, so that he can model himself according to what he's been shown. It's not enough to tell the child what he has done wrong. He should be told what he should have done, or shown how he could have done it better. This is especially true if the child is quite young. It's not unreasonable to expect a twelve-year-old to be able to do a little reasoning on his own, unless the parents expect miracles, but the toddler needs to be shown and directed very explicitly. You want the child to sit down and be quiet for fifteen minutes? Good. Show him how. Demonstrate what he can do for fifteen minutes that would be considered quiet. When fifteen minutes is up, tell him how great he was and reward him.

SUBSTITUTE CARETAKERS

I wasn't at all sure where to include a discussion of substitute caretakers, but this is as appropriate a place as any. While the parents may have had some trouble with substitutes to care for the difficult infant, getting and keeping adequate substitutes from now on is going to be a lot of fun.

I have had many interesting, though slightly maddening, experiences with substitute caretakers: There have been some who drove the child into hysterics—I don't know why; some who thought he should watch TV all day—he didn't; some who didn't want to or couldn't expend the energy he required—*they* wanted to watch TV all day; some who could not get him to do anything they wanted him to do—he hated them; and there were a few who thought that watching him meant being physically present in the same house—he tore the place apart. My experience has been that substitutes either enjoyed the child and established successful relationships, staying on with us for a long time, or they really didn't like him and stayed for a very brief time. It never took very long to establish whether or not it was going to work. If the child was happy and smiling, if the substitute was calm and unruffled, if the house hadn't been ransacked, and if there had not been any major catastrophes, I could be fairly sure that minor difficulties would resolve themselves.

For a start, parents can omit the very young and the very old as substitute caretakers. One hasn't the experience, and the other hasn't the stamina.

Parents should make an effort to explain what is required of a substitute in a very formal, frank, direct manner. Certainly, the difficulties shouldn't be maximized, but there's no point in beating around the bush and evading the problem.

Especially if the substitution is more than occasional, the caretaker should be appraised of parental management techniques—what's expected, what's acceptable, and what's not. Parents who simply walk away and let a substitute take over without detailed instructions can expect the worst kind of repercussions.

Instructions should include a schedule, methods of management, methods of parentally approved rewards and punishments, the rules of the house (what is permissible what is not, and what is totally forbidden), and anything else the parents feel would be helpful.

I like to put things in writing, so there can be no misunderstanding, and parents may find a written list of regulations helpful. It's to be expected that substitutes will have ideas of their own and will probably not follow the parents' directions completely. So the more formalized directions are, the more effective they are. The following is a list we used when Benjamin was three and his brother, David, was four.

1. Boys are dressed and perform all morning functions before the TV set goes on. This includes morning Sesame Street at 9 A.M.

2. Dressing includes hair combing and teeth brushing.

3. Boys and supervisor spend 10 minutes putting bedrooms in order. They jointly pick up clothes and toys, arrange toys neatly, make beds, etc.

4. Boys set the table for meals, taking turns.

5. Boys help clear the table after eating.

6. Boys help pick up toys after they have finished playing with them.

7. Toys are put back together and placed on shelves or in drawers or wherever they belong.

8. Books are kept on shelves. They are replaced after use. They are not left on the porch or in the yard.

9. Lost pieces of toys are searched for. Everyone looks for them until they are found or until supervisor decides the search is futile.

10. Outside toys, such as bikes and wagons, stay outside.

11. Inside toys, such as cards, games, and dolls, stay inside.

12. Boys are assigned other chores. They are expected to help supervisor with minor chores, such as dusting, putting clothes in the hamper, making beds, and putting dishes away.

13. Praise for good behavior is immediate and specific.

14. Punishment only deters bad behavior until a better behavior can be introduced. An acceptable form of behavior is always demonstrated immediately.

15. The best punishment is isolation for 10 to 15 minutes.

16. Spanking is a last resort. Casual hitting or slapping is forbidden.

17. People sometimes need time by themselves. Playing alone in one's room is not always punishment. It can be extremely soothing.

18. Arguing is permissible; punching, slapping, and calling each other names is not. Ever.

19. Bickering is easily stopped by separation.

20. Quarreling is more likely to occur on "inside" days. A good bit of supervised, directed activity and some time spent apart alleviates irritation.

21. Quiet times and rest periods are enforced.

22. Ben is encouraged to play quietly. (No nagging, please.) He is praised for doing so.

23. Crying because of injury is permissible. Crying because of frustration is mostly ignored. Crying because of major frustration is talked out.

24. Nagging and whining are not permissible and are discouraged by ignoring—walking away if necessary.

25. Tattling is discouraged by ignoring the tattler.

26. There is no point in trying to find the guilty party in a dispute. The matter is resolved in the best and most rational manner, without encouraging the boys to implicate each other in misdeeds.

27. Small children do not understand sharing. They should be encouraged, not forced, to share. Prolonged bickering or arguing about possession of a toy will result in the toy being removed from both boys' possession.

28. Watching TV all day is forbidden. One hour in the morning and one hour in the afternoon, if there is nothing else to do, is permissible. Soap operas are not suitable for small children; neither are game shows.

HOW MUCH TO EXPECT

Up until the age of two and a half or three, parents should expect to have to spend a lot of time watching and supervising. Children are simply not capable of assuming responsibility for themselves until they acquire certain levels of attainment, which are both learned and maturational. A bright child can get into a lot of trouble because he seems so advanced that adults tend to expect too much of him. The child with advanced motor skills is similarly expected to perform on a level with his motor development, although his emotional and intellectual level may not equal his physical abilities.

Children will break their backs, and their spirits, trying to live up to parental expectations. Why saddle them with unreasonable goals at a time when they really have no control over the goals established for them?

For interested parents, the Gesell maturational norms give indications of the kinds of abilities, achievements, and attainments that can be reasonably expected, with a modicum of flexibility, that is. They should be valuable in helping parents evaluate their expectations on the basis of what is possible and what is not.

Reducing expectations because of passive acceptance of hyperkinetic behaviors is just as bad as raising them beyond the child's attainment. If parents believe the child is capable of little or nothing, and signal their expectations, the child will probably attain exactly what the parents expect. Striving is a very good, positive thing to have to do. Striving in vain only gives people ulcers. Not having to strive makes them incompetent. To avoid ulcers or incompetence, avoid unrealistic expectations.

A hyperkinetic child is neither like every other child, nor is he a monster. He will always be highly active, perhaps emotional, and perhaps distractible, to some degree. He may have learning disabilities which will impede him in certain endeavors. He may not make it as an engineer if he has visual problems. He won't be a great athlete if he has motor problems. But he has so many assets that I can't accept that he will be what one author has called a "failure in living."

10 Preschool Problems

When my daughter was about three, I decided I was going mad. So, I charged into our family doctor's office and astounded him by saying, "I want you to do something. You have to calm her down. Give her something." He looked at her and then he looked at me, and he said very quietly, "No." I replied, "Why not? She's making a nervous wreck out of me." He said, "There's nothing wrong with her. She's fine. She doesn't need anything." That seemed reasonable, so I said, "Okay, there's something wrong with me. Give me something to calm me down." He replied, "No."

I usually was very fond of this man, who was uniformly kind and patient and who was interested in and cared about the families who were his patients, but momentarily I could have shot him. After a short discussion he asked, "Do you drink?" Now, that's a tricky question, so we had to clarify what was meant, and I finally admitted to being an occasional drinker. He then recommended that I go home and have a nice, tall drink and relax. I suggested that, if I had a drink every time the child upset me over the next few years, I would be well on my way to being an alcoholic. He said he didn't think I had the makings of an alcoholic, but I certainly seemed to be upset. And I said, "Well, if you could see what she does, you'd be upset, too." He then wanted to know what the child did that could upset me so much. So, I mentioned several incidents, including her imitating a trapeze artist—dangling by her knees from the crosspiece of the swing set—which had come close to giving me a heart attack. He then said, "Don't look so much." "What do you mean 'don't look,' I said, "What am I supposed to do—just let her run and not watch her? That's the darndest thing I've ever heard!" "Oh, no," said the doctor, "You'll have to watch her. Just don't look so much."

I felt a deep and penetrating confusion, but since I didn't have anything to show for my time and money except advice I didn't comprehend, I thought I owed it to myself to think about it. It took me a while to realize that I was indeed "looking too much," and I eventually resolved that I would refrain from looking, while continuing to watch the child to see what was going on. My nerves improved, and so did my relationship with my daughter.

I've never figured out why my doctor choose to be obscure. Maybe he was smart enough to realize it's not polite to tell a patient that she should be less critical and less demanding—that she really ought to ease up because she's becoming a first-class, grade-A harridan.

The ability to "not-look" is not a natural asset but must be acquired by long, patient practice. Not-looking has several factors: the ability to observe without involvement, the ability to decide what behaviors require intervention or correction, and the ability to walk away quietly without intervening. My grandfather possessed this talent to a high degree. I remember his occasionally coming to my defense and saying, "Leave the kid alone. She's not doing anything."

The hyperkinetic child is a child who gets into so much that there is pressure on the parents to correct, chide, threaten, forbid, and generally overcontrol him. In practice, overcontrol is not productive. After a while, the child becomes so used to the sound of his parents talking to him or shouting at him that he doesn't pay attention to the words, thereby eliminating any possibility of effective management.

Which brings us back to structure and limits. Intervention is necessary when behavior is unacceptable—when it is beyond the limits that are permissible. Without a predetermined set of limits, how will parents know when to intervene and when not to? Parents will have to decide individually where to draw the line—when it's time to intervene. The rest of the time, they should not-look.

FAMILY-STYLE FRACASES

Having a hyperkinetic child in its midst places quite a burden on family structure. No family member, including the child, gets a really fair deal. Families become enmeshed in the problems of the hyperkinetic child, and much of the family activity, attention, and time is concentrated on these problems. It doesn't take very long before a family is in serious trouble.

A lot of crazy things can happen when these problems dominate the family's life: Parents become estranged; one parent shifts total responsibility onto the other, who can't carry the burden alone; other children are neglected or are relegated to roles of secondary importance; parents have no time, patience, or energy to give to other children; parents have no time or energy for themselves; other children assume the parents' negative attitudes and responses, compounding the problem; families bicker and fight over the child; parental negative responses are generalized to include other children; and generally, there's a lot of tension, frustration, and anger which becomes the central theme of family life.

One of the major sources of family tension is the destructive interaction patterns that can develop between the hyperkinetic and his brothers and sisters, younger or older. Intersibling relations can degenerate to the point where they become a constant interchange of direct and open hostility. The reasons are obvious. The child is just more than another child can tolerate: He bothers them, disrupts them, distracts them, takes away their toys, and gets into their belongings; he is not compliant and does not accede to their plans and wishes; he is not particularly considerate; and often other children simply can't keep up with his physical pace. Added to this, he causes the parents to be angry and hostile, he gets more than his share of parental attention and concern, his behavior often results in negative or punitive actions against his siblings, and he is a source of parental disharmony. In all honesty, if you were the child's sibling, how would you feel about him?

I read somewhere that the best thing to do is for the parents to describe in detail the problems of the child to his siblings, explaining why they must devote so much extra time and effort to him and why they can't give the other children as much. Understanding the reasons for the situation is supposed to make the other children feel better about it. This kind of reasoning, however, shows a limited grasp of the facts of life and limited knowledge of the feelings of children. Rarely do two- or twelve-year-olds base their feelings on philosophical or theoretical assumptions. I fail to see how such an explanation will modify justified feelings of resentment, jealousy, and anger on the part of other children. Pointing out the hyperkinetic's differences might give them really good weapons to use against him, however.

There are several things the parents need to think about in connection with family interrelationships. First, how good or bad are intersibling responses? What are some direct, concrete steps the parents can take to improve those responses, modifying and correcting them? Second, how can the parents arrange their time so that other children get a fair, or fairer, share? Are the parents expecting too much from the other children in the way of acceptable behavior, compliance, understanding of the child, and suppression of anger and resentment? Are the other children expected to make fewer demands on parental time and attention, and how much less? Are they permitted and/or encouraged to express their feelings constructively? Third, are the parents in agreement in their management of the child? Are they supportive of each other, or are the problems that are child-centered creating a breach in their relationship? How do they view each other in relation to the child? Does one see the other as being essentially incompetent, punitive, rejecting, or too permissive, and how do they resolve their differences? (Do they resolve their differences?)

IMPROVING FAMILY RELATIONSHIPS

Obviously, family-type problems are pretty complicated, and it's hard to find even a starting place to improve or modify the situation. The only thing everybody agrees on is that nobody's particularly happy; they don't like what's happening, and they would do something about it if they only knew what to do.

Let's take it a step at a time and try to isolate separate, correctable factors.

What's wrong with the family? It could be that the parents are angry too much of the time, the parents are punitive too much of the time, the other children are sullen and resentful, or the home atmosphere is not happy or pleasant enough; or any other generalized problem could exist.

What factors created the problem? There are many possibilities and variables. The parents must decide which are the major influences: parental attitudes, improper management, difficulty with the hyperkinetic, absence of relief from anger-provoking situations involving him; the other children behaving badly when the hyperkinetic is out of control, the parents being too critical of the other children, etc.

Whose attitudes, responses, or behaviors need to be changed? Probably, all members of the family are involved to some degree. Separate attitudes, behaviors, and responses have to be identified for each member, along with his most noticeable or apparent faulty attitude or response.

For instance, the father's attitude may be one of avoidance, and he has thrust the responsibility for the child onto his wife. The mother is very inconsistent in her management and needs to define limits, acceptable and unacceptable behavior, and the consequences of each. An older sister has become openly antagonistic and relates to the child through a continuing series of sarcastic, belittling remarks. A younger brother is constantly frustrated in his relationship with the child, who attempts to control and bully him, resulting in squabbling, bickering, fighting and other negative interactions that irritate the parents.

What more appropriate or improved interactions are possible? Under the circumstances, it might be decided that the father will assume more direct management of the child. The mother will establish parameters for unacceptable, acceptable, and more-or-less neutral behavior and predetermine how she will respond to each. The older child will be encouraged to modify her negative interactions, and the parents will initiate systematic modification techniques to increase positive interaction between the younger children, while decreasing negative response.

How can the desired goals be reached? This depends entirely on the reasons things have been going wrong but might include the father setting aside some time each day to spend with the child and the mother deciding which behaviors are unacceptable and making up a list of punishments for their occurrence, meanwhile verbalizing more often her approval of acceptable behavior. The older sister will be encouraged to talk out her feelings with her parents, who will attempt to react nonjudgmentally, and she will be encouraged to reduce negative remarks and increase positive or neutral remarks by a system of privilege rewards. The parents will initiate a system of modification in regard to the younger children, including rewards for the younger brother and the hyperkinetic child when they join in cooperative play. Much of the minor squabbling will be ignored by both parents, and major incidents of fighting will be followed by isolation of both children.

Further, the parents have enrolled in a parent effectiveness training (PET) course, which they hope will help them modify their critical and angry verbal responses, and the father agrees to assume total responsibility for all children one evening a week, no matter what, to give the mother some relief.

PARENT EFFECTIVENESS TRAINING

Basically, I would categorize PET as a systematic method for modifying parental response, especially verbal response, and parental attitudes toward things like misbehavior, expectations, reinforcing appropriate behavior, communications, punishment, and rewards. It's a very good, sound approach to handling many situations but, like many other techniques and therapies, the results are only as good as the input. If parents put some effort into applying the techniques, using the workbooks and diagnostic tools usually included in the source, even if the methods seem foreign and unnatural to them, PET can modify parental behaviors and attitudes.

The concepts of PET are quickly understood, which may not be as much of an asset as it appears to be at first glance. Some of the concepts incline to cliche-ism, probably because PET is pretty much a commonsense, everyday approach and is presented in everyday, commonsense language. It's easy to say, "Oh, sure, I know that! So, why are you telling me something I already know?" and miss the important part—putting the commonsense approach into practice.

The ideal PET course has several characteristics. It helps parents become familiar not so much with the concepts but with the practices of effective parenting, it helps them feel comfortable with the methods, and it gets parents to evaluate honestly their own practices and then make improvements in those methods. Parents must first make a commitment to follow the program outline, however, before any positive results are likely to occur.

One of the better things to come out of PET is the

idea of "natural consequences," which is something all children must inevitably learn and which many hyperkinetic children can't learn because parents tend to overcontrol, overprotect, and deflect them from the natural consequences of their behavior.

LEARNING ABOUT CONSEQUENCES

By the time the hyperkinetic child is about three, despite what everybody says about his impulsiveness and inability to reflect, there is something he must begin to learn: For every action or lack of action, there is a consequence. Rewards, punishments, and a lack of rewards are consequences. This does not mean that every time the kid does something wrong the consequences are that he will be smacked. That's the worst kind of overcontrol and will not teach him anything about real, honest consequences. Repetitive punishment will eventually make the parent, not the child, responsible for his behavior. Unless the child is taught to assume responsibility for his own behavior, he is not likely to behave appropriately when he is in situations where there is no adult figure to assume responsibility for him. Based on this assumption, it's obvious why so many hyperkinetic children misbehave in free-play, unstructured situations and in the absence of an authority figure they feel is able to impose limits. Helping the hyperkinetic child acquire a sense of responsibility for his behavior requires stamina, persistence, and endless patience.

While it's usually fairly simple to figure out what the consequences are, allowing them to happen naturally is a horse of another color. Consequences can be bothersome, cumbersome, and a lot of trouble to other people. (Punishment is more direct, easier to administer, and less bothersome.) What are the consequences of the child disrupting the family's dinner? He will be allowed to (1) eat elsewhere, (2) eat before or after the family, or (3) just go away and stay away from the table. What are the consequences of running beserk in a supermarket? He will be removed from the market and taken home. What are the consequences of fighting in the car while the family is heading for a special outing? He will be taken home and left there. It would be nice if other family members could continue the planned activity, but it may be impossible if no substitute caretaker is available.

Obviously, consequences are troublesome, interfering with the plans and schedules of others, infringing on their rights, and causing complications. The younger the child, the more troublesome the consequences tend to be. Like liquor, spanking is quicker, but the parent will find that spanking tends to perpetuate more spanking, while complying with consequences tends to reduce unacceptable behavior rather more efficiently.

Last summer, Benjamin behaved miserably while we were driving to a big, bang-up family outing–picnic–cookout. I turned around, dropped him at home, and then drove off, leaving him standing in tears on the porch. I then spent the next four hours worrying about what he was doing, what it was possible for him to do, and what I could expect when I got home. Upon arrival, we found him sitting quietly on the porch, as meek and mild as a lamb. He helped us unpack the picnic things and, after asking a few questions about what he had done with his afternoon, I never mentioned the episode again. However, his behavior in the car has improved tremendously. (I have occasionally offered to return home with him when his behavior was not acceptable, at which proposal his behavior immediately improved.)

There are many, many consequences evident on the basis of the preschooler's behavior: being restricted to the house if he wanders, being removed from play groups when he fights, being restricted to his room when he gets into things that are forbidden to him, having toys and other objects removed from his immediate possession when he doesn't pick them up, eating in the kitchen if he cannot be nondisruptive at the dinner table, having privileges withdrawn if his behavior is not acceptable, being left at home if he does not behave properly at special events or family outings, etc. Note that all these consequences should have a specific duration: The toys are removed for one day, for instance, or he is removed from a play group for a half-hour. He is excluded from family outings once, because of one incident of misbehavior, but not for the rest of his life.

PEACE AND QUIET

While teaching the preschooler about natural consequences, parents ought to begin teaching the child some inhibitory processes: quiet time, cooling-off periods, and the like.

Enforced isolation periods, meted out as a consequence of unacceptable behavior, are not the same as quiet time or cooling-off periods and should be treated as separate entities.

Quiet times can be defined as periods during which the child is encouraged to perform some restful or relaxing activity: sleeping when he's very young, resting and reading when he's a little older. The hyperkinetic preschooler is in need of both the periods of relaxation and the acquired ability to avail himself of nonstimulating periods of time.

For the young, very active, and easily distractible child, the duration of quiet time has to be brief. What's important is not the length of the time but maintenance of the relaxed atmosphere. The child should be encouraged to sit or lie down, look at books, close his eyes and think of happy events, or snuggle with a doll or teddy bear; or the parent may participate by talking quietly, reading a book to the child, or just holding the child on his lap. The more restless the child, the more parental help he will need to maintain quiet, even briefly.

Regular, scheduled quiet times and unscheduled periods that follow an unusually stimulating occurrence are, I believe, extremely beneficial to both parent and child. The child should, of course, be reinforced for successful completion of inhibitory action. "You sure were quiet." "I feel much better now, I'll bet you feel better, too." "You could win a prize for being quiet! In fact, you did. Have a cookie."

Cooling-off periods or getting-control-of-yourself are a little like isolation, the main difference between them being that the parent attempts to inculcate the idea and techniques of cooling off: "When I get angry, I need some time to cool off, so that I don't stay mad. I need to get away by myself for a little while. Everybody needs to cool off when they're angry. I think it would be a good idea for you to play in your room for ten or fifteen minutes. It would give you a chance to cool off and not be angry any more." When the child is very upset or angry, he ought to be allowed an opportunity to leave the anger-provoking or upsetting situation and have some privacy in which to put his control mechanisms back in working order. It's only fair to the child to help him develop his own system of control. It's admittedly easier for the parents to do it for him, but he will never learn how to do it himself if they constantly intervene.

OVERCONTROL AND OVERPROTECTION

The parents of hyperkinetic children face an interesting dilemma: The child is released from blame for his actions, because he simply cannot inhibit or control much of his behavior or activity; on the other hand, he must learn to internalize the principles of responsibility, consequences, and autonomy. Where is the fine line between what the parents can expect in the way of responsibility and control and the inability of the child to inhibit or reflect on his actions?

I'm afraid that a lot depends on the child, the techniques of the parents, their attitudes toward the child, their child-rearing practices, and about 9000 outside influences that nobody can predict. Each individual instance will have to be judged on its merits, and the parents will have to determine where their child is able to be responsible and where he simply cannot.

Parents who choose to overcontrol the child and thereby assume total responsibility for his actions, behaviors, and failures, are likely to be parents who overprotect him from consequences later on. (Unfortunately, too many parents are accused of being overly protective when they intervene in situations where they know the child has no hope of succeeding, which is not the same as being overprotective.)

Once the child learns the rules of the game, he will only infrequently find it convenient to rebel against parental overcontrol. Only when it suits him.

It would behoove parents to examine closely the messages they are sending to the child. Are they telling him that he is an adequate, capable, responsible person who will one day become an autonomous adult, or are they informing him that, because of his difficulties, he is inadequate and incapable of assuming responsibility for himself, now and forever? Of course, the parent can send the "You're inadequate" message in early childhood, and then reverse himself and send a message that says the child "must" become adequate, capable, and achievement-oriented in later years. If the child has been prompted to learn to be irresponsible, however, suddenly insisting upon responsibility, achievement, and purpose is bound to result in severe conflict.

Overcontrol has a pernicious effect on parents, too. Every time the child fails, every time he does not control his behavior, and every time he does not achieve, it is the *parents who fail,* who are inadequate and incapable of achievement, not the child. Having assumed the child's responsibility, and leaving him free to behave acceptably or unacceptable, to fail or succeed, and to do as he damn well pleases at the moment, parents should not be surprised if the child doesn't worry unduly about his responsibilities. I suspect that children frequently use the mechanics of overcontrol to their own advantage, allowing their parents to be punished or getting revenge on their parents for parental misdeeds, real or imaginary.

As I said before, a lot of learning is acquired before the child is six, and some of it concerns how to get around good old mom and pop, how to get even with them for being meanies, and how to play games like overcontrol.

ANGER

At some point, frequently when the child is between the ages of four and seven, parents may find that they are chronically angry with him, or at least that they're angry too often or too explosively. Of course, the big push to "socialize" the child (make him and his behavior acceptable to society) doesn't usually start until the child is about three years old. Before then, many of his minor obnoxious and troublesome behaviors are, if not condoned, at least overlooked. However, when the child, after lengthy efforts by the parents, continues to demonstrate aberrant behaviors and seems to resist the process of socialization, the parental reaction is, as likely as not, going to be anger.

Only quite recently, and with a small degree of success, has our culture allowed expressions of anger. Much time and effort is spent in teaching children—and adults—to repress anger and to deny it exists. Anger is the "wrong" emotion, often interpreted as a symptom of a defective personality rather than the expression of a reality-oriented emotion. Anger is rarely seen as being situation-specific.

The fact remains that both children and adults get angry, sometimes justifiably and sometimes not. So, what can one do with his anger when he's angry? He can't punch anybody, although he might like to, because he'll get arrested. He can't tell them off, using obscene words and expressions that have nothing to do with the situation, because that's not acceptable. He's prohibited from throwing things, stamping his feet, slamming doors, bellowing, pounding his chest, or doing any other nice, clean, direct things to vent his anger. All these methods are childish and would make the angry person a subject of ridicule or loss of esteem and respect. It may be just as well that we can't do some of these things to vent our anger, but what *does* one do with anger, especially if one is frequently provoked?

Anger is a very destructive emotion, particularly accumulated anger. The parents and the hyperkinetic child (and other siblings, if there are any) are likely to get caught up in a corrosive whirlpool and, having been caught up, find it difficult to find a way to temper their emotions.

For the child's part, his proclivities for lability (quick swings of emotion) frequently result in provoking situations, compounded by his problem with control or impulsiveness. Acting very impulsively, he reacts to provocation by starting a fistfight. Since reactions become habits, by the time the child is four or five or six, he has certain expectations as to how the world will treat him. Likewise, the world has certain expectations as to how he will act.

On the parental side of the slate, which is often none too clean, there being residues of anger left over from other contexts such as interfamily or work-related situations, and the major and minor frustrations of modern American life, there is the lack of satisfaction with the child, the difficulties in management that are frequent, repetitive, and never-ending, and the sense of frustration that accompanies parental failures at control.

Parents of hyperkinetic children inevitably feel some sense of guilt, and the degree probably depends on how they view themselves in relation to the child (as prison wardens, as controllers of behavior, as loving guides, as interpreters of the world, as responsible parents, as parents of an uncontrollable child, as ineffective managers, as being somehow responsible for the hyperkinesis through some act or some omission, etc.) and how they view themselves (as inadequate, as conscientious, as loving, as efficient, as tolerant, etc.) which has nothing to do with the child personally but is often exacerbated by the child's behavior or lack of response to parental management.

And last but not least, is the fact that there are a lot of anger-provoking incidents (and the anger is pretty well justified from any adult's point of view). The child does do things that other children don't do, or do less frequently. The parent is justifiably angry when the child, contrary to direct and concrete instructions, does something that is disobedient, destructive, and downright dangerous to himself.

A mitigating factor, on the child's side, is that most of

the anger-provoking acts are not premeditated, which doesn't help one bit once the act has been committed and the parents are incensed. The hyperkinetic child must come to view the world as a pretty angry place—because he does not quite comprehend the causal link between what he did and the adult anger directed toward him.

This is true, quite possibly, simply because the causal link isn't really very rational. In other words, there is no relationship between the magnitude of the adult anger and the seriousness of the child's misbehavior. There is one factor that has a tremendous effect on the amount of anger generated, which the child can neither be aware of nor understand, namely, the amount of effort the parents have invested in modifying or prohibiting some of the child's behaviors.

Another important factor is the accumulative effects of repetitive, frequent, anger-provoking incidents. Parents of hyperkinetic children are more apt to find themselves in irritating and/or infuriating situations more frequently than is conducive to maintaining a placid personality.

Anger that's dissipated (vented appropriately) is anger that is done and over, more or less. A parent faced with numerous provocative incidents, daily, weekly, and yearly, cannot effectively dissipate anger. It must build up and accrue. Thereafter, any provoking action can trigger a deluge of anger in an amount not justified by the event.

Anyway, parents and children are left in a most uncomfortable position, with neither of them able to fully ventilate their feelings without injuring the other either emotionally or physically.

If it seems that everybody is getting the short end of the stick, it's true. Adults have longer short ends. There are adult methods for venting anger that are not approved for children. As an example, one parent comes home from work in an exceedingly "bad mood." The work situation has been thoroughly discussed several times and is regarded by all as being unsatisfactory as such; the parent's supervisor is seen as incompetent and uses the parent as a scapegoat.

The parent (P) walks in, letting the door slam slightly, throws down his briefcase, and, without greeting anyone, heads for the bar and pours himself a stiff drink. The other parent (OP) immediately picks up the cues and responds correctly:

O.P.: Hi. Had a bad day?

P.: Oh, boy, have *I* had a bad day? Let me tell you! That son-of-a-bitch really did it this time! (It should be noted here that the entire family knows exactly who the "son-of-a-bitch" is. He is always referred to by this title.)

O.P.: Oh, dear. What did he do?

P.: You wouldn't believe me if I told you. You simply wouldn't believe that miserable bastard could pull such a dirty, rotten trick on me.

O.P.: Oh, yes, I would. What did he do?

The parent responds by filling in the ghastly details of whatever happened, and the other parent responds by listening fairly sympathetically and by generally being supportive.

Let's pretend the hyperkinetic child comes home from school. He's in first grade and is having serious problems with his teacher, who is not sympathetic to the child and, in fact, overeacts to minor disturbances and infractions. He stomps in, slamming the door, and drops his books on the floor.

P.: I've told you a million times, don't slam the door. Why did you throw your books on the floor? Pick them up.

C.: Oh, mom, I'm so mad. Do you know what that son-of-a-bitch did today?

P.: Don't you dare use that kind of language! I'll wash your mouth out with soap!

C.: Mom, the teacher was really mean to me. She picked on me all day.

P.: Well, what did you do to make her pick on you?

Need I go any further? For the spouse who has a miserable supervisor, the parent responds with empathy. For the child who has a miserable supervisor, the parent's expectations are that the fault is somehow the child's. Further, the child is prohibited the same actions and vocabulary that the adult might use to ventilate anger.

What might be the reaction of the parent if the other parent had said, verbalizing a fantasy, "I'd like to catch him in a dark alley some night. I'd punch his face in!" How would the adult react if the child said, "I really hate her! I'd like to chop off her head!"? The response to the other adult might be, "Yeah, really, he deserves it." The response to the child is more apt to be, "You know you shouldn't say things like that about your teacher!" Why not?

The parents should take action to plan and implement a program for decreasing unacceptable expressions of anger and increasing acceptable expressions, for themselves, the child, and the other siblings. Unacceptable forms of anger are hitting, punching, exploding, abusive language, destructiveness aimed at the offending person, breaking things, temper tantrums, kicking, etc. Acceptable forms of expression are reasonable verbal statements of anger, exerted physical activity, directed physical action, and fantasy.

Parents are sometimes surprised by the deluge of angry feelings that permitting expressions of anger uncorks. If the child has been repressing his anger and frustration, it's only natural that there is some bottled-up accumulation of anger that is bound to emerge when prohibitions against expression are removed. The deluge should subside in time. If it does not, there may be some serious problems that the parents should evaluate and investigate.

The parent who violently overeacts with anger when the child explodes in bursts of anger is telling the child it's all right to explode, even if he's verbalizing sanctions against such outbursts. While anger is permissible, explosions are rarely acceptable. (Everybody gets very angry occasionally, and it's not reasonable to expect otherwise.)

Helping other children in the family express their feelings toward this child is a very important part of parenting. The parents will have to adopt the attitude that it's all right for his siblings not to like the hyperkinetic but, since they all have to live together, everybody will have to try to maintain order and civility. Other children can sometimes offer some interesting and imaginative suggestions for improving relationships, although parents should disregard advice to farm the hyperkinetic out.

NURSERY SCHOOL

Should the hyperkinetic be sent to nursery school? Is he ready for the challenge? Is he ready for the transformation? Can he inhibit his behavior appropriately? Can he respond to the changed environment?

Yes and no. Much depends on the nursery school itself and what it expects and demands of the child. More depends on the individual teacher and/or supervisor. The child is probably ready for some changes in expectations and for the mental stimulation provided by nursery school. Whether or not he can behave acceptably is up to the individual abilities of the child, his state of development, and what's expected of him.

The Montessori method of instruction has become tremendously popular in the last two decades, and I suggest that parents become familiar with its concepts and practices. Among other things, parents should be aware of the capabilities and abilities Montessori felt appropriate and reasonable for nursery-school-age children. Particularly interesting should be the physical, everyday routines that preschool children are quite capable of doing.

I'm not at all sure that Montessori methods are effective with hyperkinetic children, since so much of the training, acculturation, and instruction is relayed from one child to another. If the child is resistant to management, has learned very negative interactions with other children, and/or is very restless and distractible, a Montessori school may not be the best kind of preschool for him. He may need a highly structured setting with a firm, consistent, understanding supervisor. However, Montessori-based instruction can be beneficial in teaching the child something of responsibility, orderliness, and cooperation.

Parents should observe the nursery school and its supervisors before placement of the child. They should also observe the child in nursery school and keep in close touch with his immediate supervisor or teacher. It may be possible to head off problems and correct them if the parents are aware of them before they become catastrophic.

A bad nursery school experience predisposes the child to approach formal education suspiciously and warily. If the parents have doubts about the suitableness of available nursery schools, perhaps it's wisest to omit the experience rather than having to cope with the unfortunate consequences of a bad experience.

TOYS

The hyperkinetic child is often accused of being hard on toys and objects; breaking, pillaging, and marauding is about the way some parents see it. Being an observer of toys, I think the accusation is somewhat unjustified. Most of the toys on the market are fragile, and it's a wonder some of them don't just fall apart on the shelf.

I have always resented cheap junk toys—and some that weren't so cheap but were still easily broken. I also resent many of the gimmicks marketed as educational toys. There are many educational toys, such as balls that help train the muscles, bicycles that promote motor skills and balance, puzzles, games, books, dolls, and a lot of other things a child uses in a learning experience. And then there's an incredible amount of junk suitable for no child and certainly not suitable for the hyperkinetic child. There are two types of toys that I recommend for this child: Either one that allows him to engage in activity, or one that appeals to his imagination. Many educational toys have one specific use and/or way in which they can be used. Parents could spend 9 million dollars on toys, trying to keep this kid amused, and he would still be bored.

Toys bought for the hyperkinetic child should be durable and rugged; the parents should look at them with an eye to whether or not the child could possibly be hurt by them (e.g., if it breaks, would he be cut on a sharp corner). Third, does the toy lend to imaginative play or is it limited in its application? Suitable toys might include a tricycle, a good set of blocks, dolls that don't break easily, sturdy cars and trucks, and a wagon or scooter.

Since it's very difficult to keep this child out of trouble when he's confined to the house by illness, bad weather, or some other unfortunate circumstance, it would behoove the parents to keep a supply of toys and materials on hand that are brought out only on house-bound occasions. What do you do when it rains for three days and everybody's got cabin fever? Well, you can pull out of your magician's hat things such as fingerpaints, dot-to-dot books, paint-with-water books, clay, and all kinds of messy things not generally available to the child and plan to spend a lot of time supervising and directing activities.

THE END OF AN ERA

The child's placement in kindergarten signals the end of an era, and the beginning of a new epoch. The child is a composite of many factors, innate and acquired, and a lot depends on his perceptual-cognitive development, his conception of his world, his motor ability, his emotional development, his language skills, his intellectual abilities, his skills in relating to others, his development of autonomy and responsibility, his level of motivation, and his physical condition in general. If the passing era has been notably successful, one can hope the next one will continue to be so, although it's not a good idea to be overconfident. If the era has been marked with hostility and rejection, poor management on the part of the parents, and deteriorating behavior on the part of the child, well, look out, because here comes trouble!

11 The Educational Experience

Parents used to be told that, if they could just get the kids off to a good start, things would be just fine after that. There might be a few minor crises but, with the strong, integrated personality the parents had already helped to establish for their children, they'd weather almost any storm. Oh, that it were true! But it's not.

Let's consider briefly a theoretical situation in which the parents provide an exemplary home situation. They are loving, consistent in their dictates, reasonable in their expectations, generous with praise, long on temper, moderate in their punishment, and all the rest. Their child, within this context, behaves admirably, rarely being disruptive, aggressive, distructive, emotional, or negative, and by and large is able to confine his hyperactive tendencies to pretty constructive behaviors. So things go smoothly at home and, when the child enters school, the parents luck out with his teachers, having been able to find a good kindergarten teacher who moved the child into a satisfactory arrangement in first grade where the child's behavior was only a minor problem and his academic achievement excellent.

Before second grade, the parents and child move into a new school district. The child's behavior has been noted as satisfactory and, rather than create a problem where one may not exist, the parents cross their fingers and hope for the best, allowing the child to be placed at random in the new school.

The new teacher, an important addition to the constellation of adults in the child's life, is not at all suitable. Let's give our hypothetical teacher some personal problems that are creating fluctuating emotional states, disrupting her organization and her teaching methods. She's a little hysterical trying to stay on top of her problems and her job, too. The child can't cope with this adult. He can't find limits, and expectations fluctuate. He becomes apprehensive, because he's looking for a semblance of structure where there is none. His behavior, within the context of this situation, begins to deteriorate. He begins acting up; he becomes disruptive, because he needs something from the teacher and he doesn't know of any other way to get her attention, much less what he needs. His behavior is negatively reinforced by the teacher, because she's already irritable. So the child responds the way anyone else would respond—his behavior worsens. In time, his feelings and behaviors will be generalized into other areas of his environment where things weren't going badly before.

The parents could exhaust themselves trying to maintain their previously peaceful and supportive structure, but since the cause of the problem lies outside their jurisdiction, outside the child, and outside any area in which they can effectively act, the problem situation cannot be remedied by parental action. They can eliminate the problem by removing the child from the situation, but they cannot alter the situation.

The second hypothetical case concerns a child whose parents are well meaning, but who have overcontrolled him, frequently punishing him for unacceptable behavior and rarely responding positively. The child has always been troublesome at home, being unpredictable and often aggressive in his behavior, hyperactive, impulsive, and distractible. He is extremely restless, moving from one thing to another continuously. He is very easily frustrated and responds to minimal frustration with outbursts of temper, crying, screaming, throwing himself on the ground, and attacking other children. After three weeks in kindergarten, the child refuses to go to school, staging emotional scenes every morning before he will permit his parent to leave him in the classroom. The teacher cannot manage the child's behavior because essentially she cannot practice the parents' techniques within the classroom context. After several months, the child is more restless, less able to pay attention, more distractible, and more frustrated than ever.

The parents are called in for conferences, but they can suggest no methods for managing the child. What are the logical consequences of the parents' management of the child? Placement in a special education classroom, if there is one available for kindergarten children.

The third hypothetical case concerns a fairly functional hyperkinetic child and a fairly functional teacher, and they just don't get along. Something is wrong with the chemistry or the expectations or something. There's really no logical or apparent reason, but it doesn't work when these two people are in the same classroom. Period.

Sometimes I feel that sending the child out to be educated is like playing poker in Las Vegas. I know I can't beat the house, but I'm impelled to keep trying.

EDUCATION AS SYSTEM AND PROCESS

I think I've said enough about choosing the right teachers, so let's talk about what actually goes on in the schools and what is going wrong. Authorities point to the many factors that are causing the educational system to fail in its basic function: to educate children. These factors are serious, multidimensional and multitudinous.

I think schools have not kept pace with the times: Practice is not as good as theoretical knowledge. Schools have therefore outgrown their usefulness and have not yet grown into new usefulness. The educational system, which was originally designed to educate the masses, never did do very much for exceptional children on either end of the scale. Schools have immemorially kept the gifted student back, hindering his growth, while they reduced the learning disabled to blithering incompetency.

Since the exceptional child is now recognized to have some claims on the system (i.e., he, too, should be educated according to his abilities), parents of exceptional children are demanding that the schools educate their children.

Education is both a system and a process. Unfortunately, the emphasis has been placed too heavily on the system, while the process takes a backseat. The system is composed of the mechanics of education: children sitting in a schoolroom, teachers making out lesson plans, so many units of English to be taught each year, and a total of so many credits required to graduate from high school. I am frequently infuriated that educators don't seem to understand that keeping the child in the system is not the equivalent of keeping him in the process (the learning experience). Many times, the child is lost to the process because educators do not make efforts to keep him in it. As long as the kid is sitting in his seat, and not disrupting the class, the educator is satisfied. Nonsense. There's no reason to keep the child in the seat if he's lost to the process and no learning is taking place. After the child is lost to the process, he might as well be kept at home, because nothing positive happens to him in the system, anyway. After he's lost to learning, the only thing the school will do is compound his failures, reinforce his poor self-image, and tell his parents that it's not the school's fault.

Let me make one thing clear. When the school loses the child to the process of education, advertently or inadvertently, intentionally or unintentionally, by pushing him out, throwing him out, squeezing him out, or by simply failing to exert every effort to keep him involved, it is most definitely the school's fault, and it's about time parents understand whose fault it is and begin to speak up and demand that educators do whatever is necessary to keep the child involved.

Most educators—teachers, administrators, authorities—are reluctant to admit that it's the school system's fault, and they like to try to shift responsibility: The child is unteachable, the child is incorrigible, the parents are overprotective, the parents are hysterical, the child is defective, deviant, and/or dysfunctional. All these reasons are so much baloney!

We have collectively made a serious mistake, I'm afraid. We've delegated responsibilities and duties to the school that the school is not capable of assuming—not that the school hasn't assumed them, they just haven't done it well. The school is becoming a combination educator–social worker–diagnostician–moral educator–psychologist–parent. No institution can serve such diverse functions well. I think we must go back and think about the purpose and function of the school and reevaluate its role in children's lives.

Broadening the concept of education is not a bad thing to do, if by broadening we mean creating new opportunities for children who did not properly fit into the educational context before, creating better pedagogical methods and better teacher-training procedures, and adding new depth and breadth to the education of all children. If by broadening the concept is meant delegating responsibilities and authorities to the school system that properly belong to others, such as parents, social agencies, and psychologists, then we're in trouble.

I, for one, will not turn my parental prerogatives over to any person or any institution unless they are willing to provide twenty-four-hour service for my children, sick or well, and to put food on the table and shoes on their feet. (And I doubt that I would do it if anybody offered me a deal, anyway.)

Parental prerogatives and school authority can be exceedingly oppositional at times. Parents are encouraged to bow to the superior wisdom and authority of the school, abnegating parental authority, and I can't figure out why they would or should. Parental authority, because it rests so firmly in parental responsibility, cannot be delegated or relegated. The parent, having assumed total responsibility for the welfare of the child, automatically assumes parental prerogatives. The school's authority derives from its function—to educate the child—and should not extend beyond its proper role.

It's disheartening for parents to have to sit on the sidelines and watch their children being lost to education, especially if the parents value the acquisition of knowledge. No matter how much parents try or what they do, they can't effectively keep the child involved in the learning process if the educator can't. Once educators lose sight of their primary goal—if indeed they ever knew what it was—and start blaming the child for failure, behaviorially or academically, in the classroom, chances are mighty slim the child will continue to be involved.

A TALE OF WOE

Having lost at least one child to the process of education, I really am fighting not to lose another. Gerry was an exceptionally bright, cheerful, slightly hyperactive child when she entered kindergarten. She had a reasonably good teacher and, while some problems arose, they were rather minor, and parent-teacher conferences were friendly, productive, and goal-directed.

The Primary Grades

Gerry had an exceptional teacher for first grade and for half of second grade. When the teacher was transferred to another grade, her substitute was adequate. Gerry learned to read rapidly, her school work was excellent, and she was always placed in the advanced reading and math group. In fact, Gerry had been taught to read a little and had learned numbers, letters, and number concepts from her older sister before she entered first grade. She had been a little disappointed that kindergarten work had been so slow and covered a lot of the material she already knew.

Since Gerry was in the "fast" group, two problem situations arose. First, since the children in this group required less active teaching time than the other groups and completed their work rapidly, they were assigned a great deal of busywork to occupy their time. These groups also completed the required work much in advance of the end of the school year, leaving considerable time to fill with repetitious, monotonous assignments.

Gerry "did things" during these times. It was obvious that she easily became bored with the repetitious busywork and during such times was inclined to become distractible and restless. Early in the first-grade year, the teacher and I had discussed what was going on, what Gerry was doing that was unacceptable (some of it was highly inventive, even if it was distracting), and what we could do to reduce these behaviors.

The teacher and I had a very good relationship, and there was never a feeling that Gerry was being blamed for her behaviors, although she was punished. I was free to admit my own difficulties with management, and the teacher was open to suggestions to improve her management.

We decided that the best possible remedy for restlessness, distractibility, and obvious boredom was to plan a program to keep the child as busy as possible with new and interesting materials. The teacher agreed to implement this program, as long as Gerry cooperated by completing the required work.

Implementation of this program achieved the desired results: a reduction of unacceptable behavior in the classroom. Gerry was not considered a behavior problem; she was happy, enthusiastic, and successful in the schoolroom, and a fine relationship developed between Gerry and the teacher.

The only complaint ever lodged was that Gerry refused to play with the girls, whose activities were confined to talking, playing with uninteresting toys and games, and sedentary behaviors, and played exclusively with the boys, running, jumping, climbing, and doing the things little boys normally do, in which she excelled. Gerry had a few special friends among the girls, but her recess periods were spent with the boys. Gerry would join the girls if they were engaged in activities like jumping rope. In both groups, she was accepted as an asset to any team engaged in active sports.

By the end of second grade, Gerry could read on a sixth-grade level. She had been encouraged to go on with reading by both of her second-grade teachers. We all felt that she became discouraged beyond this level by the difficulty of the concepts being presented. She created a new mathematical system and flunked her final math test. The teacher gave me the paper and asked me if I could figure out why she had gotten every problem wrong. After an hour's study, her system of mathematics became apparent. I pointed out to the teacher that Gerry had solved the problems on the basis of her personal system.

During the summer we moved to Pennsylvania, and we struck out in school. Gerry, going into third grade with excellent grades, excellent recommendations, and excellent achievements, was placed in a "slow" section of third grade, because everybody knows that school children in the South are not comparable to school children in the North.

I did not see the move as being traumatic and did not foresee the possibility that something could go wrong with the classroom situation. When I became aware that something was wrong, my first thought was to blame everything on the move, but conversations with Gerry led me to believe that things were going wrong in school. I requested a conference with her teacher, during which the teacher spent the first half-hour listing a series of infractions of rules and misdemeanors, not to mention personality defects. Gerry was not permitted to be present at this meeting, so I had very little knowledge on which to base comments or refutations. I merely sat and shook my head on the diagonal, which was a mistake since it was taken to indicate my agreement.

After talking to Gerry, and it was quite difficult to elicit details and appraise her view of the situation, I requested another teacher conference in which I hoped we would be able to correct some of the problems.

The teacher began by complaining about Gerry's aggression toward other children and cited numerous examples. The teacher said that Gerry did these things "for no reason." I recognized that I had a very serious problem on my hands. The teacher obviously disliked the child and was going to do everything in her power to prove her case.

When pressed, Gerry admitted to fighting and stated that she did so because some of the other children called her "bad names." When further pressed, with great reluctance, she repeated those names. Now, Gerry had come from a southern community where most adults did not go beyond the infrequent use of mild expletives. The names to which Gerry reacted were not mild.

I requested a conference with the principal and the teacher. The teacher did not deign to be present for the meeting, and it was also stipulated that Gerry should not be present. I outlined the problem as I saw it—Gerry reacted very badly to the kind of name-calling that was going on. The principal suggested that Gerry should not hit anybody no matter what they called her. I suggested that if anybody called me those names, I would be inclined to smack the offender myself. This was not considered a "healthy" attitude.

Eventually, I suggested that the teacher consider moving Gerry into a group of more-or-less well-behaved children. This move would cut down on episodes of irritation and aggression. The teacher certainly did move her—as far away and out of the class as the walls permitted. She gave instructions to the class that no one was permitted to talk with the child. It's called ostracism, scapegoating, and a couple of other names, and it is the most odious technique a teacher can practice.

I was incensed. I contacted the principal and informed her that the teacher had gone too far, and suggested that the child be placed in another classroom. The teacher informed the principal that Gerry could not be placed in another classroom because she could not do acceptable work. I had another conference with the principal who actually attempted to make me sympathetic to the personal problems of the teacher who was, in effect, persecuting my child. Oh, yes, the teacher had some severe problems because of a recent personal calamity. But what that had to do with her inexcusable behavior toward the child was not my concern.

I was also the ungrateful recipient of a lot of advice to the effect that Gerry would eventually have to learn to cope with unpleasant situations, that I could not protect her forever, and that the best thing I could do was let her learn to solve her own problems. (Which she certainly did—she learned to tune-out because her own thoughts were a lot more satisfactory than school. After several years of practice, tuning out became as automatic as breathing.)

By applying pressure to the principal, minor modifications were made between the teacher and the child, and we lived out the rest of the school year in very uneasy circumstances marred by occasional outbreaks.

Gerry was enrolled in another school for the fall term, and we hoped to make the best of it. The teacher gave her very poor marks, although a school achievement test at the end of the year indicated that she had made a little progress. (Don't forget, she was already working well above grade level before entering third grade.) I pointed this discrepancy out to the principal, who informed me she could not do anything about the grades given by a teacher.

I had hoped the new school environment would prove beneficial, but many of the problems continued to persist. Gerry's school work was mediocre at best, at about a "C" level. The fourth-grade teacher, in a conference with me, listed complaints about fighting with peers, lack of attention in class, lack of preparation, failure to complete assigned homework, and interruptive behavior in the classroom.

Gerry made some adjustment to school in due course, and though peer relationships, academic achievement, and restlessness were always a problem, she was not thought to be markedly deviant.

Junior High School

We moved again, just before Gerry started seventh grade. Junior high school was a debacle and disaster from the very beginning. The situation deteriorated so badly that Gerry was eventually placed in the "zoo," a supposedly "regular" classroom composed chiefly of troublemakers, nonachievers, and other "undesirables." At which point, I decided I really had had enough of teachers, guidance counselors, and such, and had Gerry evaluated. Since no one would believe she was intelligent, creative, and *not* emotionally disturbed, I thought perhaps I would be able to force them into some action by proving she was all of those things. Gerry's verbal scores on the Wexler Intelligence Test were slightly above average. Her scores on the performance (nonverbal) section of the Wexler were outstanding. The combined scores put her in the superior range. Her achievement scores were something else again, and achievement is what is seen in the classroom. In ninth grade Gerry achieved a ninth-grade level in reading. (Since she was reading on a sixth-grade level at the end of second grade, it only took her seven years to improve her reading ability by three grade levels. This was supposedly Gerry's fault. No one suggested that it might be inadequate teaching.)

Confronting the school authorities with the evidence proved to be the most frustrating experience of my life. Upon being pressured, coerced, argued with, and subjected to my unkind remarks, the authorities had to admit that, yes, I was right, but they didn't know what to do with the child and didn't have any place for her, anyway. But I did get her out of the zoo.

I had to come home and confront Gerry and admit that there was nothing more I could do. I had done everything I knew how to do, and I had failed. We wound up with my fourteen-year-old child comforting me because I was reduced to tears of frustration.

High School and College

We decided that the best placement for Gerry in high school was in the now defunct "Alternative West," an experimental, liberal high school. I expected it would turn out to be a playground for Gerry and my goal was to remove all the useless and destructive pressures to which she was constantly subjected: "She could do better if she tried." "She should study harder." "She shouldn't fight." "She would get better grades if she were attentive." "She would get better grades if she did her homework." On several occasions, I had talked her into making an effort, which lasted as long as three weeks. It is unreasonable to expect such efforts to continue beyond a few weeks if teachers do not immediately recognize them. Believe it or not, I once pointed out to a teacher that Gerry had completed every assignment for the previous three weeks, a fact of which the teacher was unaware.

The next thing that happened within the school context surprised me no end. About halfway through the term, I had occasion to talk with the assistant principal of the alternative school on another matter. She began talking about Gerry in glowing terms. I was so shocked that I had to ask her if she knew whom she was talking to. When I was assured that she was talking to the right parent about the right child, I asked her to continue—at length. I later discovered that previous records of children who attended the school were not transferred and perused by teachers who were ready to categorize and arm themselves against their students. Nobody expected Gerry to be a behavior problem, and when she wasn't one on the first day of school, nobody bothered to recognize her as such.

I had hopes that the new situation would go a long way to correct the old patterns, behaviors, and expectations. It did, but I realized that the child had been lost somewhere along the way and that all the good and positive achievements, recognition, and success in the world could not alter that fact. Gerry spent about a year and a half in college, and she hated every minute. She freezes when the words "learn," "school," "homework," "grades," or similar words are mentioned and becomes totally incapacitated, although she is normally an adept and adequate person.

Looking back, I can't help but feel that one understanding, sympathetic teacher in fourth, fifth, or sixth grade—maybe even in junior high school—might have made the difference. I had to admit that I could not help. I could promote learning outside the classroom situation but, within the classroom, I was helpless to influence the child's behaviors or attitudes.

THE SAME BALL GAME

So much concern about education has recently been expressed that I had rather hoped things would be different for my son Ben. But it's the same old ball game. Most of the hitting and running seems to be done by the hyperkinetic child. Most of the errors are probably made by the adults who are supposed to educate him.

Benjamin is in third grade and I have a sinking feeling that he's going to be lost to the process of education and that it's going to be difficult for both of us to keep him in the system. If not this year, he may be lost next year, or the year after that. I keep saying—to the child and to school personnel—the same old things, over and over. Sometimes I get tired hearing myself. Sometimes I just get tired and I don't feel I have whatever it takes to make the effort. Ben won't be lost because he can't learn or doesn't want to learn or isn't motivated to learn. He probably won't be lost because his behavior is so unacceptable. He'll be lost because crazy things happen and parents are powerless to counteract them.

By now, I've mentioned certain events and episodes from Ben's school experience, but maybe the whole story should be told.

Ben started kindergarten as a bright, energetic, not particularly troubled child who was eager to learn but not so sure he wanted to go to school to do so. I rather hoped somebody there would convince him school was a good place to be educated, but several people appeared to conspire to teach him otherwise.

Three weeks after school started, I began getting calls from Miss S. Her major complaint was that she could not "control" Ben. His most disturbing behavior was his tendency to put his hand on the doorknob three times a day and threaten to leave school and go home. I saw this as mildly provocative, nonthreatening and, after the first week, a trifle boring.

In due course, Ben refused to cooperate with any of her suggestions or directions, and this behavior was quite disturbing to the class. Miss S. then called upon the principal and guidance counselor for help (see Chapter 4 for *that* interview).

It became apparent that Ben was very unhappy, confused, frightened, and convinced that the problem was centered in his terribly deviant behavior. I was aware that Ben eventually became angry with adults who could not or would not set limits and enforce those limits. I suspected the teacher was incapable of defining structure adequately for a child like Ben.

Eventually, Ben was removed from school, "cooled off" for two weeks, and enrolled in a private kindergarten to which I had been referred. The teacher had been informed in detail of Ben's misadventures and probably expected a two-headed monster to appear. Instead, she got the Benjamin I knew. There were a few minor "tests" and a few bad days; there were some problems, but the "emotionally disturbed" behavior miraculously disappeared. His final report, indicating progress in learning skills, conversation skills, and group living, included the following: "Overall, I am most pleased with Ben's progress and am happy to have him share our kindergarten experience."

After lengthy discussions between the teacher and myself—and visiting almost all the local private schools—we choose a primary school that was some distance away because the atmosphere and attitudes were impressive, the staff was impressive, and the first-grade teacher that I observed was impressive. We were so pleased that we made arrangements to send both boys to this school. David, who has had no school-related problems, benefitted tremendously.

Shortly after school opened, there was a informal picnic meeting of parents and teachers. I had asked Gerry to accompany me, since I wanted her opinion of the teacher.

To our amazement, the first-grade teacher I had met had left, and the new teacher was a sweet, young thing who could barely speak above a whisper. And she was going to spend her first year as a full-fledged teacher with Benjamin? My daughter and I looked at each other in despair and disbelief, and I said, "I think I'm going to kill myself. I think I just blew 1500 bucks."

It wasn't too long after this that I began to get indications that things were not going well. A series of meetings commenced during which we discussed what Ben was doing. (Mostly, he was *not* doing anything. He spent a lot of time crawling around under her desk—he didn't threaten to leave because he knew he couldn't get home without a school bus—and the poor teacher couldn't get him to come out and participate in classroom activities.) She was very earnest, very sincere, and she wanted help from me. How could I tell her to modify her whole personality? How could I explain that the best way to get him out from under her desk might be to grab him and physically drag him out, plop him in his seat, and tell him he would damn well stay out from under her desk because it was damn well not permitted and he would damn well not do it?

It was eventually decided, without my concurrence, that Ben was too immature for first grade and should be placed, on trial, in a K-one class, whose teacher just happened to be a particularly dynamic person with twenty year's teaching experience. I had observed this lady and noticed how she rolled right along through her classes without ruffling a hair on her head. I said, "Oh, he's going to do beautifully. Yes, indeed, he will. The first time he pulls any nonsense, she'll pound him right into the ground, nicely and sweetly, of course. He'll never give her any trouble again. He'll do exactly as she wants him to do. He'll be Mr. Perfection personified." He was. After two weeks, reports proclaimed the good news—extraordinary improvement in behavior and maturity and academic skills!

The school authorities felt this trial proved their point: Ben's immaturity. I felt it proved my theory of teacher-child personalities. We finally had a meeting with all parties concerned (I coerced my daughter to represent her brother's interests and give his side of the story—something like expert testimony) to decide Ben's fate. After agreeing that the child was doing much better, I explained my theory of personalities, which met with its usually skeptical response. The director of the school pointed out to me that I was angry, to which I concurred, and pointed out that I was angry because it appeared to me that three parties had entered into an agreement—the school had agreed to educate the child, the child had agreed to be educated, and I had agreed to pay—and so far I was the only party who had fulfilled his contract. Therefore, the contract was null and void. In other words, I was calling a halt to the proceedings. The director suggested that I was being punitive. I agreed that it was a distinct possibility, but that I was doing my best to make a fair and equitable decision based on my best efforts to be rational. On that basis, Ben would be taken out of private school *immediately* and be placed in public school on Monday morning—in first grade.

The director and other school personnel were truly concerned for Ben. I felt my appraisal of his abilities was probably more realistic than theirs, simply because I knew him a lot better than they did. I was a lot angrier about the situation than at any party connected with the situation, and I would have considered another first-grade placement had one been available.

My comments to the principal of the public school were brief. I explained that I wasn't satisfied with Ben's progress and felt he needed a more structured environment. Ben was placed with a tremendously capable first-grade teacher, and I kept my mouth shut and my fingers crossed.

I arranged to accidentally meet the teacher about two weeks later and asked how things were going. She mentioned some problems with "settling" in a new school but felt it was to be expected when a child entered a new class. She expressed concern about Ben's apparent lack of academic achievement and I suggested that he would catch up. Her last words were, "I wouldn't worry. He'll settle in and do fine." I walked away, smiling to myself, thinking,

"Oh, yes, he certainly will settle in. I'll just bet you'll settle him in."

Ben settled in, more or less, and his academic achievement was more than satisfactory. There were behavior problems in unsupervised situations and there were some problems with Ben's independent work habits, but on the whole, it was a good year.

The teacher chose her successor carefully. Most fortunately, a truly marvelous team taught the combination second-third grade, Mr. O. and Mrs. S., who probably had the most beneficial impact on Benjamin that any teachers could have. Why? Because Ben's homeroom teacher, Mr. O., almost unflappable and very secure in his role of adult mentor, was able to distinguish between child and problem behavior, working on the behavior while encouraging and giving approbation to a child he found essentially likeable.

Amazing things began to happen. Ben began to see himself and his so-called problems as manageable. He began to act positively in relation to his peers and other adults. Other teachers began to see the child in a different light. By the middle of the year, Ben began to develop a good, sound relationship with Mrs. S. He began to feel pride and a sense of accomplishment. Ben became able to talk about his difficulties and could devise strategies to overcome them.

A system of rewards for acceptable behavior was initiated. When Mr. O. and I discussed the program, we thought we could start with a deferred-reward system and, if it didn't work, modify it to make it more immediate and situation-specific. I insisted that rewards be kept within the school province, but it was difficult to find an appropriate reward since Ben was already being reinforced for completion of his work with free library time. The plan finally emerged: Ben would receive one chip per day for adequate (not perfect) behavior. Five chips could be traded for ten minutes of gym with the student teacher assigned to the regular gym teacher. (It should be noted that neither the teacher nor I thought this plan was workable, since the reward was so long-range. But it did.)

The guidance counselor worked with Ben and some of

the other children with whom he had fights and arguments, talking things out. More and more people got involved. The music teacher occasionally provided the reward when neither gym teacher was available. Other teachers offered encouragement on the playground. The principal lent his support to both teachers and child. And the child blossomed.

I thought we had finally solved our problem. Ben would go on to a third-grade class taught by his second-grade math teacher, Mrs. S. He would have a lot of contact with Mr. O., probably being placed in his language classes. He would be surrounded with people who accepted, encouraged, and liked him and who were proud of his achievements and ready to help him build on them.

In June, the authorities officially closed our local school. While Ben's teachers were within the school district, he was denied access to the school where they were to teach. I am firmly convinced that another year or so would have seen his own sense of adequacy and worth safely established.

After much discussion and a million phone calls, Ben was placed in another school in the fall. In October, things began to go wrong. I contacted the guidance counselor and alerted her. I thought somebody should intervene before the situation got out of hand. Six weeks later, Ben was at home, being medicated for stomach cramps, diagnosed by our doctor as due to some kind of pressure.

I have made another request for a transfer, to which I have had no reply except silence, which I take to mean a negative response. In the meantime, I have spent considerable time and effort trying to find out from the child what went wrong and then conveying these messages to school personnel. In this regard, Ben wrote an incredible letter to his teacher. "You give me too much to do at one time. You give me too much work."

It has become apparent that Ben's own evaluation of the problem was correct: The teacher assigned too much work at one time, with too many instructions. She put a lot of emphasis on marks and grades. Ben was the recipient of a whole stack of papers marked with "Es." He internalized the grades as his inability to do the work. The teacher assigned a good bit of homework, some of a long-term nature. Ben stopped doing homework. His need to complete all work and finish it at once prevented him from seeing a week-long assignment as five or seven easy steps.

There were many new children in the school, and the playground situation became a threatening and devastating experience for both boys, with fights, abuse, challenges, etc., a regular noontime occurrence.

After a prolonged absence and several meetings with school personnel, Ben went back to school. Do I think it's going to work? Let me put it this way: The teacher has been asked to correct some of the obvious problems in her techniques and methods. She has been informed by me that Ben cannot cope with the pressure of her expectations, which are not reasonable and are high for third-grade children. She has agreed to modify her methods somewhat. She will omit the letter grade from his papers. She will attempt to assign his work in smaller segments. However, the same afternoon Ben reentered school, the teacher informed Ben that he had missed a lot of time and consequently had a great deal of work to catch up on.

I personally have no desire to modify the teacher's personality, methods, or expectations. I just wish I could get Ben into a more hopeful situation.

In the meantime, having learned the rules of the game, Ben is playing the game all-out. He's realizing the potential of being a "victim" of hyperkinesis. A lot of the time he and I are together is spent maneuvering: he tries to maneuver me into accepting his distractibility, impulsiveness, and restlessness as part and parcel of his "symptoms"; I try to maneuver around his role playing. It would be too easy for me to step in and control too much of his life. It's very difficult to have to watch everything I say and do, so that I insist on the kinds of behavior and performance of which he is quite capable without my being punitive and excessively irritated.

12 Dropping Out at Ten

There's been a lot of talk and a lot written about dropouts. The standard dropout is depicted as a sixteen-year-old failure, headed for delinquency, who finally has the opportunity to absent himself physically from the school environment. The long series of mistakes, errors, omissions, and commissions that led to his embarkation are usually played down, if mentioned at all. The causes for dropping out are often attributed to socioeconomic factors; that is, dropouts come from deprived, depressed, marginal homes. Well, there are a lot of dropouts from good homes, with good parents who really care about them, no matter what the socioeconomic background is.

Currently, great concern is being expressed about the future of dropouts—how to make them integral, contributing members of society and how to help them find themselves, etc. By the time the child reaches standard dropout age, though, it's too late. Remediation may help. Reconstruction is out of the question. The time when somebody should have started to worry about the child dropping out was when he first began to tune out—when he was nine or ten. If we expect him to stay in the system until his education is completed, then the time to work with him is when he's still willing to work in the system. We need to work with the nine- or ten-year-old with academic problems or behavior problems whose difficulties will plague him and increase with each year until he is forced to concede his failure in the system. The third, fourth, or fifth grader is probably still readily amenable to any change that will bring him success within the educational context. I don't think that can be said for the failing and disillusioned high school student who is ready to drop out.

THE TEACHER'S ATTITUDES

How the child's classroom performance is evaluated, whether he is a "success" or not, is greatly dependent upon the teacher's attitudes. Deviance in the classroom is the bane of all teachers. How accepting the individual teacher is—and how tolerant of certain kinds of deviance—is strictly a function of teacher personality. It's an accepted fact that the abnormally quiet child, even when academically nonachieving, will often receive approval—and promotion—from teachers. The abnormally unquiet child is more apt to bring down on his head teacher censure and disapproval, which often has a way of being translated into grades and promotions. In other words, good behavior or no behavior is equated with good grades.

If parents find that the teacher's attitude toward their child is essentially negative, with the teacher registering blanket disapproval and negatively reinforcing unacceptable behavior (by the absence of positive interactions), the parents can attempt to modify the teacher's attitudes by (1) enlisting his cooperation, (2) pointing out the child's good points, and (3) letting him know, *tactfully,* that they are aware of his attitudes and will be watching him.

There will be many things the parents will find to say in the child's favor. (If not, their attitudes are in grave need of modification.) They should, if possible, explain the mechanisms that keep the child from successful or acceptable behavior. They should not feel constrained from disagreeing with statements that reflect the teacher's negative attitude. For instance, if the teacher says that the child is not at all able to pay attention and the parents feel the child is able to concentrate for even a brief period of time, five or ten minutes, they should politely point out that the child can indeed pay attention for so much time and humbly suggest that the teacher try to adjust his teaching methods somewhat in view of the child's "short attention span."

The likelihood of enlisting the teacher's cooperation is a function of the teacher's attitude—whether or not he views the child favorably and is willing to modify his methods and practices to suit the abilities of the child.

MODIFYING CLASSROOM PROCEDURES

It would be nice if parents whose children are having school-related problems knew something about theories of education and learning. Maybe what's needed is a crash course for parents. Since that's a little impractical, and the subject can't be covered here, let me try to point out some possible problem areas and how they can be improved or modified.

Teaching has two basic components: the scheduling of presentation of required learning material, and the scheduling of reinforcement for successful learning of the materials. (That's a terrible oversimplification!) Problems can arise in one of two general areas: the behaviorial or the academic. Or both, because one affects the other.

There are a zillion articles in current educational journals that are directed to teachers, and explicate programs, plans, theories, and practices for improving or modifying academic or behaviorial performance. Most of these are based on behavior modification principles, which is fine as far as it goes. But there may be other factors, such as a poor self-image or a lack of motivation to succeed that can influence behavior.

There are two areas in which modifications of the teacher's practices can be made: the scheduling of lessons and the reinforcement of successful or acceptable behaviors. Parents often can give valuable suggestions (carefully worded, of course) in either of these areas.

As an example, if the child has a problem concentrating for extended periods, it may well be that he can acquire most of the necessary learning in the first ten or fifteen minutes of instruction provided he is paying attention during that time. And so the teacher should be requested to modify his methods so that the bulk of the material is presented at that time.

If the parents feel that they are unable to make valid suggestions for modification of teaching practices, they might consider consulting remedial teachers or specialists in the field of education. In other words, a parent-sponsored Individual Education Program (IEP) may be a valuable tool for convincing a teacher and showing him how to modify his methods.

Sometimes unacceptable behavior gets in the way of proper reinforcement for academic success. The child is able to complete the learning assignment successfully, but in the meantime does something for which he is reprimanded, and the success is ignored and unrewarded or reinforced. Asking the teacher to set up a reinforcement schedule, with appropriate rewards for success, may meet with resistance, because such procedures require time and thought.

Since the teacher already has a lesson plan for the day, he might be asked to set up a reinforcement schedule based on successful completion of certain time-limited segments of the lesson plan. For instance, if reading and math are the targeted areas, the teacher might consider reinforcing the child, either verbally or with a token, for successful completion of the first twenty (fifteen, ten, or five) minutes of the teaching period, whatever the child can manage. This would at least open up the possibilities for two positive reinforcement opportunities. If the initial time limit is established at ten minutes, it can be increased later when success is demonstrated.

Behavioral problems often interfere with learning, and a negative downward spiral commences, with the child achieving less and less success. Sometimes, this is conveyed in the form of bad marks, and three months of continued bad marks will convince most children they are failure-prone. Perhaps the teacher can be asked to omit grades and marks for some established period, while attempting to initiate a schedule of reinforcement.

If the parents are aware that the main problem in the classroom is the child's behavior, not his academic achievement, suggestions for handling that behavior are in order. One would presume that the teacher has learned somewhere along the line that negative reinforcement tends to increase and prolong the very behaviors it is intended to decrease and extinguish. If the parents gently remind the teacher of this fact, it should not come as a revelation.

Parents who have been able to deal successfully with the child's behavior at home naturally should be able to relate their methods and practices and point out those that seem to work best. Usually, a campaign to eliminate frustration and failure, and at the same time increase positive interaction between the teacher and child, results in improved school behavior.

If the parents meet with the teacher and discuss school-related problems, rather than generalizations, the teacher will as a matter of course become aware that they are keeping an eye on what is happening in the classroom, especially if they do not permit blame to devolve on the child's head.

I am not, by temperament, very good at playing a "Big Brother" role and watching other people, a fact I've made clear to my children on many occasions. I don't like to have to watch other people to see if they're doing what they should be doing, and I'm resentful when called upon to do so. However, there are times when it's necessary.

For example, a modification program that isn't producing results is being sabotaged by somebody and requires close parental supervision, which is not an easy task since the parents don't sit in the classroom with the child. If there are no changes in the child's attitudes, feelings, behavior, or grades, investigate the matter immediately.

Keep in mind that if positive reinforcement works on

the child, it also works on the teacher. Expressing parental appreciation and understanding for the teacher's efforts and help, even when it's minimal, enhances the possibility that the teacher will cooperate.

Pointing out the things that the teacher does right, which of his methods and practices are most appropriate and successful, and telling him that the child is responsive to their positive interactions are as important as pointing out new approaches and methods.

Parents know first hand how difficult it sometimes is to cope with the child. Why not tell the teacher when he copes successfully? When and if the parent-teacher meetings result in modification of the child's behavior and improved academic work, the teacher should be informed of the parents' whole-hearted support and cooperation.

PERSONALIZED EDUCATION

Remember when I said there are many professionals out there who are really great people? One of these is Lee Brubaker, who has a rather interesting background in special education, administration, and psychology and implements and administers one of the better special education programs in Pennsylvania. I asked him how many school placements, which are pretty random and really aren't based on the child's abilities and the teacher's personality, really work. "About eighty-five percent," he replied. "We have to individualize placement for about fifteen percent of our children. (That means about 900 of a school population of 6000.) As a matter of fact, I have some parents coming into my office this morning to talk about moving their boy into another school. There are only two sixth-grade teachers in his school, but there are eighteen in the district. One of them has got to be right. It's pretty late, almost half the year is over, so we're going to have to move him right away."

So I tossed out my theory about the differences between the system and the process, and Dr. Brubaker concurred. There is a lot of difference between keeping the child in a schoolroom seat and teaching him anything. Brubaker's goal is to keep the child involved in learning, and he'll place him in as many schools as necessary, handpicking the teacher as he goes along, and trying to match the child and teacher personalities.

This theory of personalities doesn't stop at the top. Brubaker's special education teachers hand-pick their successors as they move children out of resource rooms and self-contained classrooms. As a very fine resource room teacher said, "The teacher can make or break the child. There are some teachers' classes I would never send a child from my class into. It would never work. There are others in whom I feel so confident, I *know* it's going to work. I try to help the regular teacher plan for the individual child and, when I can make the right placement, they never come back here [to special education]."

Why, I wanted to know, was there such resistance to moving a child out of a specific teacher's classroom? Couldn't we just accept the fact that some people can't get along with other people and leave it at that, without assigning blame and going through all this rigmarole about what the child is doing, and how he is doing, and how good the teacher is? According to Brubaker, there are several factors in school politics that hinder such a realistic assessment.

Usually, parents first approach the principal of their school, whose dual responsibilities do not make him the ideal person to make decisions about specific placements. Of course, the principal has a certain responsibility for the education of the child, but he also has the responsibility of supporting and upholding his staff. His job would probably be a little easier if removal of the child from a teacher's classroom were not regarded—by many teachers—as a combination personal affront and negation of their abilities. It is considered a sign of failure on the part of the teacher. (Never mind what is happening to the child. He may be failing every day, but what is inferred is that it is better for a child to face repeated failure than for an adult to do so. The adult can quite obviously manipulate the situation to make himself look better, while the child cannot. Such manipulation must therefore be seen as approvable and commendable behavior on the part of adults.)

Other school administrators have certain responsibilities to the principal and teacher to uphold them in confrontative or refutative situations. Even when the parent makes every effort to avoid dealing in personalities and tries to focus on problems and solutions, he will make little headway against the bureaucratic support system. It's simply not good enough for parents to say, "Look, it just doesn't work. Let's do something else." School administrators, principals, and teachers will then attempt to make it work, principally by modifying the child, not by trying to change the teacher's behavior or attitudes.

If parents can't resolve the problem within the school itself, they should talk to the director of pupil personnel services, who usually is a person "without an ax to grind." Try to explain the situation as briefly and concisely as possible and see what alternatives the director can propose. Among other things, he can endorse placement changes and recommend placement in resource rooms and learning disability classes, request an IEP, etc. Directors of pupil personnel services usually have a somewhat different attitude toward children, possibly because of their own special roles within the school structure. (The actual responsibilities and authority of each director, of course, will depend on the local school district structure. Some directors have great autonomy and authority. Others have less, and a few have very little.)

THE INDIVIDUAL EDUCATION PROGRAM

Because of federal legislation, the IEP has become a new factor for adminstrators to deal with. Brubaker has about 1000 IEPs to prepare, administer, and supervisc each year.

An IEP is a systematic teaching approach for all children who are designated exceptional: the handicapped, the retarded, the gifted, the learning disabled, and the emotionally disturbed. It attempts to define the abilities and disabilities, achievement and lack of, and year-by-year progress, with clear-cut directions to individual teachers concerning the specific areas of deficit or faculty.

The IEP is a pretty cumbersome apparatus. It requires a preliminary consultation among school personnel, the writing of an IEP, a second consultation among school personnel, teachers, and parents, the use of various testing and measuring devices, and a computerized system to keep track of scores, progress, etc. All in all, preparing an IEP is time-consuming; putting it into practice is probably even more so. However, it is the best method for individualizing the process, and system, of education that's been devised.

Some time ago, theories of individualizing education were pronounced rather grandiloquently. Very little of that theory has seeped down into the classroom, except through the application of IEP's, and it took federal intervention to get IEP's systematized and operable.

SPECIAL EDUCATION CLASSES

A child should be removed from the regular classroom only when the situation becomes intolerable for him. I would argue with my last breath that another regular classroom—or remedial instruction—should be tried before any child is placed in special education classes. I would argue that an IEP should be made as a matter of course before such placement, and I would argue that all resources should be exhausted before such a move is contemplated, much less made.

Many learning disability classes are excellent, and many of the teachers are qualified people who have chosen to work with these children and who do so with kindness, patience, encouragement, and gratifying results. However, in many school districts there is still a stigma attached to the child in special education. Alternatives should be explored—first. Even if preschool screening has led to an evaluation of the child, parents should find out what opportunities are available, such as resource rooms and the possibility of remedial instruction from "itinerant" teachers, who divide their time among the various schools in the district. No child should be placed in a special education classroom because of a disability in one remediable area, such as a correctable visual or motor problem.

For the child who is already in school and starts to have problems in the classroom, the place to begin is with the teacher. *All* possibilities should be explored. Perhaps moving the child to a resource room for a period or two during the day will help alleviate the problem. Perhaps the services of an intinerant teacher can help the child overcome some specific academic problem. Sometimes, simply having a IEP prepared will help the teacher make plans to help the child overcome some deficit.

A word of caution about IEP's and consultative-type resource rooms is in order here. It is not unusual for teachers to be, to some degree, resentful when advice on management and teaching methods is tendered by "experts." As one disgruntled teacher commented about the services of a consulting resource teacher, "Oh, sure, she sat in that room and wrote out remedial plans for the kids. She didn't have a room full of kids to cope with all day. She didn't tell me how to work with one child when I was trying to teach twenty-five."

Although there are as yet no published statistics, conversations with teachers and administrators lead me to believe that the resource or itinerant teacher who not only devises remedial plans but actively works with individual children, tutorially or in small classes, is a more acceptable alternative than asking the teacher to implement individualized programs within the classroom. Gratifyingly, many of the children who are taken out of the classroom only for special instruction or remediation manage to pretty well hold their own while they are in the regular classroom.

When alternatives have been exhausted, parents must

take a realistic look at special education, particularly classes for the learning disabled. The essential purpose of learning disability classes is to prepare the child for a return to the mainstream—the regular classroom—in due course. Special education is not the proper dumping ground for all children classroom teachers can't teach for one reason or another. The focus of special education for learning-disabled children is remediation. There will be, of course, some children with academic and/or behavior problems that persist. Does that mean they can never go back into a regular classroom? Probably not. It means they will continue to need help, remediation, and support during their school years and, with adequate help, will probably be able to reenter regular classes, at least in some areas of competence, within a couple of years. As Brubaker says, the goal is that no child remain in learning disability classes *longer than three years.* If a child remains in special education longer than that, than one must seriously question the efficacy and potential of the special education system itself.

GETTING BY

All too frequently, the hyperkinetic child learns to get by in school by assuming inappropriate or unproductive roles: the underachiever, the class clown, the dumb one, the inept one, the walking disaster area, the bully, or the predelinquent. By assuming one or more of these roles, he attempts to minimize the frustrations of his personal failures. While the assumption of such roles is gradual, they are usually pretty well fleshed-out by third or fourth grade and, except for adding on artifacts and new mannerisms, the child will maintain the facade at least until the end of his school career.

The assumption of such demeaning roles is visible proof of the child's acceptance of his failure and deviance. However he elects to get by, he has dropped out of the process. He may choose to fantasize, to seek negative interactions with his peers, to set up negative interactions with his teachers, to keep the class amused and thereby win some popularity and recognition, or attempt to control his peers—and teachers—through physical aggression. Proficiency in any of these roles will not prepare a child for assumption of his adult roles and responsibilities—unless the class clown elects to go on stage as a comedian.

As a role grows, the child's ability to get outside the role decreases. He no longer has other expectations for himself, is no longer motivated to seek other methods of behavior, and no longer has much chance of changing adult expectations.

If the parents reflect a negative self-image for the child, his acceptance of the school evaluation will be almost automatic. He will presume that the school, by iterating his parents' opinions and attitudes, is perfectly justified in its conclusions. The parents will reiterate the school's judgments, completing a perfect and vicious circle.

If the parents have reflected a fairly positive self-image, the messages of the school and the parents conflict and the child may be in trouble. As the child grows older, he is more likely to accept the attitudes of other adults—and peers—as being realistic and honest, and reject the positive attitudes of his parents. If he accepts the attitude that he is "bad," he will resist and challenge efforts to modify or correct his behavior.

A child who is receiving conflicting messages may be in need of the attitudes and opinions of a third party, to help him deal with the arbitrary evidence and his own feelings about himself. A good therapist who is supportive and accepting may be able to direct the child's attention to his talents and abilities, modify his acquired role and habits, and help him see himself in a more positive perspective.

13 School Problems at Home

Meanwhile, back at the ranch, the parents are having their own problems coping with child behaviors they find particularly aggravating and irritating. Since a lot of the child's outside attitudes and behaviors carry over into the home, the parents are often confronted with increased negativism, frustration, anger, disgruntlement, and apathy. After all, have you ever tried explaining to any child why he or she shouldn't try out on you the same techniques that have proved successful in other situations?

Why do children come home to have their fears about themselves confirmed by unwitting parents? I don't know, but they frequently do. Parents should be wary about what they are actually confirming in confrontative situations. No child ever came to his parents and said, "Hey, look folks, my teacher thinks I'm incorrigible? What do you think?" Instead, he comes home and tries out the same behaviors on his parents that made his teacher climb the walls and declare him totally uncontrolled and uncontrollable. The unwary parent who reacts naturally and angrily may find that he has confirmed somebody else's opinion of the child, an opinion he does not share.

There is a tendency for parents to deemphasize the child's responsibility, especially at home, and to tolerate more unacceptable behavior when the child is experiencing school problems. This is probably a mistake, especially when and if the only opportunities for successful assumption of responsibility and reinforcement of acceptable behavior occur in the home. This doesn't mean that parents shouldn't relax the structure and limitations on a particular day when the child comes home in hysterics. But it does mean that parents must make a special effort to maintain limits, consistency, and the semblance of structure. Understanding the child's problem makes it very easy for parents to excuse the child's responses and reactions, even when they are unacceptable, which really doesn't go very far to make the responses and reactions less irritating or less provoking for the parents. It's better to maintain discipline than to relax it until the parent is thoroughly provoked and angry: "That's the end! I won't take any more!" and the parent proceeds to chastize the child for infringements the parent has permitted for the previous two weeks.

PARENTAL SUPPORT

If the child is having trouble in the classroom or on the playground or in any other situation, the last thing he needs is to find his parents have become his enemies—blaming him, angry at him, refusing to support or help him in difficult situations, and generally withdrawing positive interactions. Of course, school problems don't usually add to parental tranquility and temperateness, so it's hard to refrain from saying, "Okay, you did it! No matter what we do, you don't try. You don't cooperate and you don't get any better. We quit. You work it out by yourself!"

Too often the hyperkinetic youngster is portrayed as a somewhat psychopathic personality and, after repeated attempts to help him correct his problems, parents are likely to begin treating him as if there were some personality defect that negates their attempts. The child may be seen as remorseless, uncaring of the hurt or injury he inflicts on others, and unconforming to socially acceptable standards of behavior; he seems to feel no sense of shame or guilt, and he is apt to be viewed as quite shallow in his emotional response. I believe such a child is supersensitive and that his apparent shallowness and carelessness is a facade—and not a terribly good one—to cover an overwhelming sense of personal inadequacy, incompetence, and anxiety. His nonchalance is assumed, not part of his personality. He is not the happy-go-lucky, devil-may-care, independent pre-delinquent he is often presumed to be. He is, instead, a child who has been, and will continue to be, hurt, baffled and embarrassed by his differentness. His lack of self-confidence, of a sense of adequacy, and of an image of a positive, achieving person capable of self-actualization prevents him from venturing beyond the narrow confines of the poor self-image he has of himself. Rather than being free of guilt, this child often internalizes an overwhelming sense of wrongdoing and the consequent fear.

Confronted with "evidence" of misconduct or failure in school, parents are inclined to rank themselves with the enemy and apply pressure to make the child conform or study or behave, rather than assuming the position of uncritical, supportive allies.

While not criticizing or belittling school personnel, the parents should make it crystal clear that they are positively and totally on the child's side. The best way to do this is to say it and keep on saying it. (Other parental attitudes, of course, should be consistent with this message.)

Parents should be sure the child knows they will do everything in their power, and maybe a little beyond, to help him. It then becomes requisite that they do as much as they can. Obviously making such a statement without the necessary backup would be not only pointless, but harmful to their relationship with the child.

It's a good time to examine parental communications and take whatever steps are necessary to improve what parents say, how they say it, what they mean, and what they wish they had never said; to become more attentive listeners, more responsive and empathetic to the unvoiced needs of the child.

It's not a good time for the parents to tighten up discipline, insist upon strict compliance to the regulations, enforce school policies, become excessively punitive or in any other way, apply pressure to "make the kid shape up."

It may be a good time for parents to think about therapy, either for themselves or for the child, especially if either or both of them need a supportive and sympathetic ear.

It's the best time to evaluate parental response and reaction and make sure that the parents are initiating or participating in positive interchanges with the child while eliminating as many negative reactions as possible.

It is the worst time to panic or be emotionally prostrate. If you insist upon your right to a nervous collapse, postpone it until a more suitable time.

The parents should look for opportunities for the child to participate in activities or pursuits in which he can succeed. No matter what the child likes to do or in what areas he's competent—hammering and nailing, helping around the house, riding his bike, reading, gardening (indoors or outdoors), taking care of pets (from a guppie to a giraffe), swimming, painting, stringing shells and beads, or doing cartwheels—the parents should direct the child toward every opportunity to prove his competency and his worth. This may mean that the parent or parents will have to set aside some time to work with the child. If the child likes plants, get him a couple of small plants and help him take care of them. If he likes to wash dishes, let him wash dishes and give him a dime as a reward. The plates may be a little greasy, but nobody ever died from a greasy plate. If he likes to read, set aside a half-hour every day and read to each other. Just don't be overly critical of his reading mistakes.

Set aside a little space for talking and confiding. Share a snack and show undivided attention to the child, accepting his comments and remarks unjudgmentally. If the child brings up specific situations and you can offer concrete, helpful advice, that's all right. Don't indulge in platitudes and cliches or false assurances and left-handed complements: "You could get better marks if you'd study harder." "You should be nicer (kinder, more friendly, etc.), and people would like you better." "If you would only try to concentrate. . . ." "If you would only try. . . ." "I know you can do better if. . . ." "Anyone as smart as you are can. . . ."

I wonder if parents are aware how often what they offer in the way of encouragement or a compliment is, in all fairness, belittling, carping, and critical. It's far better to reflect the feelings of the child without adding "encouraging" remarks, unless the comments are realistically honest and reassuring. "I really like you," is a nice, friendly sentiment. "I really like you when you behave," translates to mean the parents don't like the child very often because he is well-behaved infrequently.

Think about both the tone and content of remarks before you make them. How would you like it if someone complimented you by saying, "You're really a very attractive person, but you'd be much more attractive if you spent more time and money on your clothes"? How about, "You really write very well. I'll bet you could be another Hemingway if you tried harder"? So don't demean the child by tagging on belittling remarks such as, "I know you're trying very hard to be good in school. I'm sure things will be fine if you try just a little harder."

It's not easy to refrain from foot-in-mouth comments when the child says, "All the other kids hate me" or "I can't do it." The automatic response is, "Don't be silly. Not everybody can hate you!" and "Of course you can do it." Both answers are automatically wrong. They are not reassuring, and they do reflect critical judgment. The reassuring answer is more like, "Oh, dear. I would feel terrible if I thought nobody liked me. How do you feel?" and "Well, let's work on it together. Perhaps together we can figure it out."

If the child mentions a specific incident that is causing him trouble, and the parent can think of an operable, goal-directed solution, such advice may be tendered with instructions and directions for its application.

For instance, the child admits he becomes restless and "gets into trouble" in school during the time between the end of one teaching session and the beginning of another. He says that during this time there's "nothing going on." The parents might suggest an activity that the child likes, and which the teacher approves of, to fill this space. Perhaps the child likes to draw and sketch, and the teacher is amenable to this idea. The parents could therefore supply materials to keep the child occupied and curtail restlessness. The teacher is asked to reinforce the quiet occupation of the child as long as it does not interfere with scheduled instructions.

Providing the parents act noncritically, goal-directed problem solving can itself be very reassuring to the child. His problem can be attacked directly, with possible successful conclusions, and can be viewed as normal, everyday occurrences subject to remedy, rather than threatening, fearsome difficulties that can't be overcome.

Sometimes what is reassuring to the child is somewhat surprising. Ben was having serious difficulties in first grade. The administrators felt he was "immature" and wanted to put him back into kindergarten, where I did not feel he belonged. After several weeks I'd had enough of the situation and everybody concerned with it. I said something like this to him: "I've had it! This is as far as I go. You, sir, are not going into kindergarten, because you don't belong there. I am taking you out of [private school] and you are going to [public school]. You are going into first grade. You will do first grade work, because you can do it. You will behave in school exactly as you behave at home. You will not do any of the things I've heard you've done. You will do as you are supposed to do, because we both know you are perfectly capable of doing them. You may con the rest of the world, sir, but you cannot con me. I know you too well and I know what you can do. You are sweet, bright, intelligent, and totally wonderful, and dammit, you are going to school and be sweet, bright, intelligent, and wonderful! That's it." This diatribe turned out to be reassuring and, while Ben was not always sweet and wonderful, he did prove he was bright and intelligent. Kindergarten was not the place for him. He would have internalized return to kindergarten as failure. While he may have liked the idea of another year to play around and not be held responsible, he was terribly proud of his achievements in first grade and internalized those as marks of success.

APPROVAL IS NOT THE ABSENCE OF CRITICISM

Every child needs his parents' approval. Conversely, parents are well aware that they "ought to" give their children the approval they need. Now, comes the big question: When and how do you give your approval to a kid who is not exactly approvable in your eyes? How do you overcome some of the natural reactions to the child, including antipathy, irritation, the desire to get away from him frequently, and plain old dislike of some of his personality traits, and give him what amounts to parental endorsement?

Let me begin to answer these questions by, first of all, classifying two kinds of parental approval: the blanket endorsement kind, which is composed of several interesting ingredients—affection, admiration, pride, and old-fashioned liking—and the situation- or behavior-specific kind that is mostly verbalized when the child has performed adequately or acceptably.

It's a lot easier to be situationally and behaviorally approving than it is to be approving in general. No matter how unacceptable the child's behavior may be at times, there will be things he does that the parents can acknowledge verbally as approvable. It's terribly important for the hyperkinetic child to know *when* his behavior finds approval, and it's just as important for him to know that some—or many—of the things he does are acceptable and/or esteemable.

Very frequently, the unacceptable behaviors of the

child get in the way of parental expression of approval. Often, when he does behave acceptably, his behavior is either unrewarded or the expression of approval is offered in a demeaning way. For instance, when the child misbehaves in the supermarket, he is told his behavior is unacceptable. When he does behave, however, either the parent does not verbally acknowledge his efforts (after all, that's the way he should have been behaving all along) or belittles his efforts by commenting on past performance ("You were very good at the store today. I don't see why you can't always behave like that"). Let me put it this way: Not getting mad at the kid and berating him for his behavior is *not* approval. Not by a long shot.

Not only does the child's behavior get in the way of parental expressions of situational approval, but it may effectively prevent the parents from demonstrating their blanket acceptance and approval.

Too often, there are just too many irritating and exasperating occurrences for the parents to cool down long enough to be able to register what is presumably their basic acceptance and affection for the child. After a long, harrowing day, when you're seriously contemplating locking the kid in the basement so you won't have to face another incident, how do you express your deep-down love and acceptance?

Let's take a hypothetical situation. The child has been especially monstrous for a couple of days, and his parents are pretty exasperated. They haven't been able to figure out what, if anything, is making the child especially difficult. One of the parents lost his temper at dinner time and punished the child harshly, which doesn't make the parent feel any better. However, the child is now rather subdued, and things have quieted down. The child approaches the more angry parent, who hasn't really gotten over being angry, and says, "Will you help me with my homework?" Now, the parent is about as eager to work with the child on his homework, which has been a source of contention before, as he is to walk into the proverbial fiery furnace. What should he do?

The parent has several choices. If he thinks he has cooled down enough, and they can work on the homework harmoniously without any more negative interactions, he can acquiesce. If he is still pretty upset and feels short of temper, he might try to explain his feelings honestly and decline the invitation: "I'm really very tired and a little out of sorts. I really don't think I can be much help to you in the mood I'm in. It would be better if you asked your father/mother right now. I'll be glad to help you tomorrow." Or he might agree to help the child with a specific problem with the homework: "You don't understand the directions? Well, let's look at them. Maybe we can figure them out." He can then limit himself to helping figure out the directions—nothing more.

Initiating positive interactions when the parent is exasperated is pretty difficult. However, there's nothing wrong with a little candor: "Look, friend, we've had a couple of really miserable days. Before it gets worse, let's you and me sit down here and try to figure out what we can do to make things better for each other. Okay?" Unless the parent uses the discussion as a forum for criticizing the child's behavior, such problem-solving dialogues can reflect parental concern and acceptance.

PREPARING FOR THE NEXT CRISIS

By the time the child is in his late elementary school years, parents should remind themselves that it's time to prepare for the next big crisis—adolescence. There are several areas, which have been discussed previously, which need to be reviewed and reevaluated.

Parental management techniques probably need to be redefined. Appropriate techniques for the seven-year old child are not necessarily appropriate for the ten- or eleven-year-old.

Parental expectations should be reevaluated with an eye to the original expectations, the ratio of success, and whether or not these expectations are still adequate and realistic.

The child's real abilities, skills, talents, and potentials need to be examined, along with his disabilities, weaknesses, and difficulties.

It's important to remember that, while expectations may be reasonable, it's quite possible the child *can't meet them because he has not been able to or has not had the opportunity to acquire a particular skill or component of a skill.* No matter what the reason may be that the child didn't learn something, it is important to help him acquire that skill if he is able to learn it now. As an example, let's presume the child's school behavior prevented him from acquiring some necessary skills in manipulating numbers. It could be something as simple as not having learned the multiplication tables. It's obvious that he will need this skill, now and in the future. The child could be tutored in math, especially in multiplication. The lack of skills may involve a complicated, sophisticated ability, such as making new friends, or the ability to work independently because the child feels doubtful about his mastery of self-discipline. Whatever the child may lack, it is not reasonable to assume he will acquire the necessary knowledge without training in the specifics. Academically, if the child is especially bright, he may "fake it," but he will probably never feel very secure about his grasp of the subject. It's difficult to fake abilities such as social skills and self-management techniques.

The child's self-concept should be evaluated. Is he aware of any feelings of alienation, isolation, doubt, anxiety, and/or despair? Does he, in fact, see himself as a potentially self-actualizing individual? Or does he see himself as some combination of both good and bad characteristics? Very often, the exceptional child must come to terms with himself far in advance of his more complacent peers. This process can be quite traumatic for the young child, who is not unaware of how society deals with deviance.

If the child is to grow, his responsibilities and limits must be broadened to include elements of independence and self-actualization. It's totally unfair to the child to have responsibility, independence, and/or consequences suddenly thrust upon him at some arbitrary age. He needs to grow into them, increasing his competence as he goes along. Unless parents are willing to gradually release control, they may find themselves abruptly confronted with a youngster who's insisting upon his rights to assume control for himself.

Parents should carefully examine their involvement with the child, evaluating the impact of their management mechanisms. Are they, in effect, restricting and inhibiting the child by heavy-handed controlling behavior or are they permitting some latitude for the child to learn self-control?

Gold stars may be appropriate for six-year-olds, but they are probably not appropriate—and valued as rewards—for preadolescents. Reinforcement devices, verbal and otherwise, should be scrutinized for efficacy and suitability. Punishments should be evaluated. Are the parents treating the child as they would normally treat a much younger child? Spanking a twelve-year-old and sending him to bed without his dinner will probably not prevent a recurrence of undesirable behavior but will cause much resentment and vindictiveness.

If they have not done so before, parents might want to consider the initiation of family conferences and discussions. It's not always easy to keep communications between parents and the hyperkinetic child open and honest, especially if the child becomes depressed and apathetic. Any structured situation may promote the interchange of opinions and ideas. If nothing else, family discussions may present an opportunity for the child to talk about his frustrations and fears.

ONE BITE AT A TIME

Parents of hyperkinetic children, no matter how serious or how mild the symptoms may be, at one time or another probably feel like they're engaged in a life-or-death struggle, fighting on many fronts and seriously undermanned, understaffed, and underarmed.

They probably feel this way because it's pretty realistic

to see the whole situation as an on-going struggle against odds: the child, the system, the school, and everybody else. Parents tend to get involved and spend a great deal of time and energy trying to solve the problem, which as a whole does not lend itself to solution.

Remember when I said to take stock of the child's positive attributes? Parents can do themselves—and the child—a big favor by taking stock of their own attributes. They usually have many positive characteristics, which they need to be reminded of from time to time. If nobody else will do it for them, they ought to remind themselves.

Someone recently said to me, "The way to eat an elephant is one bite at a time." Maybe all parents should have that motto framed and hung in a prominent spot. The problems of hyperkinesis are not, as a unit, amenable to solution, but they can yield to change and modification, one at a time.

14 More on the Home Front

Here and there, a good bit has already been said about responsibility, rights, structure, consistency, dependence, and independence. But there areas are so important that they need to be dealt with more systematically.

Many authorities are now writing about the subjects of responsibility and rights, in an attempt to give parents some guidance. I recently read something to the effect that attitudes toward children had changed as a result of increased liberation for everybody else. I'm not sure that attitudes have changed very much, but I wish they had. While our society appears to be highly child-oriented, I've never been convinced we like children very much. I don't really think we're very accepting of children and childishness, and I don't think you have to look very far to see how children are basically excluded from supposedly adult society, adult interactions, and adult activities.

I have always believed the so-called generation gap was an artificially contrived barrier created by adults to avoid the difficulties of coping with relaxing parental control while maintaining a supportive attitude and building a new relationship. My older children have pointed out to me that, whether I like it or not, it is a creation of the society in which we live, and it does, therefore, exist. However, I continue to refuse to endorse the notion.

I have begun to suspect that, in reality, things change very little, if at all. Our viewpoint may change, but parents probably confront the same problems that parents have always confronted, and the way parents deal with problems probably hasn't changed much either, including tearing their hair out, getting angry, being baffled and perplexed, and threatening to give up.

I tend to agree with the viewpoint of current writers who distinguish between management and control, and between responsibilities and rights, and who suggest positive reinforcement and modification of management techniques rather than becoming involved in theories of personality.

RESPONSIBILITIES AND RIGHTS

Parents generally have the responsibility to provide structure and consistency for the child. Within the context of structure and consistency, the child is responsible for his choice of actions.

Rights and privileges accrue from the acceptance of responsibility and the performance of responsible actions. The parent who does not provide structure and consistency for a hyperkinetic child has no right to demand acceptable behavior from the child. The child who chooses to act irresponsibly cannot fairly demand privileges.

Parents of hyperkinetic children tend to assume more control and more responsibility than is healthy for parents or child. The responsibility-free child becomes more and more dependent on his parents to control both himself and his environment. The unhappy consequence of this assumption of responsibility is usually an absorption of the child's personality by the parents, and the parents' personalities by the child, with all parties losing their separate identities and independence. The child becomes the problem, and the parents become the problem bearers, with no other identities except those created by the hyperkinetic symptoms.

One of the rights that follows from responsibility is the inalienable right to make mistakes, to suffer the consequences of personal mistakes, to learn from those mistakes, and to make the same mistakes if one is not willing to face the consequences.

The parent who has assumed responsibility for his child doesn't permit the natural flow of consequences. He may substitute illogical consequences—nagging, punishment, deprivation of privileges and rights—but he ignores logical consequences because they don't suit him. The consequences may be logical, suitable, fair, just, and consistent with reality, but the parent denies their inevitability.

One of the hardest things for a parent to do is to sit back, with his mouth tightly closed, and let logical consequences catch up with his child. Especially as the child gets older and the parents see him making dumb, avoidable mistakes, it's very difficult not to give advice. But, as my older children keep telling me, everybody has a right to make his own mistakes. And I keep on saying, "Yes, I know, but could you at least try to make smarter mistakes?"

On the other hand, fear of being overprotective prevents parents from intervening when the child is in over his head and floundering. Intervention is overprotection when the goal is to prevent the occurrence of natural, logical consequences. But intervention is not overprotection when the goal is to modify a factor or situation that is not tolerable for the child. For example, if the child is failing academically, trying to subvert the proof of failure is overprotection. Trying to modify the situation so that the child can succeed is not overprotection.

CONFLICT AND CONFRONTATION

Under the best circumstances, there are at least 50 million chances for rousing parent-child confrontations. When the child tends to be highly active, strong-minded, intelligent, assertive, and volatile, the chances are increased proportionately to the extent that the child has one, some, or all of these characteristics.

Confrontations are no more and no less than power struggles, and there isn't any way for parents to win them unless they are willing to beat the kid into the ground. If that's what they consider winning, okay. I have managed to learn two things: it's better not to get involved in power struggles, and it's impossible to avoid them all the time.

Testing his power to manipulate, control, and manage other people is an essential activity for the child, unless the parent intends for him to grow up believing he is totally powerless—hence inadequate, dependent, and a hopeless nincompoop. I suspect most children, if they had the verbal capacity, would be able to give fairly accurate estimates of their own power. Power games between parent and child exercise the child's ability and not necessarily the parents'—and like the bicep, the more power is exercised, the more it grows. By and large, adults tend to overreact to children's power games. They are regarded as threatening to the adult's conception of his own power, prestige, or self-image, or the adult would not become so upset and angry when confronted.

There are three methods of avoiding or getting out of confrontative situations. The first, and hardest, is to try to avoid setting up situations that will naturally result in confrontations. The parent says, "You get in here and clean up the mess you made, or else!" And the kid thinks, "Oh, boy, I'm not cleaning up *that* mess. I'll take my chances with 'or else!'" And they're off and running.

Any threat can lead to a confrontation. If the parent feels the need to include a threat in an admonition, he'd better be pretty sure he can back it up. If the threat is unrealistic, the child will almost always decide to engage in a power struggle.

Some adults, including some parents, apparently like to set up situations in which they exercise their power over a seemingly less powerful individual. This is a dangerous practice for two reasons: The adult may come to take his own contrived power plays seriously, and children are not always the safest opponents. So, if you want to play power games, pick on a peer. If you win, you'll have something to boast about, and if you lose, you won't feel so bad.

Parents often unthinkingly walk into confrontations that they really didn't set up and didn't expect. Once nose to nose in confrontation, the only way out is to back off or back down. Either verbally recognize the confrontative situation and refuse to participate, or agree to lose.

Some time ago, I realized I had walked into a devilish situation, and I wanted to get out of it quickly. I said to Ben, "Oh, no. I won't let you turn this into a confrontation," to which he replied, "I don't even know what that means." Thinking I could sidestep the issue, I said, "Good! Go away until you find out." "How can I find out?", he inquired. "Go look it up in the dictionary," I said. About five minutes later, Ben came back with the dictionary and asked me how to spell "confrontation." "Hey, have you ever looked at any of the pictures in here? Boy, they have some of the neatest pictures. Look. Here's an Indian tomahawk. And here's a picture of all kinds of teeth. See, you have teeth like these, the incisors. They're the one's right in front, here. The canines are right here. See, and the premolars. . . ."

With age, the child is not so readily diverted, which means the parent will have to deal with confrontation more directly. Telling the child that you have recognized the tenor of the situation and that you refuse to play the confrontation game may work—if you refuse to play and refrain from anything provocative.

On rare occasions, in complete bewilderment, I have said, "I don't know what you're doing, and I don't know why, and I don't care. You'd better go and think about what you're doing and what you hope to gain. When you figure it out, come back and tell me and I'll decide whether or not I'll give you what you want." The first time I gave this speech off the top of my head and the child actually spent some time thinking about what was going on, I realized its efficacy. I've used it since, polished, refined, and made it situation-specific. I realized that one of the important things it did for me was to get me off the hook.

With older children ("older" probably means any age above four), agreeing to lose is an effective, though sneaky way to back down, and I have suggested the technique to my children to use in confrontations. Even if the other person realizes that you really don't agree with them, there's not much they can do about it if you refuse to argue the point.

Avoiding confrontations, of course, never settled differences or solved the problem that resulted in them to begin with. It's very important to make it clear to children that parents are willing to discuss problems and listen to complaints as long as they are presented reasonably and not belligerently.

Apparently, I have been able to get the idea across to at least one of my children. David recently had a justified complaint. I had been provoked by Benjamin and had lost my temper and yelled at him; I then turned around and yelled at David, mostly because he happened to be around at the wrong time. I stalked off to my room and proceeded to read a book, before I did anything else wrong. David waited about fifteen minutes, which was excellent timing on his part, and then came into my room and said quite reasonably, "I wish you would tell me something. How did I get involved in all this? I didn't do anything."

Of course, David was right, and what he did and the way he did it was admirable. His actions gave me not only the opportunity to admit my error and apologize to him, but also a chance to tell him that his behavior showed remarkable maturity, clear-sightedness, and self-confidence and that it made me feel very good to know he could handle himself so well.

TEACHING CHILDREN TO LIE

It's been pointed out that, for one reason or another, hyperkinetic children deviate from the truth quite frequently. I can understand that. They are in trouble with adults so often that lying is often seen as their only means of defense.

There's an excellent technique for teaching your child to lie: Confront him angrily and demand an explanation or an admission of guilt. I have found this method to be almost foolproof. The child will inevitably, because of fear and/or guilt, try to extricate himself. Even if he's not guilty, he's scared by the angry adult and will say something that, almost inevitably, gets him in deeper. Of course, hearing half-truths, evasions, lies, and protestations, the parent becomes more incensed.

When the parent confronts the child, and the child is able to avoid repercussion by evasions, half-truths, and lies, the parent has successfully taught him an effective, even if unethical, method for avoiding penalties. In other words, the parent has reinforced the value of lying, which is not exactly what he meant to do.

I think it's reasonable to presume that parents don't want to teach their children to lie. So they shouldn't set up situations in which the child only has two options: to admit guilt and accept punishment, or to extricate himself by denying the truth. Faced with the Inquisitor General and the possibility of being burned at the stake, would you admit to being a heretic? I wouldn't.

WORDS AND MORE WORDS

The parent–hyperkinetic child relationship sometimes become a one-sided harangue, a torrential flow of admonitions from the parent directed to the child in an effort to control and correct the child's behavior; it almost seems the parents are trying to raise a sound barrier between the child and his unacceptable behavior.

It doesn't work. At least, it doesn't do what the parents hope it will do—it doesn't correct the child's behavior, and it probably makes it worse.

The main point of structure is to help the child establish limits, expectations, goals, and areas of competency and independence. It's reasonable to assume that, if the structuring is fairly consistent, the child will internalize and remember the limits, expectations, and goals, without being reminded of them every thirty seconds. Continuous direction also voids the concept of consequences. If acceptable and unacceptable behaviors result in the same consequences—a torrent of continuous admonitions—there is no reason to perform in any particular way. Instead of clear-cut rules and regulations, with specific penalties and rewards for performance or nonperformance, there is issued a complicated and often conflicting series of directives: "Pick up your toys. I told you not to throw your toys on the floor, didn't I? How many times have I told you not to throw your toys on the floor? Pick them up. Now, hurry up. No, no, that's not where the teddy bear goes. You know better than that. Put it over there where it belongs. Now, come on. You're taking too much time to clear this up. If you didn't make such a mess, you wouldn't have to clean it up."

Admonitions should be infrequent and straightforward. They should be directed at a specific action, not at a hypothetical situation: "You know you're not allowed to play ball in the house." And not, "Oh, dear, you can't bounce your ball in the living room. What if you broke something? You know how mad mommy would be if that happened."

When David threw a ball and broke a globe on a lamp in the living room, he was afraid I would be angry. I faked him out. I just looked rather bored and said, "You knew you weren't supposed to. Now what?" He said, "I'm sorry. I didn't mean to break it." And I said, "Well, sorry doesn't fix the lamp. I think you had better buy a new globe for it, don't you?" David is very careful of his money, so I'll bet he doesn't play ball in the house again.

Parents who have a tendency to vent their grievances with 3 million words, and that includes me, may find they have to walk away from a situation to avoid excessive verbiage. Parents shouldn't be ashamed to pick up cues from their children. I get fish-eyed looks and Ben will occasionally say disgustedly, "Oh, mommy!" This enables me to stop, take stock of what I've said, what I'm going to say, figure out what my point is (if there is one), say it concisely, and get out before I make a fool of myself. I have found their reactions are quite reality-oriented. If they accept my verbiage, it's usually because they are aware of misdeeds. If they look at me strangely, I am probably going too far.

Sometimes a younger or older sibling of the hyperkinetic child becomes the constant critic, issuing frequent comments, criticisms and derogatory remarks which lead to bickering and fighting. While parents can expect some squabbling among siblings, they should watch interactions so that the relationship does not become one of estrangement and antagonism. When and if most interactions become negative, critical, and antagonistic, parents should intervene to modify the relationship.

Constantly admonishing other people, also known as nagging, never won Brownie points for anybody. If we can believe fairy tales, it never did very much for the nagger's personality, either.

PRAISE AND ENCOURAGEMENT

If you believe that people are basically self-actualizing, and have a positive growth potential, you also must believe that children tend to strive for the sake of striving and grow for the sake of growing. When they perform correctly and adequately, they should be told they have, so that they are assured of their direction and capabilities. That is encouragement.

Praise, however, tells the child he has performed in accordance with parental expectations. Praise is often non-goal-oriented and frequently belittling. To be told that one has performed adequately is quite different from being informed that one is a "nice" or a "good" boy. What is a "good boy"? Presumably, one who has done exactly as his parents expected him to do. He is worthy in so far as he lives up to their expectations and receives praise.

It should be pointed out that academic achievement, as translated into good grades, honor roles, and such, tends to limit the worthiness of the individual child to his ability to get such marks of recognition. The child who cannot, for one reason or another, get good grades or make the honor role, is seen by his peers and himself, and perhaps by some adults, as having less value as a person and being worth less. This is an extremely pernicious practice, and parents should take care not to make such value judgments on the basis of school achievement.

Encouragement is more goal-directed and more reality-oriented. It deals primarily with observable actions and behaviors. When the parents comment on the child's behavior, do they mean to say he's a "good boy" or do they mean he has "behaved adequately or acceptably"? Encouragement can be a lot more honest and direct, too. If the child has behaved well in the supermarket, it's more honest to say, "I appreciate the way you behaved in the store. It makes it much easier for me to shop," than to say, "You were such a good boy."

Encouragement is applicable to troublesome or problem situations, whereas praise is not. How can you praise a child for making a mistake? Instead, by encouragement, the parent can offer support, counsel, and guidance, besides allowing the child to work out his feelings about the situation. When the child says, "I can't do my math. I don't understand it," it's not very helpful for the parent to say, "Of course, you can. You're very good at math." It's more helpful to say, "Let's take a look at it. Maybe we can figure it out."

I don't think it's especially harmful to comment on a child's attributes or personality, if it's not excessive. I don't see any great harm in telling a person that I think he is generous, affectionate, loyal, intelligent, beautiful, or charming—occasionally.

CONFLICTS AND COMPROMISES

Conflict, like some other concepts, has become a questionable quality. One should not be in conflict or engage in conflict. Really? I don't know how to avoid conflict unless one decides to absent himself from the rest of the world, in which case he may feel very ambivalent about hermitry.

I presume one should disapprove of sharp and/or prolonged conflict. As long as parents and child share a relationship (I was going to say "live together," but conflict arises even when they live apart), there are bound to be times when they do not agree, want to go in separate directions, want the other person to do something he does not want to do, hold opposing opinions, don't see eye to eye, and a lot of other things that can be summed up as conflict.

Conflicts probably aren't basically bad, but are often handled badly. Conflict that is turned into confrontation is precarious. Conflict that's discussed, weighed and measured, and resolved by compromise or some other solution can be just as positive, healthy, and acceptable as any other parent-child interaction.

If parents proceed to act rather democratically, don't inform their children that children are inferiors, and that their opinions, wishes, and activities are less important than those of adults, the possibilities for differences of opinion and conflicts are enhanced.

Arbitration, discussion, decision making, and compromise will be what the democratic parent will have to rely on to resolve conflictual situations. It should be clear, however, that the final authority and responsibility belong to the parents. The child's needs, wishes, activities, opinions, and attitudes may be as important as those of the parents, but judgments, based on a fair evaluation of the situation, are for the parents to make.

If my children are making a lot of engine noises, playing with their cars in the playroom, and I am next door reading a book, if the noise bothers me, I probably should move myself to quieter surroundings. After all, they are playing where they are supposed to be playing, they are playing cooperatively, and "racing cars" normally makes a lot of engine noises. However, if my children are playing and making a lot of noise, and I am next door to them working at my typewriter and can't move, the children must modify their activity to comply with my wishes.

Group discussions are kind of a pain in the neck. They agreements, contracts, and the like, can noticeably reduce conflict and confrontation. As may be evident, I believe in making up lists, formalizing rules and regulations, and contracting for certain responsibilities and privileges. Itemizing rules and regulations makes them easier for everybody to remember, makes reinforcement and privileges more accessible, and prompts me to enforce penalties.

Group discussions are kind of a pain in the neck. They are time-consuming and require your full attention, and it would be a lot easier to make arbitrary, unilateral decisions. However, group endorsement of policies and procedures, even if the parents make the final decision, seems to elicit more cooperation from those who are expected to cooperate.

Agreements, which are similar to contracts (I distinguish them for my own purposes) are reciprocal vehicles for solving specific, goal-oriented problems, whereas contracts can cover many factors. Ben and I have made numerous agreements. Ben agreed not to buy junk foods and go off the Feingold diet, and I agreed to make a special treat, such as fudge, popcorn balls, or peanut brittle, once every two weeks. Ben agreed to try not to disturb me when I was working for a maximum of two hours. I agreed to spend a maximum of a half-hour with him when I completed my work (or my time ran out).

Contracts can be used to cover several behavior areas, or all the details of a particularly troublesome area, for example, morning routines. Depending on where parents and child are starting from, contracts can be highly specific or more generalized, but rewards and penalties are always spelled out.

For one reason or another, getting Ben up and out in the mornings has often been a hassle, probably because he doesn't want to go to school and face the difficulties. We set up a point-system chart, listing the specific behaviors that needed to be corrected to make the morning routine pleasanter and easier for everybody. Penalties are loss of points. A major altercation or argument leads to a forfeiture of all points earned up to that point for the day (e.g., if a fight starts at breakfast, all previous daily points are lost). A reminder means a loss of one point. Points can be traded

	Possible points	Mon.	Tues.	Wed.	Thurs.	Fri.
Getting up promptly when called	2					
Getting dressed quickly (approximately fifteen minutes)	2					
Brushing hair (without being told)	1					
Brushing teeth (without being told)	1					
Being downstairs at 8:00 A.M.	1					
Feeding animals quickly and doing a good job	3					
No fighting or arguing with brother	2					
No arguing or complaining to mother	2					
Being inside again at 8:30 A.M.	1					
Eating quickly and quietly	1					
Being ready to leave, with all necessary belongings, at 9:00 A.M.	2					

for cash at month's end or saved for a specific purchase.

Obviously, minor complaints about someone's behavior or a little chafing should be overlooked, and some flexibility is permitted. If the child is really trying and gets downstairs at 8:01 A.M., he should get his point.

"CHILD LABOR" AND MATURITY

My children have long bemoaned my strange ideas on child labor. I was never too keen on doing things for other people that they could do perfectly well for themselves, especially pick-me-up-and-put-me-away kinds of chores. I also explained to them that being mature meant that one could do anything and everything that was necessary to maintain one's self, and that included cleaning, cooking, minor repairs, keeping clothes clean, taking care of plants and animals, and taking out the garbage. I told them that one day they would be pleased to find they could do all these wonderful things without too much effort, since they had learned to do them efficiently and well through practice. No one was ever impressed with my explanation, but that doesn't matter. My job is to turn out a reasonably functionable adult, not to make everybody happy with me all the time.

My opinions solidified when I saw the Vineland Maturity Scale, which equates common, everyday activities and capabilities with certain age levels. I said to myself, "Ha! I've not only been right, I wasn't right enough!" and proceeded to reexamine my expectations, which included both more responsibility and more independence.

It has been said repeatedly that hyperkinetic children are irresponsible. If so, irresponsibility, or what looks like irresponsibility, is likely the result of several factors: The parents assume too much control and take over the child's responsibilities; the child is given to distractibility and the task is too complex, has too many facets, or is too prolonged; the child is not positively reinforced for successful completion of the task, so there is no point in doing it adequately; the task involves skills and abilities the child does not have; the child does not understand the separate components of the task at hand; the child is not aware of the consequences of not doing the task; or the parents are inconsistent in enforcing compliance in performance of the task.

All children take well to orderliness, responsibility, and independence as long as they are not inundated, and the hyperkinetic child is not an exception. As a matter of fact, a great deal of disorder, a lack of responsibility (based on the assumption that the child cannot assume any), and the curtailment of independence seem to frustrate and irritate the child.

All responsibilities and privileges, including a measure of independence, must be matched with the child's abilities. It's unreasonable to expect a highly active, distractible eight-year-old to clean up his room without a detailed description of the steps involved in the process. He's bound to get distracted somewhere, especially if he doesn't know how to proceed.

Any problem can look monumental to a person who does not readily have available the techniques to make the solution quick and easy. It's really not unusual for an imaginative child to magnify difficulties and make a problem appear insurmountable. After all, the conceptual and logical mental processes that make problem solving less difficult are not operating until the child is between ten or twelve, and certainly not operating efficiently until much later than that. To make things worse, hyperkinetic children sometimes *do* have problems in planning and projecting alternatives. It is frequently apparent that a child feels rather overwhelmed by the complexity, size, and/or duration of a task (e.g., reviewing 120 spelling words or putting together a complex model). (It appears that this is the result, at least partially, of that inner need to hurry or to do everything at once.) Parents should help the child enumerate the components of a complex or large task, such as cleaning up his room.

Working with the child, one step at a time, establishing the following kind of procedure might help an eight- to ten-year-old child clean up his room:

Cleaning up your room (Time limit: forty-five minutes)
Make the bed
Put toys away in toy box
Put games away on wide shelves
Put books away on bookshelves
Pick up any dirty clothes and put them in the hamper
Check drawers to see if they are neat
Straighten up work table
Get a clean cloth and dust furniture
Shake out the throw rug beside bed
When the room is all cleaned up, I will run the vacuum cleaner

The following privileges are granted on the basis of performance:

Perfect job: Everything is put away neatly; drawers are not jumbled; nothing is left under the bed; the room is very tidy: two hours of bike-riding on Saturday.

Good job: Shelves are a little disorderly; drawers are not neat; a few toys are left scattered around; too many things are left out of place; one item on the list has been omitted. One hour of bike-riding on Saturday.

Poor job: Job took too long; too many reminders of things left undone; things are not put away neatly; or two or more items on the list have been omitted. No bike-riding on Saturday. Better luck next time!

There has to be a time limit, obviously, or a routine task could become a lifetime vocation. A fair allotment of time should be granted, based on how long it takes to do the job with adult help. If it takes a half-hour to do the job with adult supervision, it shouldn't take much more than forty-five minutes to do it by oneself.

The reward or reinforcer, of course, need only be as much as it takes to elicit good performance. If the child will clean his room for a cookie or verbal reinforcement, so much the better.

There are also routine weekly chores that may be alotted to children, providing they are specified. We now use a combination schedule and contract:

MONDAY	
Empty trash baskets; take trash to curb	Ben
Clean upstairs cat pan	David
Clean downstairs cat pan	Ben
Boy Scouts at 4:15	David
Feed inside animals (cats, dog)	David
Homework	
TUESDAY	
Water downstairs plants	David
Water upstairs plants	Ben
Homework must be done by 4:30	Ben and David
Feed animals inside (cats, dog, guppie)	Ben
Dancing at 6:15	Ben and David
WEDNESDAY	
Give rabbits Tetramycin in water	David
Clean baby rabbits' hutches	Ben
Feed inside animals (cats, dog)	David
Homework	
THURSDAY	
Empty trash baskets; take trash to curb	David
Clean upstairs cat pan	Ben
Clean downstairs cat pan	David
Boy Scouts at 4:00	Ben
Feed inside animals (cats, dog, guppie)	Ben
Homework	
FRIDAY	
Clean all other rabbit hutches	David and Ben
Homework	
Feed inside animals (cats, dog)	David
SATURDAY	
Clean your rooms	David and Ben
Clean your hallway	Ben
Clean your bathroom	David
Ceramics class at 11:30	David
Whatever Ben wants to do for two hours	Ben
Feed inside animals (cats, dog, guppie)	Everybody

Other work may be assigned as the week progresses, but listed tasks are to be done no matter what else happens—without reminders and without arguments. Participation in outside activities is somewhat contingent upon performance. If rooms are not satisfactorily cleaned on Saturday mornings, the taxi service (me) becomes unavailable. If I choose to alter the schedule, unfulfilled requirements become my responsibility. If outside factors alter the schedule (e.g., inclement weather preventing the cleaning of the hutches), then a specific time is set aside for that task.

It's convenient to list events and happenings, such as special TV programs, so that everybody is aware that there are time limits for the performance of tasks.

NOT-DOING

The graceful art of not-doing is painfully acquired. It often results in logical and natural consequences occurring to the child that are not particularly pleasant. Not-doing has one decided advantage: It removes the parent somewhat from the role of great white ogre—the one who punishes and inflicts penalties and pain.

Having gotten the hang of it, I found that not-doing became easier with practice. The big discovery was, however, that it was more effective as a modifier of behavior than all my anger, yelling, punishing, and penalties put together.

Not-doing, unfortunately, lends itself well to spite, humiliation, and other bad practices, although that's not what it's meant to do. Basically, not-doing is a kind of negative agreement between parent and child: "If you will not clean your room, I will not furnish transportation for your activities, because *we* will be cleaning your room." To provide taxi service for the child and then come back and clean up his messy room is asking for more of the same treatment.

Parents tend to get wrapped up in their own routines

and schedules and continue to do what they think they are supposed to be doing long after they should have quit trying.

Assertiveness training courses have become quite popular, as people have begun to recognize the importance of saying, "No, I really can't do that," and "No, that's not fair to me," *before* they get mad. Not-doing is a nonverbal way of saying "No!" to your children before you get mad, or in place of getting mad.

Not-doing is hard to describe. It is bringing the child back home when he misbehaves in public places, rather than being hassled and fighting with him. It's withdrawing privileges and desired activities. It's walking away from a provocative, argumentative child without being drawn into the argument. It's refusing to turn on the TV until homework and chores are completed.

Not-doing should not be confused with passive-aggressive behavior, because the two have nothing in common. The passive-aggressive person does things for revenge, even if they are detrimental to himself. Not-doing often requires the nondoer to figure out what would be the best thing for *him* to do in a given situation.

Not-doing can relieve parents of the burden of trying to make the child do certain things and puts the responsibility for actions and behaviors on the child, where it belongs. Of course, it's possible to make a child do what you want, if you're willing to go to all the trouble and accept mediocre results. (You can't make anybody do a good job when he doesn't want to.)

Not-doing is also stepping back and allowing other people to resolve their differences, make their own decisions, and solve their own problems. It's amazing how capable children can be when their parents refuse to do these things for them.

It's impossible to not-do when you're angry, upset, or involved, because the decision to not-do is pretty cold-blooded. It's also mostly fair, just, and nonarbitrary.

To be able to decide what to not-do, the parent must be willing to accept the fact that he has limitations, such as not being able to do three things at once, not being able to function in the midst of chaos, not being able to give continuous support and assurance, and not being able to control himself in the face of continued provocation.

Hyperkinetic children make excessive demands on parents, and I think parents need to evaluate their limitations: which demands they can meet, which they can sometimes meet, and which they can't cope with at all. Excessive demands are usually dealt with harshly and/or punitively. They are better modified by lack of response or not-doing, which is often an overt form of refusal to reinforce negative behavior.

15 The Terrible Teens

To achieve not only the status but the reality of adulthood (self-actualization), with its many positive benefits and many responsibilities, the child must pass through several major stages. The logical progression is from total dependence to independence to mature interdependence.

Without achieving independence, the child will not be able to make the transition to adulthood. It's really a very simple concept. It's the achieving part that is often not so simple—the achieving which, under better circumstances with more docile, less impetuous, and less negativistic children, can drive parents over the deep end. For the hyperkinetic teen, the process is more likely to be tempestuous, protracted, and highly emotional.

The reasons the progression is more turbulent are, on the whole, quite logical and rational. They follow naturally from what has happened before. The parents have had to exert more control. The child is still more impulsive. No matter how good the parental management has been, the child is bound to have some deeply felt, and totally rational, negativistic feelings about his own abilities and his relationships with others. He has had to learn that his judgmental abilities are not always sound. He has had to cope with his differentness, and whether or not he has been able to accept and justify his deviance to himself is questionable.

What's especially ironic is that good parental management may make the separation of parent and child more traumatic. If the child has learned to rely on parental judgment and support, his quest for independence can be further complicated by his dependence on his parents.

Nevertheless, despite parental doubts that the child will ever reach maturity, he indeed must do so—or remain in protective custody, of one kind or another, for the duration of his life. Unless the parents intend to supervise the child indefinitely, or allow societal custodians, such as jailors or attendants to do so in their place, they must not hold him back, must relax their control, and must support his efforts to be independent.

THE NEED FOR INDEPENDENCE

What is independence? Basically it is the total sum of capabilities and skills that allows an individual to take charge of himself. It includes being able to earn enough money to pay one's way—to provide shelter, food, clothing, and other basic necessities—and to acquire the things one wants in the way of amenities and pleasures. One should be able to afford to buy and maintain a car if one wishes, to raise a family, or to buy and maintain a house or an elaborate stereo set, or to do any of the other things people do simply because it suits them. The word "maintain" is important here. It's in learning to take care of, or maintain, oneself and one's possessions that the individual learns how to take care of and maintain other people who are important to him. It's not buying the car that's important, it's keeping the car in good repair—at least until all the payments have been made.

I hope it's clear now why I have made such an issue of teaching the child to do routine, mundane tasks, to schedule himself, and to assume responsibility. Of course, all children must learn the techniques for taking care of themselves, and most of them do. It is particularly hard for the hyperkinetic child to understand the structures—and strictures—and to internalize them to the point where they become automatic habits and responses. It is particularly hard for him to foresee the consequences of his impetuous behavior.

Impulsive behavior is not conducive to a rational, orderly life-style. Impulsiveness tends to result in highly chaotic independence, which cannot be equated with success in any form. A chaotic life-style does not even permit one to earn the most elementary kind of living. If the parents made the child get up every morning and go to school, whether he wanted to or not, who's going to assume the responsibility for making the adult get up and go to work when he doesn't want to? Adults usually go to work because of some remote, long-range plans that have little to do with the work situation, although paychecks are a good inducement. How does one explain to a hyperkinetic young adult that he should go to work today, because he may want to do something in three years that he won't be able to do if he loses his present job?

The achieving of independence is likely to be a prolonged process for the hyperkinetic. While his so-called rebellious years often begin a little later than for his contemporaries, the process tends to last longer, with the child slipping back and forth between an adult role and child role. One day, the child acts reasonably adult and makes a decision the parents can applaud. The next evening, the child is anxious and dependent, actively seeking guidance from his parents. Having given their advice, the parents are challenged by their suddenly transformed adult-again, belligerent progeny who is resentful because not only have the parents acted like parents but because he has also acted like a child. Unfortunately, the parents cannot know to which state of maturity they are responding—until it's too late and they are wrong again.

Besides being protracted, this transitional stage is often very tumultuous. Nobody seems to have made an extensive study of this particular problem, but certain things happen to the child that make speculation possible.

EMOTIONAL PROBLEMS

A far greater proportion of hyperkinetics evidence emotional problems as teenagers than they did as children. (In junior and senior high schools, special education classes for the emotionally disturbed far outnumber those for the learning disabled. The opposite is true at elementary school levels.) The few authors that write about hyperkinetic teenagers usually depict them in bleak terms of emotional trauma.

There seem to be several major factors that produce this teenage dilemma. The first, and most important, is the child's negative self-concept, which has been discussed previously. I think I've made it clear that the hyperkinetic child nearly always, somewhere or some time, picks up negative feedback.

During adolescence, the hyperkinetic child often becomes very depressed. Much of this "I'm no good" syndrome is attributable to the devaluation of the child as he experiences proof of his academic and social incompetence. It is very difficult for parents to cope with this sense of isolation, despair, and distrust, since many of the causes can be reality-oriented. Parents may want to consider therapy for the child at this point, especially if the depression is prolonged or profound.

The second factor is the child's attacks on the parents' self-esteem and values, probably caused by an increased awareness of the problems. It's not so uncommon for people to blame other people for things they either didn't do or were beyond their control. Undoubtedly, the parents will have made a lot of mistakes and have been spiteful, angry, and hostile to the child to some degree, so some of the accusations may be just. However, the parent will hardly be able to maintain his serenity when every mistake he's ever made—and some he hasn't—are thrown in his face like a dead fish, particularly when the one doing the throwing is a child who has been and is dearly loved. Parents' feelings will be hurt, they will feel unjustly abused, and they will try to justify their actions. Their natural response, however, is apt to lead into a battle royal. The child screams, "You've never been fair to me," and the parent says, "Yes, I have!" and the child says, "No, you never were. Not ever. I remember, when I was in third grade, when the teacher said I broke the window. I didn't do it. But you wouldn't believe me. You never believed me. You always believed the other person! You never would believe anything I said!" This is not the time for the parent to justify his behavior and explain why he never could quite put complete faith in what the child said when confronted with accusations of misbehavior.

I think that most parents will agree that having the child devaluate and demean one's best efforts and achievements is a very hurtful and provocative experience. These dreadful confrontations can't be completely avoided, but they can be minimized by the parent refusing to argue. Discuss, yes; argue, no.

The third factor is something that's been mentioned in connection with the child. The person who does a lot of things has to, statistically, do more wrong things than the person who does less. It follows that parents who are more involved with the child, actively exert more control, and are faced with more problems make more mistakes than passive parents. The parent who relinquishes control of the child early and sits back and lets the kid go on to do what he wants and then face the consequences on his own makes only one big mistake. The parent who interacts frequently has the opportunity to make mistakes every day. Therefore, numbers are definitely on the side of the parent who throws up his hands and says, "I can't do anything with this kid! I give up!" and means it.

While there is no guarantee of success, however, I'll put my money on the parent who works with the child. It may not be much consolation in the midst of turmoil, but chances are heavily weighed that, with maturity and understanding, the parent-involved child will eventually come to terms with himself and his parents.

It's not easy to remember, but one of these days the hyperkinetic child will be twenty-five years old, then thirty-five, and then. . . . The child's ability to become a self-actualizing adult is the goal for which the parents have actually been aiming since the child was born.

THE PROCESS OF MATURATION

It used to be commonly thought that children "outgrew" hyperkinesis, and that some process of maturation gradually alleviated the symptoms and the child became just like every other child during adolescence. This is not quite true.

Nobody has been able to document the physiological changes that tend to reduce restlessness and motor activity. It's just as logical to presume that the child is somehow learning to inhibit these behaviors. By the time activity decreases, however, the child is abysmally weighed down by a great many problems he's acquired along the way. The impulsivity, which is more a cognitive style than anything else, and the emotionality are only slightly tempered, if at all. I'm not sure there aren't a lot of parents who would welcome a return of motor activity if they could trade off the child's acquired anxiety, frustration, hostility, negative self-concept, depression, irritability, inaccessibility, and general apathy.

My own experience makes me believe that something dramatic happens within the hyperkinetic adolescent that eventually proves to be growth-oriented, questing, positive, and productive. Whatever it is, it is extremely *fragile.* Hypothetically, it may be a combination of newly acquired abilities to deal with abstracts and conceptual insights, emerging emotional maturity, and a striving for integration of the personality. The child is able to examine his difficulties, reflect on them, analyze them, produce conceptual solutions and, tentatively, put them into practice. It has occurred to me that it takes a monumental amount of courage for the child to even hesitantly try new approaches—new solutions, to old, old problems. It is entirely possible that the teen-aged hyperkinetic does the right thing for the wrong reasons. My daughter once said, "Nothing could get any worse than it was. So it didn't matter what I did, as long as I did something. I couldn't stand the way things were any more."

While the child may be able to modify his behavior somewhat, without apparent or parent-produced cause, the process of maturation cannot be expected to supply the necessary knowledge and skills, social, academic, or personal, that the child has not been able to acquire. His negative expectations will further prohibit him from acting in positive and productive ways. If the child has not learned social skills before adolescence, for instance, he may be able to observe his peers and, to some extent, model his behavior accordingly. But his feelings of ineptness and worthlessness will make him hesitant, unsure of the outcome, and too ready to withdraw the tentative overtures he makes to other people.

There are at least 200 reasons for a parent not to approach his child with the statement, "Hey, look. I see what the problem is. You never learned to make friends in first grade. You haven't learned the social skills. Let's teach you how to do it, and everything will be fine!" No matter how well-intentioned or helpful the parent may be, he is doomed to a quick and final rejection for his proposal.

I think parents of hyperkinetic adolescents are in a mighty precarious position: walking a very fine line between support and intrusion, between parental control and child management, and between building a new relationship with the child and losing him to outside influences.

THE DIPLOMA: CHALLENGE OR THREAT?

For achievers, high school is a challenge. For underachievers, such as the hyperkinetic child is apt to be, academia is a real threat. Even if parents have had to accept the sad fact that the child cannot or will not reach the educational levels they had hoped for him to achieve, the problems involved in keeping him in school, getting him there in the morning and keeping him there all day, can be harrowing.

The hyperkinetic child often begins to express his attitudes toward education, either verbally or by overt actions. He begins talking of dropping out of school as soon as he legally can, or he cuts classes. What can a parent do to keep the child in school? How can parents keep the child involved when the school system has obviously failed?

I think the only solution is for parents, working with the child, to develop practical, feasible alternatives that implement the goals of both parents and child, if possible.

Because of his difficulties, the hyperkinetic adolescent is rarely able to visualize for himself long-range, productive goals. He cannot conceptualize himself as self-actualizing because of the many prohibitions and problems he's experienced. He's more inclined to be aware of what he doesn't want to do and what he can't do than of what he really wants to do and his actual abilities.

Parents and child need to sit down calmly and outline goals, the methods for attaining goals, and the necessary efforts and/or abilities that may be called for. For example,

1. What are the individual's long-range goals (five years from now)?
2. What are the short-term goals (the next year)?
3. What kind of occupation does the individual think possible for himself?
4. If he had his choice, what would he like to do most?
5. What are his special interests, hobbies, etc.?
6. What does the individual think his limitations are (can't do math, hates to sit in one place all the time, etc.)?
7. How much education is necessary to achieve his goals?
8. Does he need a high school diploma?
9. Does he need post-high school education?
10. What is the best way for him to get the education

he requires (remedial instruction, summer school, work-study programs, alternative schools, specialized training or education, etc.)?

11. What are the consequences of not reaching his goals?

Let's presume that the hyperkinetic adolescent is really having trouble with academic subjects because of a uncorrected reading problem. After much prodding, he finally says that he's thought about a skilled trade, like carpentry. As for short-term goals, he wants to get out of school next year, without completing high school. He sees himself as a total washout academically; he feels he can't learn and is quite stupid. However, he has always demonstrated proficiency with tools and has always enjoyed physical labor.

After investigating the possibilities of an apprenticeship program and the academic alternatives, the parents and adolescent compromise on the following plan: The child will remain in school if at all possible. The parents have brought pressure to bear, and he will receive remedial instruction. In his junior year (in seven months) he will be able to participate in a work-study program. The parents will try to arrange a job for him as a carpenter's helper. Parents and child agree on the importance of high school graduation. The parents are supportive of the child's efforts to become a carpenter and agree to do whatever they can to help him in this endeavor.

ALTERNATIVE EDUCATION

The movement to create alternatives to the conventional high school environment has not been as successful as it could be. Our local alternative school has just closed as a result of decreased enrollment. The concept of alternative schools has always met with resistance from parents and school administrators—even students.

The idea that not all high school students can, should, or want to compete academically has been recognized for some time. However, the pressure to achieve, the insistence on compliance with academic standards, and the promotion of personal value judgments based on academic abilities have not noticeably been reduced in recent years.

If it is true that the world is populated with many different personalities, with many abilities and skills, then why is it still so important that all children and all adolescents be constrained to fit some preconceived, standardized mold? What is the great difference between the carpenter and the lawyer? Currently, it doesn't appear to be the ability to make money. As for power and prestige, have you tried to retain the services of a carpenter lately?

When my daughter was ready to enter high school, I choose to allow her to go to an alternative school. Why? It was apparent that she was already lost to the educational process, and I could see no point in permitting her to undergo the long series of frustrations, devaluations, pressures, and rejections she would probably experience in an academically pushy school system.

When she announced she planned to quit school when she was sixteen (she was fourteen at the time), I suggested that she could graduate a year early if she did some tricky maneuvering and went to summer school. This plan was immediately censured by the school administrators, which enhanced it greatly in her eyes. Among other things, she was told she couldn't stick to such a tough, tight schedule. Their disapproval probably did as much as any approval on my part to ensure her successful performance.

HONESTY—THE BEST POLICY?

Parents of exceptional children, including the handicapped and hyperkinetic, normally develop many hostile feelings toward their children in the course of raising them. They may also develop some positive feelings—love, affection, caring, tenderness, admiration, respect, and enjoyment. Nevertheless, the child will undoubtedly be most aware of parental negative attitudes.

Total honesty between people—saying whatever comes into your mind at all times—is a quick way to end a relationship. Lying about one's feelings may keep the relationship going, on a false basis, a little longer, but it will inevitably end in collapse.

By the time the hyperkinetic is in his teens, there's no point in not sharing your feelings with him, because he *already* knows how you feel. Telling him that there are occasions when you are so angry you'd like to clobber him will probably come as no shock. It may also encourage the adolescent to talk about his own feelings toward his parents—he may often feel resentful and angry toward them, too.

Sharing your angry feelings is not indulging in a vicious, destructive attack on the child's personality. It means talking about exasperating situations, behaviors, or events. A two-hour harangue can only make the teenager more resentful. Expressing disapproval of certain behavior and asking for an explanation of the behavior or compromise or modification can be quite constructive.

Adolescents are quick to pick up contradictions delivered by their parents—and so are children! The parent who says one thing while sending a contradictory message is not on the way to establishing a relationship with his child. It's possible to mean both messages, but the one that is more effective is the unspoken one. The parent who says, "I want you to get good grades in school because I really care about you," but whose message is being received as, "You miserable brat! I want you out of school, out of my house, and out of my life—*now!*" needs to make a choice: Either resolve the conflict in his statements or let the kid alone.

It may sound very harsh, but when the parents don't like the child, when their anger has overcome all other feelings, and when they can no longer perform in a constructive manner, the best thing they can do is to leave him alone, at least until the parents can handle their feelings more constructively. It is in no way beneficial for parents to allow the child to believe that he can, through some action, modification, or improvement, attain their approval, love, or acceptance, if this is not true. Living in a state of armed truce may not be the pleasantest way to live, but it's a lot better than living with shells exploding around your head.

Since a lot of the friction between parents and hyperkinetic adolescents is the direct effect of parental overcontrol, punitiveness, and distrust of the child's abilities, it is not surprising that a hands-off policy sometimes indirectly benefits the parent-child relationship.

Since adolescent opposition is an accepted fact, and since hyperkinetic adolescents are often quite oppositional, parents should be prepared to deflect opposition.

When my children were in junior and senior high school drugs were a big, big issue. The school authorities kept informing parents "that they had the situation under control." My children kept telling me the most hair-raising stories about drug use and abuse. I, quite naturally, believed my daughters, who, in this specific case, were perhaps better informed than the authorities.

I was concerned that Gerry would experiment with drugs, and there were many discussions, in school and at home, on the subject. Finally, with my teeth clenched and heart palpitating, I managed to say to her, "I would prefer, if you must experiment with drugs, that you do it here. I would feel a lot better. At least, you wouldn't get hurt, raped, or arrested. I'll do my best not to get upset. I can't promise anything, except that if I find you're using drugs behind my back, I'll kill you." (I don't know if I would have acted rationally if she had taken me up on my offer. I think I would have had a heart attack.)

Five years later, Gerry told me how my dictum on drugs had affected her. She had believed me—and believed in me—and realized that a lot of her peers used drugs because of parental prohibitions. She further realized she could get "high" on her own natural ebullience and that drugs were a one-way street.

It isn't always easy for an adult, with a great deal of life experience, to be able to see things in the same perspective as the adolescent, who has had little real experience. It's a lot easier for the parent to override the opinions, wishes, and attitudes of the child. After all, it may be true that the parent does "know best." Until the time that the sum total of parental knowledge can be transferred painlessly to the child, however, the adolescent will have to acquire his own knowledge.

The last thing the hyperkinetic adolescent needs is a daily series of confrontations with his parents. It's not particularly beneficial for the parents, either. Just remember, achieving adulthood will be a lot easier for the child if parents have been steadily working toward the child's assumption of responsibility, liability, and independence.

16 Is It Worth It?

Over and over again, the prognosis for hyperkinesis is pictured as bleak. Authorities point to the high incidence of psychoses and neuroses, personality problems, delinquency, lack of job success, and other marks of failure as proof that the hyperkinetic child cannot or does not outlive his difficulties. Nonsense! These examples of failure just prove that you can't beat a child over the head for twenty years without causing some damage. It's a prime example of circuitous, muddled thinking.

Hyperkinesis in any degree, however symptomatic, does not result in emotional illness or personality disorder. The life experiences of the hyperkinetic, the way he has been treated, the world's response to him, and his reaction to the world, can produce very serious disorders.

If the difficult child becomes the difficult adolescent and adult, the delinquent, the mental patient, or the prison inmate, it's because an adult, or two or three, or many, didn't do what they could or should have done when the child was malleable and amenable to remediation. It's because the child was not permitted to grow, within the context of his own personality, in positive, self-achieving ways and has been thwarted, defeated, and crippled. Maybe the learning-disabled child's disability will prevent him from being an engineer. But who's to say that, through remediation, he can't acquire enough compensatory skills to enable him to be an engineer? Who dares to close the doors of opportunity on seven- and eight-year-old children? Not I.

It's not fair to expect parents to do a superlative—not to say, adequate—job raising a hyperkinetic child, especially when so many of the problems and situations they encounter are adverse and self-defeating. Parents will have to do the best they can, get as much help for themselves and the child as is available, and hope for a successful outcome. A successful outcome is what child-raising is all about.

Can parents of hyperkinetic children hope for success? You better believe they can! Someone recently accused me of being very negative. To which, I replied, "Nuts! I'm one of the least negative people I know. You're confused. I'm a fighter, and you think that's negative. It's not. Recognizing there's going to be a fight and planning to win it are very positive steps. And I always plan to win!"

I had hoped this book would be cathartic for me, and that I could get rid of a lot of aggravation, frustration, and anger in the writing. Instead, I'm more aggrieved, more involved, and more aggravated today than I've been in twenty years. The problems of hyperkinesis have had to be analyzed during the writing, and I'm not happy about many of the things I've read, seen, heard, and talked about.

A lot of people are going to be displeased with what I've said and how I've said it. Too bad. A lot of those people are exactly the ones who need to be upset and made to confront their contributions to the situation as it exists. Anybody who wants to prove I'm wrong may feel free to do so. Anybody who wants to show me how the problems of hyperkinesis are being handled effectively, efficaciously, and advantageously (i.e., to the advantage of the hyperkinetic child and his family) should by all means present the evidence. It would certainly do me a lot of good to know that positive, productive things are happening in an area beset by confusion, hyperbole, pessimism, and a lot of plain old prejudice.

So, what's going to happen next? The field appears to be pretty well divided into two groups: those who speak positively and encouragingly—and rationally, I might add—about the hyperkinetic and his possibilities, and those whose main thrust appears to be ostracism, medication, and negation. Then there are a few fanatics who would like to blame all the ills of society on the hyperkinetic: all delinquents, all sociopaths, all psychotics, all prison inmates, all welfare recipients, all ne'er-do-wells are hyperkinetics. To this group of wonderful people, I would like to present my goose-stepping, funny-little-mustache award of the year.

To what end all the research, writing, and discussion will lead is anybody's guess. One can hope the guys in the white hats will win, as they frequently do in fiction, but the white hats don't always triumph in real life.

Three or four hundred advocates for the hyperkinetic child aren't enough. Parents of hyperkinetics are going to have to get up and get out; they must start speaking out, advocating, insisting, and persuading, not only on behalf of their individual child but also as advocates of all children. Parents, individually and in groups, are going to have to start speaking positively and productively in reference to the hyperkinetic child, refusing to accept the labels, stigma, ostracism, and limitations imposed on him. No parent should accept devaluation of his child. No parent need accept such a verdict.

My daughter Gerry is twenty years old, and the outcome is still unsure. I believe she will become a reasonably productive, self-actualizing adult. To doubt her is to doubt myself and my accomplishments as a parent and as a person, and such doubts lead to destruction. My son Ben is eight, and I have no idea how the experiment will turn out. I'm not making the same mistakes I made before—not all of them, anyway—but I'm making new ones, of course, and the effect of these new mistakes is unpredictable. My optimism is based on two facts: I now know a lot more about the problem than I did before and I sure *do* like that kid an awful lot. I think he's tremendous, fabulous, great, superlative, wonderful and beautiful. So, he has some limitations. So does everyone.

Final chapters are supposed to be conclusive. That is, issues and situations are supposed to be resolved. I have no resolution of the issues. I'm afraid child-raising is an ongoing experience and there can be no final resolution. As a matter of fact, what I hoped to do was to expand the issues and raise new questions. I would like to leave the prognosis, if you don't mind, wide open to possibilities and optimism.

Since my children feel I should end on a positive note, here it is: Quite some time ago, I felt I was being oppressed and treated very badly by a particular person. The situation erupted into a confrontation, during which, of course, I became very angry and threw out some founded and unfounded accusations about what the other person was doing or not doing, and eventually shouted, "If you think I'm going to curl up and die, you're crazy! I won't die even if you kill me!" My inadvertent contradiction of terms has since become my motto. I found repeating this slogan to myself had a very salutary effect on the days I felt like leaving home, abandoning my children, burning my house down, or any other rather drastic measure.

Not too surprisingly, having repeated my motto frequently over the past ten or fifteen years, I find I have come to believe it.

When things are really bad, and the situation is completely out of hand, take the child, look him in the eye and start saying, with great conviction. "We won't die, even if they kill us."

Bibliography

The following is a general sampling of the material researched. Because the size of the bibliography grew to such proportions, many repetitive journal articles were not included. Articles and books which may be of particular interest to parents are noted with an asterisk.

Aarskog, D., et al. The effect of the stimulant drugs, dextroamphetamine and methylphenidate on secretion of growth hormone in hyperactive children. *Journal of Pediatrics,* **90,** 136–139, 1977.

Alabiso, Frank. Inhibitory functions of attention in reducing hyperactive behavior. *American Journal of Mental Deficiency,* 77, 259–282, 1972.

Alexander, Theron. *Children and Adolescents.* New York: Atherton, 1969.

Allen, Richard, et al. Effects of psychostimulants on aggression. *Journal of Nervous and Mental Disease,* **160,** 138–145, 1975.

Aman, M. G., and Werry, J. S. Methylphenidate in children: Effects upon cardiorespiratory function on exertion. *International Journal of Mental Health,* **4,** 119–131, 1975.

Anderson, Camilla. *The High Cost of Minimal Brain Damage in America.* New York: Walker, 1972.

Anderson, Robert P., et al. Measurement of attention distractibility in LD children. *Academic Therapy,* **9,** 261–266, 1974.

Appleman, Michael A. Three recent developments relating to the legal issues involved in the use of drugs on hyperactive children. *NOLPE School Law Journal,* **5**, 22–24, 1975.

Arnold, L. E. Control of aggression by advanced grade placement: Criteria and case history. *Journal of School Health,* **42**, 458–459, 1972.

Arnold, L. Eugene. Is this label necessary? *Journal of School Health,* **43**, 510–514, 1973.

Arnold, L. Eugene. Causes of hyperactivity and implications for prevention. *School Psychology Digest,* **5**, 10–22, 1976.

*Axline, Virginia M. *Play Therapy.* New York: Ballatine Books, 1969.

Ayllon, Teodoro, and Rainwater, Nancy. Behavioral alternatives to the drug control of hyperactive children in the classroom. *School Psychology Digest,* **5**, 33–39, 1976.

*Ayllon, Teodoro, et al., Eliminating discipline problems by strengthening academic performance. *Journal of Applied Behavior Analysis,* **7**, 71–76, 1974.

*Ayllon, Teodoro, et al. A behavioral-educational alternative to drug control of hyperactive children. *Journal of Applied Behavior Analysis,* **8**, 137–146, 1975.

Ball, Thomas S., and Irwin, Aubrey E. A portable, automated device applied to training a hyperactive child. *Journal of Behavior Therapy and Experimental Psychiatry,* **7**, 185–187, June 1976.

*Bannatyne, Alex. *Counsel for Parents.* Springfield, Ill.: Charles C Thomas. 1974.

Bannatyne, Alexander. *The Spatially Competent Child with Learning Disabilities (SCLD): The Evidence from Research.* Bannatyne Children's Learning Center, Miami, Fla. 1975. Pamphlet.

Barkley, R. A., et al. Do stimulant drugs improve the academic performance of hyperkinetic children? A review of outcome research. *Clinical Pediatrics,* **17**, 85–92, 1978.

Barkley, Russell A. Predicting the response of hyperkinetic children to stimulant drugs: A review. *Journal of Abnormal Child Psychology,* **4**, 327–348, 1976.

Barkley, Russell A. The effects of methylphenidate on various types of activity level and attention in hyperkinetic children. *Journal of Abnormal Child Psychology,* **5**, 351–369, 1977.

Barkley, Russell A. A review of stimulant drug research with hyperactive children. *Journal of Child Psychology, Psychiatry, and Allied Disciplines,* **18,** 137–165, 1977.

Barkley, Russell A., and Ullman, Douglas G. A comparison of objective measures of activity and distractibility in hyperactive and nonhyperactive children. *Journal of Abnormal Child Psychology,* **3,** 231–244, 1975.

Battle, Esther S., and Lacey, Beth. A context for hyperactivity in children over time. *Child Development,* **43,** 757–773, 1972.

Bax, Martin. The active and over-active school child. *Developmental Medicine and Child Neurology,* **14,** 83–86, 1972.

Bendix, Selina. Drug modification of behavior: A form of chemical violence against children? *Journal of Clinical Child Psychology,* **2,** 17–19, 1973.

Berkowitz, B. T., and Graziano, A. M. Training parents as behavior therapists: A review. *Behavioral Research and Therapy,* **10,** 297–317, 1972.

Berne, Eric. *Transactional Analysis in Psychotherapy.* New York: Grove Press, 1961.

Berne, Eric. *Games People Play.* New York: Grove Press, 1964.

*Bettleheim, Bruno. *Love is Not Enough.* New York: Avon, 1950.

*Bettleheim, Bruno. *Truants from Life: The Rehabilitation of Emotionally Disturbed Children.* New York: Free Press, 1955.

*Bettleheim, Bruno. *Dialogues with Mothers.* New York, Avon, 1971.

Block, Gerald H. Hyperactivity: A cultural perspective. *Journal of Learning Disabilities,* **10,** 236–240, 1977.

Block, J., et al. Comment on the Kagan-Messer reply. *Developmental Psychology,* **11,** 249–252, 1975.

Bloom, Robert B. Teacher pupil compatibility and teachers' ratings of children's behavior. *Psychology in the Schools,* **13,** 142–145, 1976.

Blunden, Dale, et al. Validation of the classroom behavior inventory. *Journal of Consulting and Clinical Psychology,* **42,** 84–88, 1974.

Boileau, Richard A., et al. Effect of methylphenidate on cardiorespiratory responses in hyperactive children. *Research Quarterly,* **47,** 590–596, 1976.

Bornstein, Philip H., and Quevillon, Randal P., The effects of a self-instructional package on overactive preschool boys. *Journal of Applied Behavior Analysis,* **9,** 179–188, 1976.

Bower, Eli M. *Orthopsychiatry and Education.* Detroit: Wayne State University Press, 1971.

Bower, K., et al. Hyperactivity: Etiology and intervention techniques. *Journal of School Health,* **45,** 195–202, 1975.

Braud, Lendell W., et al. The use of electromyographic biofeedback in the control of hyperactivity. *Journal of Learning Disabilities,* **8,** 420–425, 1975.

*Brazelton, T. Berry. *Infants and Mothers.* New York: Dell Publishing Co., Inc., 1969.

*Brazelton, T. Berry. *Toddler and Parents: A Declaration of Independence.* New York: Delacorte Press, 1974.

Bremer, David A., and Stern, John A. Attention and distractibility during reading in hyperactive boys. *Journal of Abnormal Child Psychology,* **4,** 381–387, 1976.

Brodemus, John, and Swanson, Jon C. The "paradoxical effect" of stimulants upon hyperactive children. *Drug Forum,* **6,** 117–125, 1977.

Broudy, Harry S. Ideological, political and moral considerations in the use of drugs in hyperkinetic therapy. *School Review,* **85,** 43–60, 1976.

*Bruck, Connie. Battle lines in the Ritalin war. *Human Behaviors,* **5,** 24–33, 1976.

*Brutten, Milton, et al. *Something's Wrong with My Child.* New York: Harcourt Brace Jovanovich, 1973.

Bugental, Daphne B., et al. Causal attributions of hyperactive children and motivational assumptions of two behavior-change approaches: Evidence for an interactionist position. *Child Development,* **48,** 874–884, 1977.

Butter, H. J., and Lapierre, Y. D. The effect of methylphenidate on sensory perception and integration in hyperactive children. *International Pharmacopsychiatry,* **9,** 235–244, 1974.

Butter, H. J., and Lapierre, Y. D. The effect of methylphenidate on sensory perception in varying degrees of hyperkinetic behavior. *Diseases of the Nervous System,* **36,** 286–288, 1975.

Campbell, Susan B. Mother-child interaction: A comparison of hyperactive, learning disabled and normal boys. *American Journal of Orthopsychiatry,* **45,** 51–57, 1975.

Campbell, Susan B. Mother-child interaction in reflective, impulsive and hyperactive children. *Developmental Psychology,* **8,** 341–349, 1973.

Campbell, Susan B., et al. Continuities in maternal reports and child behaviors over time in hyperactive and comparison groups. *Journal of Abnormal Child Psychology,* **6,** 33–45, 1978.

*Cantwell, D. P., ed. *The Hyperactive Child.* Holliswood, N.Y.: Spectrum, 1975.

Cantwell, Dennis P. Early intervention with hyperactive children. *Journal of Operational Psychiatry,* **6,** 56–67, 1974.

Cantwell, Dennis P. Genetics of hyperactivity. *Journal of Child Psychology and Psychiatry,* **16,** 261–264, 1975.

Christesen, Donald E. Effects of combining methylphenidate and a classroom token system in modifying hyperactive behavior. *American Journal of Mental Deficiency,* **80,** 266–276, 1975.

Clements, Sam D. *Minimal Brain Dysfunction in Children: Terminology and Identification.* NINDB Monograph no. 3, U.S. Department of Health, Education, and Welfare, 1966.

Cohen, Stewart, and Comiskey, Thomas J., eds. *Child Development: Contemporary Perspectives.* Itasca, Ill.: F. E. Peacock, 1977.

Cole, Sherwood, et al. Stimulants and hyperkinesis: Drug use or abuse? *Journal of Drug Education,* **5,** 371–378, 1975.

Cole, Sherwood, et al. The hyperkinetic child syndrome: The need for reassessment. *Child Psychiatry and Human Development,* **7,** 103–112, 1976.

* Conference on the Use of Stimulant Drugs in the Treatment of Behaviorally Disturbed Young School Children. *Journal of Learning Disabilities,* **4,** 523–530, 1971.

Conners, C. Keith. Symptom patterns in hyperkinetic, neurotic and normal children. *Child Development,* **41,** 677–682, 1970.

Conners, C. Keith. Recent drug studies with hyperkinetic children. *Journal of Learning Disabilities,* **4,** 476–483, 1971.

Conners, C. Keith. Drug and cognitive studies in disturbed children. *Psychopharmacological Bulletin,* **10,** 60–61, 1974.

Conners, C. Keith, et al. Food additives and hyperkinesis: A controlled double-blind experiment. *Pediatrics,* **58,** 154–166, 1976.

Connor, James P. *Classroom activities for helping hyperactive children.* New York: Center for Applied Research in Education, 1974.

Conrad, Peter. The discovery of hyperkinesis: Notes on medicalization of deviant behavior. *Social Problems,* **23,** 12–21, 1975.

*Conrad, Peter. *Identifying Hyperactive Children: The Medicalization of Deviant Behavior.* Lexington, Mass.: D. C. Heath, 1976.

Conrad, Peter. Situational hyperactivity: A social system approach. *Journal of School Health,* **47,** 280–285, 1977.

Costello, C., ed. *Symptoms of Psychopathology: A Handbook.* New York: Wiley, 1970.

Cott, A. Megavitamins: The orthomolecular approach to behavioral disorders and learning disabilities. *Academic Therapy,* **7,** 245–258, 1972.

Craig, Eleanor. *P. S., You're Not Listening.* New York: New American Library, 1973.

Cratty, Bryant J. *Perceptual-Motor Behavior and Educational Processes.* Springfield, Ill.: Charles C Thomas, 1969.

Cruickshank, W. M., ed. *Psychology of Exceptional Children and Youth.* Englewood Cliffs, N.J.: Prentice Hall, 1971.

Cruickshank, W. M., and Hallahan, D. P., eds. *Perceptual and Learning Disabilities in Children: Research and Theory,* Vols. I and II. Syracuse, N.Y.: Syracuse University Press, 1975.

*Cruickshank, W. T., et al. *A Teaching Method for Hyperactive and Brain Injured Children.* Syracuse, N.Y.: Syracuse University Press, 1966.

Cruickshank, William M. Field of learning disabilities. *Journal of Learning Disabilities,* **5,** 6–7, 1972.

Cullinon, Douglas, et al. Modification of impulsive tempo in learning disabled pupils. *Journal of Abnormal Child Psychology,* **5,** 437–444, 1977.

David, Oliver J., et al. Lead and hyperactivity. Behavioral response to chelation: A pilot study. *American Journal of Psychiatry,* **133,** 1155–1158, 1975.

David, Oliver J., et al. Lead and hyperactivity: lead levels among hyperactive children. *Journal of Abnormal Child Psychology,* **5,** 405–416, 1977.

Davids, A. An objective instrument for assessing hyperkinesis in children. *Journal of Learning Disabilities,* **4,** 499–501, 1971.

Denckla, Martha Bridge. Research needs in learning disabilities: A neurologist's point of view. *Journal of Learning Disabilities,* **6,** 441–450, 1973.

Denhoff, Eric. The responsibility of the physician, parent and child in learning disabilities. *Rehabilitation Literature,* **35,** 226–230, 1974.

Denhoff, Eric, et al. The child at risk for learning disorder: Can he be identified during the first year of life? *Clinical Pediatrics,* **2,** 1972.

Denson, R., et al. Hyperkinesis and maternal smoking. *Canadian Psychiatric Association Journal,* **20,** 183–187, 1975.

Denton, Claire L., and McIntyre, Curtis W. Span of apprehension in hyperactive boys. *Journal of Abnormal Child Psychology,* **6,** 19–24, 1978.

Dinkmeyer, Don, and McKay, Gary D. *Systematic training for effective parenting: Parent's handbook.* Circle Pines, Minn.: American Guidance Service, 1976.

Divoky, D. Toward a nation of sedated children. *Learning,* **1,** 7–13, 1973.

Dobson, James. *Dare to Discipline.* New York: Bantam Books, 1977.

Donofria, Anthony F. Parent education vs. child psychotherapy. *Psychology in the Schools,* **13,** 176–180, 1976.

Dougherty, Edward and Anne. The daily report card: A simplified and flexible package for classroom behavior management. *Psychology in the Schools,* **14,** 191–195, 1977.

Douglas, V. I. Are drugs enough to treat or train the hyperactive child? *International Journal of Mental Health,* **4,** 199–212, 1975.

*Douglas, Virginia I. Research on hyperactivity: Stage two. *Journal of Abnormal Child Psychology,* **4,** 307–308, 1976. (This entire issue was devoted to the subject of hyperactivity.)

Douglas, Virginia I. Stop, look and listen: The problem of sustained attention and impulse control in hyperactive and normal children. *Canadian Journal of Behavioral Science,* **4,** 259–282, 1972.

Douglas, Virginia I., et al. Assessment of a cognitive training program for hyperactive children. *Journai of Abnormal Child Psychology,* **4,** 389–410, 1976.

Dubey, Dennis R. Organic factors in hyperkinesis. *American Journal of Orthopsychiatry,* **46,** 353–366, 1976.

Edelson, Richard I., and Sprague, Robert L. Conditioning of activity level in a classroom with institutional retarded boys. *American Journal of Mental Deficiency,* **78,** 384–388, 1974.

Edson, Thomas. Physical education: A substitute for hyperactivity and violence. *Journal of Health, Physical Education, and Recreation,* **40,** 79–81, 1969.

Eisenberg, L. The clinical use of stimulant drugs in children. *Pediatrics,* **49,** 709–715, 1972.

Eisenberg, L., et al. The effectiveness of psychotherapy alone and in conjunction with perphenazine or placebo in treatment of neurotic and hyperkinetic children. *American Journal of Psychotherapy,* **117,** 1088–1093, 1961.

Eisenberg, Leon. Future threats or clear and present dangers? *School Review,* **85,** 155–165, 1976.

Ellis, M. J., et al. Methylphenidate and the activity of hyperactives in the informal setting. *Child Development,* **45,** 217–220, 1974.

Epstein, Michael H., et al. Implications of the reflectivity-impulsivity dimension for special education. *Journal of Special Education,* **9,** 11–25, 1975.

Erickson, Marilyn T., and Williams, Ben, eds. *Readings in Behavior Modification Research with Children.* New York: MSS Information Corp., 1973.

*Erikson, Erik H. *Childhood and Society,* 2nd ed. New York: Norton, 1963.

Fairchild, Thomas N. *Managing the hyperactive child in the classroom.* Austin, Tex.: Learning Concepts, 1975.

*Farber, Adele, and Mazlish, Elaine. *Liberated Parents, Liberated Children.* New York: Avon, 1975.

*Feingold, Ben F. *Why Your Child Is Hyperactive.* New York: Random House, 1974.

Feingold, Ben F. Hyperkinesis and learning disabilities linked to the ingestion of artificial food colors and flavors. *Journal of Learning Disabilities,* **9,** 551–559, 1976.

Feingold, Ben F. Food additives and hyperkinesis: Dr. Feingold replies. *Journal of Learning Disabilities,* **10,** 122–124, 1977.

Feldhusen, John F., et al. Prediction of delinquency, adjustment and academic achievement over a 5 year period with the Kvaraceus delinquency proneness scale. *Journal of Educational Research,* **65,** 375–381, 1972.

Fisher, Mary Ann. Dextroamphetamine and placebo practice effects on selective attention in hyperactive children. *Journal of Abnormal Child Psychology,* **6,** 25–32, 1978.

Flynn, Nona M., and Rapoport, J. L. Hyperactivity in open and traditional classroom environments. *Journal of Special Education,* **10,** 285–290, 1976.

Freeman, Frank S. *Theory and Practice of Psychological Testing.* 3rd ed. New York: Holt, 1962.

Freeman, Roger D. Drug effect on learning in children: A selected review of the past 30 years. *Journal of Special Education,* **1,** 17–44, 1966.

Freeman, Roger D. Review of medicine in special education: Another look at drugs and behavior. *Journal of Special Education,* **4,** 377–384, 1970.

*Freeman, Roger D. Review of medicine in special education: Medical-behavioral pseudorelationships. *Journal of Special Education,* **5,** 93–99, 1971.

*Freeman, Roger D. Minimal brain dysfunction, hyperactivity and learning disorders: Epidemic or episode? *School Review,* **85,** 5–30, 1976.

Fremont, Theodore S., and Deifert, David. What you should know about hyperactivity. *Mental Health,* **60,** 11–13, 1976.

Friedland, Seymour J., and Shilkret, Robert B. Alternative explanations of learning disabilities: Defensive hyperactivity. *Exceptional Children,* **40,** 213–215, 1973.

Friedlander, B. Z., et al., eds. *Exceptional Infant: Assessment and Intervention,* Vol. 3. New York: Brunner/Mazel, 1975.

Gadow, Kenneth D. Psychotropic and anticonvulsant drug usage in early childhood special education programs. III: A preliminary report: Parent interviews about drug treatment. Paper presented at the Annual International Convention of the Council for Exceptional Children, Atlanta, Ga., 1977.

Gallagher, James J., ed. *Teaching Gifted Students.* Boston: Allyn and Bacon, 1965.

Gallagher, James J., and Bradley, Robert H. Early identification of developmental difficulties. In *Early Child Education,* 75th yearbook of the National Society for the Study of Education. Chicago: University of Chicago Press, 1972.

Gardner, R. The mutual story-telling technique in the treatment of psychogenic problems secondary to minimal brain dysfunction. *Journal of Learning Disabilities,* **7,** 135–143, 1974.

Gardner, Richard A. Techniques for involving the child with MBD in meaningful psychotherapy. *Journal of Learning Disabilities,* **8,** 1975.

*Gardner, William I. *Children with Learning and Behavior Problems: A Behavior Management Approach.* Boston: Allyn and Bacon, 1974.

Gesell, Arnold, and Ilg, Frances L. *Infant and Child in the Culture of Today.* New York: Harper & Row, 1943.

Gesell, Arnold, and Ilg, Frances L. *Child Development.* New York: Harper & Row, 1949.

Gittleman-Klein, Rachel, ed. *Recent Advances in Child Psychopharmacology.* New York: Human Sciences Press, 1975.

Gittleman-Klein, Rachel, and Klein, Donald F. Are behavioral and psychometric changes related in methylphenidate-treated, hyperactive children. *International Journal of Mental Health,* **4,** 182–198, 1975.

Gittleman-Klein, Rachel, et al. Relative efficacy of methylphenidate and behavior modification in hyperkinetic children: An interim report. *Journal of Abnormal Child Psychology,* **4,** 361–379, 1976.

Glueck, Sheldon, and Glueck, Eleanor. *Predicting Delinquency and Crime.* Cambridge, Mass.: Harvard University Press, 1959.

*Goodman, Paul. *Growing Up Absurd.* New York: Vintage Books, 1960.

Goodwin, Sally E., and Mahoney, Michael J. Modification of aggression through modeling: An experimental probe. *Journal of Behavior Therapy and Experimental Psychology,* **6,** 200–202, 1975.

Gottlieb, Marvin I. Pills: Pros and cons of medication for school problems. *Acta Symbolica,* **6,** 35–64, 1975.

Gracenin, Carolyn T., and Cook, Jimmie E. Alpha biofeedback and LD children. *Academic Therapy,* **12,** 275–279, 1977.

Graham, Ada, and Graham, Frank. Lead poisoning and the suburban child. *Today's Health,* **52,** 38–41, 1974.

Green, A., et al. Child abuse: Pathological syndrome of family interaction. *American Journal of Psychiatry,* **131,** 882–886, 1975.

Greenberg, Jerrold S. The use of drugs to calm kids. Paper presented at New York State Federation of Chapters of the Council for Exceptional Children. Buffalo, N.Y., 1974.

Greenberg, Jerrold S. Hyperkinesis and the schools. *Journal of School Health,* **46,** 91–97, 1976.

Greenberg, L., et al. Pharmacotherapy of hyperactive children: Current practices. *Childrens Hospital, National Medical Center, Clinical Proceedings,* **27,** 101–105, 1971.

Greenberg, L. M., et al. Effects of dextroamphetamine, chlorpromazine and hydroxyzine on behavior and performance in hyperactive children. *American Journal of Psychiatry,* **129,** 532–539, 1972.

Greenberg, Lawrence M., and Yellin, Absalom M. Blood pressure and pulse changes in hyperactive children treated with imipramine and methylphenidate. *American Journal of Psychiatry,* **132,** 1325–1326, 1975.

Grinspoon, Lester, and Singer, Susan B. Amphetamines in the treatment of hyperkinetic children. *Harvard Educational Review,* **43,** 515–555, 1973.

Groover, Robert V. The hyperkinetic child. *Psychiatric Annals,* **2,** 36–44, 1972.

Gross, Beatrice, and Gross, Ronald, eds., *Will It Grow in a Classroom?* New York: Dell Publishing Co., Inc., 1974.

Gross, Mortimer D. Growth of hyperkinetic children taking methylphenidate, dextroamphetamine, or imipramine/desipramine. *Pediatrics,* **58,** 423–431, 1976.

Hackett, Regina. In praise of praise. *American Education,* **11,** 11–15, 1975.

Halverson, C., and Waldrop, M. The relations of mechanically recorded activity level to varieties of preschool play behavior. *Child Development,* **44,** 678–681, 1973.

Halverson, Charles F., Jr., and Waldrop, Mary F. Relations between preschool activity and aspects of intellectual and social behavior at age 7½. *Developmental Psychology,* **12,** 107–112, 1976.

Hargreaves, David H., et al. *Deviance in the Classroom.* Boston: Routledge & Kegan Paul, Ltd., 1975.

Harlin, Vivian K. The hyperkinetic child: His management in the school environment. *School Health Review,* **4,** 9–13, 1973.

*Harris, Thomas A. *I'm OK, You're OK.* New York: Harper & Row, 1967.

Harvard, Janice. School problems and allergies. *Journal of Learning Disabilities,* **6,** 492–494, 1973.

Havighurst, Robert J. Choosing a middle path for the use of drugs with hyperactive children. *School Review,* **85,** 61–77, 1976.

Hawley, Claude, and Buckley, Robert. Food dyes and hyperkinetic children. *Academic Therapy,* **10,** 27–32, 1974.

Hawley, Claude, and Buckley, Robert. Hyperkinesis and sensitivity to the aniline food dyes. *Journal of Orthomolecular Psychiatry,* **5,** 129–137, 1976.

Hine, R. Jean. Hyperkinesis and food additives: A review of current research. *Bureau Memorandum,* **17,** 10–12, 1976.

*Hobbs, Nicholas. *The Futures of Children.* San Francisco: Jossey-Bass, 1975.

Hogg, J., and Maier, I. Transfer of operantly conditioned visual fixation in hyperactive severely retarded children. *American Journal of Mental Deficiency,* **79,** 305–310, 1974.

*Holt, John. *How Children Fail.* New York: Penguin Books, 1969.

Horowitz, F., ed. *Review of Child Development Research,* Vol. 4. Chicago: University of Chicago Press, 1975.

Huessy, H. R., et al. 500 children followed from grade 2 through grade 5 for the prevalence of behavior disorders. *Acta Paedopsychiatrica,* **39,** 301–309, 1973.

Huessy, H. R., et al. 8–10 year follow-up of 84 children treated for behavioral disorder in rural Vermont. *Acta Paedopsychiatrica,* **40,** 230–235, 1974.

Huessy, Hans R., and Cohen, Alan H. Hyperkinetic behaviors and learning disabilities followed over 7 years. *Pediatrics,* **5,** 4–10, 1976.

Jacob, Rolf G., et al. Formal and informal classroom settings: Effects on hyperactivity. *Journal of Abnormal Child Psychology,* **6,** 47–59, 1978.

*James, Muriel, and Jongeward, Dorothy. *Born to Win.* New York: New American Library, 1978.

Johnson, Richard A. et al. Developing school policy for use of stimulant drugs for hyperactive children. *School Review,* **85,** 78–96, 1976.

Jones, Nancy, et al. The hyperkinetic child: What do teachers know? *Psychology in the Schools,* **12,** 388–392, 1975.

Juliano, Daniel B. Conceptual tempo, activity and concept learning in hyperactive and normal children. *Journal of Abnormal Psychology,* **83,** 629–934, 1974.

*Juliano, Daniel B., and Gentile, J. R. Will the real hyperactive child please sit down: Problems of diagnosis and remediation. *Child Study Journal Monographs,* 1–38, 1974.

*Kagan, J. Reflection-impulsivity: The generality and dynamics of conceptual tempo. *Journal of Abnormal Psychology,* **71,** 17–24, 1966.

Katz, Sidney, et al. Clinical pharmacological management of hyperkinetic children. *International Journal of Mental Health,* **4,** 157–181, 1975.

Keele, Darman K., et al. Role of special pediatric evaluation in the evaluation of a child with learning disabilities. *Journal of Learning Disabilities,* **8,** 40–45, 1975.

Keogh, Barbara K. Hyperactivity and learning disorders: Review and speculation. *Exceptional Children,* **38,** 101–109, 1971.

Keogh, Barbara K., et al. Functional analysis of WISC performance of learning-disordered hyperactive and mentally retarded boys. *Psychology in the Schools,* **10,** 178–181, 1973.

Kinsbourne, Marcel. School problems. *Pediatrics,* **52,** 697–710, 1973.

Klein, Donald F., and Gittleman-Klein, Rachel. Problems in the diagnosis of minimal brain dysfunction and the hyperkinetic syndrome. *International Journal of Mental Health,* **4,** 45–60, 1975.

Klotz, S. D. *Making the Child Accessible for Teaching-Learning: The Role of the Internist and Allergist in Learning Disabilities.* St. Petersburg. Fla.: Johnny Reads, Inc., 1973.

Kohl, Herbert R. *The Open Classroom.* New York: New York Review, 1969.

Krager, John M., and Safer, Daniel J. Type and prevalence of medication used in treating hyperactive children. *New England Journal of Medicine,* **291,** 1118–1120, 1974.

Krippner, Stanley, et al. Stimulant drugs and hyperkinesis: A question of diagnosis. *Reading World,* **13,** 198–222, 1974.

Krumboltz, J., ed. *Learning and the Educational Process.* Chicago: Rand McNally, 1965.

Kvaraceus, W. C. Forecasting juvenile delinquency: A three-year experiment. *Exceptional Children,* **27,** 429–435, 1961.

Lambert, Nadine M., and Windmiller, Myra. An exploratory study of temperament traits in a population of children at risk. *Journal of Special Education,* **11,** 37–47, 1977.

Lambert, Nadine M., et al. Hyperactive children and the efficacy of psychoactive drugs as treatment intervention. *American Journal of Orthopsychiatry,* **46,** 335–352, 1976.

Langhorne, John E., et al. Childhood hyperkinesis: A return to the source. *Journal of Abnormal Psychology,* **85,** 201–209, 1976.

Laufer, Maurice W. Long-term management and some follow-up findings on the use of drugs with minimal cerebral syndromes. *Journal of Learning Disabilities,* **4,** 518–522, 1971.

Ledebur, Gary W. The elementary LD Process Group and the school psychologist. *Psychology in the Schools,* **14,** 62–66, 1977.

Lennard, Henry L., et al. *Mystification and Drug Misuse: Hazards in Using Psychoactive Drugs.* New York: Harper & Row. 1972.

Leuba, C. Toward some integration of learning theories: The concept of optimal stimulation. *Psychological Reports,* **1,** 27–33, 1955.

Levine, Melvin D., and Liden, Craig B. Food for inefficient thought. *Pediatrics,* **58,** 145–148, 1976.

Lloyd, John. The pedagogical orientation: An argument for improved instruction. *Journal of Learning Disabilities,* **8,** 17–21, 1975.

Loney, Jon. The intellectual functioning of hyperactive elementary school boys: A cross-sectional investigation, *American Journal of Orthopsychiatry,* **44,** 754–761, 1974.

Loney, Jon, et al. Parental management, self-concept and drug response in MBD. *Journal of Learning Disabilities,* **8,** 87–190, 1975.

Loney, Jon, et al. Responses of hyperactive boys to a behaviorally focused school attitude questionnaire. *Child Psychiatry and Development,* **6,** 123–133, 1976.

Long, Kate. *Johnny's Such a Bright Boy, What a Shame He's Retarded.* Boston: Houghton Mifflin, 1977.

*Lupin, Mimi, et al. Children, parents and relaxation tapes. *Academic Therapy,* **12,** 105–113, 1976.

Maccoby, E. E., et al. Activity level and functioning in normal preschool children. *Child Development,* **36,** 761–770, 1965.

Mantione, Frank F. *A comparison of the effects of muscular relaxation and rest on the behavior of grammar school children described as hyperactive.* Buffalo: State University of New York, 1975.

Marwit, Samuel J., and Stenner, A. Jack. Hyperkinesis: Delineation of two patterns. *Exceptional Children,* **38,** 401–406, 1972.

Matheson, Roger. Management of hyperkinesis by medication: A review of the literature. *Remedial Education,* **7,** 23–25, 1975.

Mayron, Lewis, W., et al. Light, radiation and academic behavior. *Academic Therapy,* **10,** 33–47, 1974.

Meier, John H. Prevalence and characteristics of learning disabilities found in second grade children. *Journal of Learning Disabilities,* **4,** 1–16, 1971.

Mendelson, W., et al. Hyperactive children as teenagers. *Journal of Nervous and Mental Disease,* **153,** 273–279, 1971.

Minde, K., et al. The hyperactive child in elementary school: A 5 year controlled follow-up. *Exceptional Children,* **38,** 215–221, 1971.

Minde, K., et al. A 5-year follow-up study of 91 hyperactive school children. *Journal of The American Academy of Child Psychology,* **11,** 595–610, 1972.

*Moustakas, Clark E. *Psychotherapy with Children.* New York: Harper & Row, 1959.

Munro, Nancy. A study of food and poverty among 113 Head Start children in Missoula. Missoula: Montana University, 1968.

Murray, Joseph N. Is there a role for the teacher in the use of medication for hyperkinetics? *Journal of Learning Disabilities,* **9,** 30–35, 1976.

Mussen, P., ed. *Carmichael's Manual of Child Psychology.* New York: Wiley, 1970.

Mussen, Paul, et al. *Child Development and Personality,* 3rd ed. New York: Harper & Row, 1963.

Nash, Ralph J. Clinical research on psychotropic drugs and hyperactivity in children. *School Psychology Digest,* **5,** 22–33, 1976.

Nestadt, Allan. A review of medication for children with specific learning disabilities. *Phoenix Journal,* **9,** 3, 5, 7–9, 1976.

*Ott, John N. Influence of fluorescent lights on hyperactivity and learning disabilities. *Journal of Learning Disabilities,* **9,** 417–422, 1976.

Painter, Marylyn. Fluorescent lights and hyperactivity in children: An experiment. *Academic Therapy,* **12,** 181–184, 1976–1977.

Palkes, Helen, et al. Improvement in maze performance of hyperactive boys as a function of verbal-training procedures. *Journal of Special Education,* **5,** 337–342, 1971.

Paternite, Carl E., et al. Relationships between symptomatology and SES-related factors in hyperkinetic/MBD boys. *American Journal of Orthopsychiatry,* **46,** 291–301, 1976.

Peters, John E., et al. Physician's Handbook: Screening for MBD. Ciba Pharmaceutical Co.

Powers, Hugh W. Dietary measures to improve behavior and achievement. *Academic Therapy,* 203–214, Winter, 1973–1974.

Powers, Hugh W. Caffeine, behavior and the LD child. *Academic Therapy,* **11,** 5–19, 1975.

Powers, Sandra M. The Vane Kindergarten Test: Temporal stability and ability to predict behavioral criteria. *Psychology in the schools,* **14,** 34–36, 1977.

Prichep, Leslie S., et al. Evoked potentials in hyperkinetic and normal children under certainty and uncertainty: A placebo and methylphenidate study. *Psychophysiology,* **13,** 419–428, 1976.

Prinz, Robert, and Loney, Jan. Teacher-rated hyperactive elementary school girls: An exploratory developmental study. *Child Psychology and Human Development,* **4,** 246–257, 1974.

Prout, H. Thompson. Behavioral intervention with hyperactive children: A review. *Journal of Learning Disabilities,* **10,** 141–146, 1977.

Quay, Herbert C., ed. *Children's Behavior Disorders: An Enduring Problem in Psychology.* Princeton, N.J.: D. Van Nostrand, 1968.

Quinn, Jim A., and Wilson, Barry J. Programming effects on learning disabled children: Performance and affect. *Psychology in the Schools,* **14,** 196–199, 1977.

Renstrom, Roberta. The teacher and social worker in stimulant drug treatment of hyperactive children. *School Review,* **85,** 97–108, 1976.

Rickard, Henry C., and Dinoff, Michael, eds. *Behavior Modification in Children.* University, Ala.: University of Alabama Press, 1974.

Ricks, D. F., et al., eds. *Life History Research in Psychopathology,* Vol. III. Minneapolis: University of Minnesota Press, 1974.

Riddle, K. Duane and Rapoport, J. L. A 2-year follow-up of 72 hyperactive boys. *Journal of Nervous and Mental Disease,* **162,** 126–134, 1976.

Robin, Stanley S., and Bosco, James J. The social context of stimulant drug treatment for hyperkinetic children. *School Review,* **85,** 141–154, 1976.

*Robins, L. *Deviant Children Grown Up.* Baltimore: Williams & Wilkins, 1966.

*Ross, Dorothea M., and Ross, Sheila A. *Hyperactivity: Research, Theory and Action.* New York: Wiley, 1976.

Ryback, D., and Staats, A. Parents as behavior therapy-technicians in treating reading deficits (dyslexia). *Journal of Behavior Therapy and Experimental Psychiatry,* **1,** 109–119, 1970.

Safer, Daniel J. Establishing boundary lines for families of children with behavior disorders. *Psychology Quarterly Supplement,* **42,** 86–97, 1968.

Safer, Daniel J. A familial factor in minimal brain dysfunction. *Behavior Genetics,* **3,** 175–186, 1973.

Safer, Daniel J., and Allen, Richard P. Side effects from long-term use of stimulants in children. *International Journal of Mental Health,* **4,** 105–118, 1975.

Safer, Daniel J., and Allen, Richard P. *Hyperactive Children: Diagnosis and Management.* Baltimore, Md.: University Park Press, 1976.

Safer, Daniel, et al. Depression of growth in hyperactive children on stimulant drugs. *New England Journal of Medicine,* **287,** 217–220, 1972.

Safer, Daniel J., et al. Stimulant drug treatment of hyperactive adolescents. *Diseases of the Nervous System,* **36,** 454–457, 1975.

Salzman, Louis K. Allergy testing, psychological assessment and dietary treatment of the hyperactive child syndrome. *Medical Journal of Australia,* **2,** 247–250, 1976.

Sandoval, Jonathan, et al. Current medical practice and hyperactive children. *American Journal of Orthopsychiatry,* **46,** 323–334, 1976.

Saraf, Kishore R., et al. Imipramine side effects in children. *Psychopharmacologia,* **37,** 265–274, 1974.

Satterfield, James H., et al. Response to stimulant drug treatment in hyperactive children: Prediction from EEG and neurological findings. *Journal of Autism and Childhood Schizophrenia,* **3,** 36–48, 1973.

Satterfield, James H., et al. Intelligence, academic achievement and EEG abnormalities in hyperactive children. *American Journal of Psychiatry,* **131,** 391–395, 1974.

Satterfield, James H., et al. Pathophysiology of the hyperactive child syndrome. *Archives of General Psychiatry,* **31,** 839–844, 1974.

Sawrey, James M., and Telford, Charles W. *Educational Psychology,* 2nd ed. Boston: Allyn and Bacon, 1964.

Schaefer, Jacqueline W., et al. Group counseling for parents of hyperactive children. *Child Psychiatry and Human Development,* **5,** 89–94, 1974.

Schleifer, M., et al. Hyperactivity in preschoolers and the effect of methylphenidate. *American Journal of Orthopsychiatry,* **45,** 38–50, 1975.

Schnackenberg, Bob C. A plea for comprehensive treatment for the hyperkinetic child. *Child Welfare,* **56,** 231–237, 1977.

*Schrag, Peter, and Divoky, Diane. *The Myth of the Hyperactive Child.* New York: Pantheon Books, 1975.

Schrager, J., and Lindy, J. Hyperkinetic children: Early indicators of potential school failure. *Community Mental Health Journal,* **6,** 447–454, 1970.

Schulman, J. L., et al. *Brain Damage and Behavior.* Springfield, Ill.: Charles C Thomas, 1965.

Scott, T. J. The use of music to reduce hyperactivity in children. *American Journal of Orthopsychiatry,* **40,** 677–680, 1970.

Shader, R., and DiMascio, A., eds. *Psychotropic Drug Side Effects.* Baltimore: Williams & Wilkins, 1970.

Shetty, T. Alpha rhythms in the hyperkinetic child. *Nature,* **234,** 476, 1971.

Silberberg, Norman E., and Silberberg, Margaret C. Hyperlexia: The other end of the continuum. *Journal of Special Education,* **5,** 233–242, 1972.

*Silberberg, Norman, and Silberberg, Margaret. *Who Speaks for the Child?* Springfield, Ill.: Charles C Thomas, 1974.

Simpson, D. Dwayne. Attention training through breathing control to modify hyperactivity. *Journal of Learning Disabilities,* **7,** 274–283, 1974.

Slater, Eliot, and Cowie, Valerie. *The Genetics of Mental Disorders.* London: Oxford University Press, 1971.

Sleator, Esther K., et al. Hyperactive children: A continuous long-term placebo-controlled follow-up. *Journal of the American Medical Association,* **229,** 316–317, 1974.

Smith, Altomease. Social dangers of treating the hyperactive child. *Urban League Review,* **1,** 30–34, 1975.

Speer, F., ed. *Allergy of the Nervous System.* Springfield, Ill.: Charles C Thomas, 1970.

Sprague, Robert L., and Gadow, Kenneth D. The role of the teacher in drug treatment. *School Review,* **85,** 109–140, 1976.

Sroufe, L. Alan, and Stewart, Mark A. Treating problem children with stimulant drugs. *New England Journal of Medicine,* **289,** 407–413, 1973.

Stedman, James M., et al. *Clinical Studies in Behavior Therapy with Children, Adolescents and Their Families.* Springfield, Ill.: Charles C Thomas, 1973.

Stevens-Long, Judith. The effect of behavioral context on some aspects of adult disciplinary practice and affect. *Child Development,* **44,** 476–484, 1973.

Stewart, Jack, ed. *Counseling Parents of Exceptional Children.* Columbus, Ohio: Charles C. Merrill, 1978.

*Stewart, M. A., and Olds, S. W. *Raising a Hyperactive Child.* New York: Harper & Row, 1973.

Stewart, Mark A. What are the problems of the hyperactive child? Paper presented at the Annual Meeting of the American Psychological Association, Chicago, Illinois, Aug.–Sept., 1975.

Stewart, Mark A. Is hyperactivity abnormal? and other unanswered questions. *School Review,* **85,** 31–42, 1976.

Stewart, Mark A., and Morrison, James R. Affective disorder among the relatives of hyperactive children. *Journal of Child Psychology, Psychiatry, and Allied Disciplines,* **14,** 209–212, 1973.

Stilwell, Anne, and Stilwell, Hart. *The Child Who Walks Alone.* Austin: University of Texas Press, 1972.

Taichert, Louise C. *Childhood Learning Behavior and the Family.* New York: Behavioral Publications, 1973.

Taylor, W. F., and Holdt, K. C. Class-room related behavior problems: Counsel parents, teachers or children? *Counseling Psychologist,* **21,** 3–8, 1974.

Telford, Charles, and Sawrey, James. *The Exceptional Individual,* 3rd ed. Englewood Cliffs, N.J.: Prentice-Hall, 1977.

Tharp, Roland G., and Wetzel, Ralph J. *Behavior Modification in the Natural Environment.* New York: Academic Press, 1969.

Thomas, A., et al. *Behavioral Individuality in Early Childhood.* New York: New York University Press, 1963.

Thomas, A., et al. *Temperament and Behavior Disorders in Children.* New York: New York University Press, 1969.

Treegoob, Mark, and Walker, Kenneth P. The use of stimulant drugs in the treatment of hyperactivity. *School Psychology Digest,* **5**, 5–10, 1976.

Treichel-Arehart, Joan. School lights and problem pupils. *Science News,* **105**, 258–259, 1974.

Trotter, Sharland. Labeling: It hurts more than it helps. *Journal of Learning Disabilities,* **8**, 191–193, 1975.

Valett, Robert. *Programming Learning Disabilities.* Palo Alto, Calif.: Fearon Publishers, Inc., 1969.

*Valett, Robert. *Psychoeducational Treatment of Hyperactive Children.* Belmont, Calif.: Fearon Publishers, Inc., 1974.

Walker, Sydney. Drugging the American child: We're too cavalier about hyperactivity. *Journal of Learning Disabilities,* **8**, 354–358, 1975.

Waugh, Kenneth W., et al. *Diagnosing Learning Disorders.* Columbus, Ohio: Charles E. Merrill, 1971.

Weiss, G., et al. Comparison of the effects of chloropromazine, dextroamphetamine and methylphenidate on the behavior and intellectual functioning of hyperactive children. *Canadian Medical Association Journal,* **104**, 20–25, 1971.

Weiss, G., et al. Long-term methylphenidate treatment of hyperkinetic children. *Psychopharmacological Bulletin,* **10**, 34–35, 1974.

Weiss, G., et al. Effect of long-term treatment of hyperactive children with methylphenidate. *Canadian Medical Association Journal,* **112**, 159–165, 1975.

Weiss, Gabrielle. The natural history of hyperactivity in childhood and treatment with stimulant medication at different ages: A summary of research findings. *International Journal of Mental Health,* **4**, 213–226, 1975.

Weissenburger, Fred E., and Loney, Jan. Hyperkinesis in the classroom: If cerebral stimulants are the last resort, what is the first resort? *Journal of Learning Disabilities,* **10**, 339–348, 1977.

Weisz, J. R., et al. Field dependence-independence on the Children's Embedded Figures Test: Cognitive style or cognitive level? *Developmental Psychology,* **11**, 539–540, 1975.

Weithorn, Corinne J. Hyperactivity and the CNS: An etiological and diagnostic dilemma. *Journal of Learning Disabilities,* **6**, 41–45, 1973.

Weithorn, Corinne J., and Ross, Roslyn. Stimulant drugs for hyperactivity: Some additional disturbing questions.

American Journal of Orthopsychiatry, **46,** 168–173, 1976.

Welsch, Ellen Bowman. You may not know it, but your schools probably are deeply into the potentially dangerous business of teaching with drugs. *American School Board Journal,* **161,** 41–45, 1974.

Wender, Paul H. *Minimal Brain Dysfunction in Children.* New York: Wiley, 1971.

Wender, Paul H. *The Hyperactive Child: A Handbook for Parents.* New York: Crown, 1973.

Weery, John S., and Sprague, Robert L. Methylphenidate in children: Effect of dosage. *Australian and New Zealand Journal of Psychiatry,* **8,** 9–19, 1974.

Weery, John S., et al. Studies on the hyperactive child. VII: Neurological status compared with neurotic and normal children. *American Journal of Orthopsychiatry,* **42,** 441–451, 1972.

Weery, John S., et al. Medication for hyperkinetic children. *Drugs,* **2,** 81–89, 1976.

West, Mina, G., and Alexrod, Saul. A 3-D program for LD children: *Academic Therapy,* **10,** 309–319, 1975.

Whaley-Klahn, Mary Anne, and Loney, Jan. A multivariate study of the relationship of parental management to self-esteem and initial drug response in hyperkinetic/MBD boys. *Psychology in the Schools,* **14,** 485–492, 1977.

Williams, N. Hyperkinesis: A behavioral and physiological comparison. *Mental Retardation,* **4,** 48–61, 1976.

Wolraich, Mark, et al. Effects of methylphenidate alone and in combination with behavior modification procedures on the behavior and academic performance of hyperactive children. *Journal of Abnormal Child Psychology,* **6,** 149–161, 1978.

Worland, Julien. Effects of positive and negative feedback on behavior control in hyperactive and normal boys, *Journal of Abnormal Child Psychology,* **4,** 315–326, 1976.

Wortman, Richard A. Learning disabilities or learning problems? *National Elementary Principal,* **50,** 48–52, 1971.

Wunderlich, Ray C. Treatment of the hyperactive child. *Academic Therapy,* **8,** 375–390, 1973.

Zahn, Theodore P., et al. Pupillary and heart rate reactivity in children with minimal brain dysfunction. *Journal of Abnormal Child Psychology,* **6,** 135–147, 1978.

Zeitlin, Shirley. *Kindergarten Screening: Early Identification of Potential High Risk Learners.* Springfield, Ill.: Charles C Thomas, 1976.

Zentall, Sydney S. Optimal stimulation as theoretical basis of hyperactivity. *American Journal of Orthopsychiatry,* **45,** 549–563, 1975.

Zentall, Sydney S. Environmental stimulation model. *Exceptional Children,* **43,** 502–510, 1977.

Zentall, Sydney S., and Zentall, Thomas R. Activity and task performance of hyperactive children as a function of environmental stimulation. *Journal of Consulting and Clinical Psychology,* **44,** 693–697, 1976.

Zentall, Sydney S., and Zentall, Thomas R. Amphetamine's paradoxical effects may be predictable. *Journal of Learning Disabilities,* **9,** 188–189, 1976.

Zrull, Joel, et al. An evaluation of methodology used in the study of psychoactive drugs for children. *Journal of the American Academy of Child Psychology,* **5,** 284–291, 1966.

Zrull, Joel P., et al. Hyperkinetic syndrome: The role of depression. *Child Psychiatry and Human Development,* **1,** 33–40, 1970.

*Zuckerman, Lawrence, et al. *Children: The Challenge.* New York: Hawthorn Books, 1976. (A parents' handbook for study is available with this book.)

Zupnick, S. A new approach to disturbed children: The medical college school program. *Psychiatric Quarterly,* **48,** 76–85, 1974.

Index